An Easy Course in Using the HP 48

AF709226

by Dan Coffin, Chris Coffin
and John W. Loux

Illustrations by Robert L. Bloch

Grapevine Publications, Inc.
P.O. Box 2449
Corvallis, Oregon 97339-2449 U.S.A.

Acknowledgements

The term "48" is used for convenience herein to refer to the HP 48SX and the HP 48S, the registered trade names for the handheld calculator/computer products of Hewlett-Packard Co. We extend our thanks once again to Hewlett-Packard for their top-quality products and documentation.

Printed in the United States of America
ISBN 0-931011-31-0

Second Printing – August, 1992

CONTENTS

[0] Start Here

What Is This Machine?

Before you start using the HP 48 (or "48" for short), here's some idea of what you can expect from it: The 48 is a calculator—a tool to give you quick answers to quick questions. Most often this means keying in a value or two, pressing a key, and reading the result in the display.

The 48 was indeed designed to work in just that way. Although it's tremendously sophisticated, *most of its operations are simply variations on the basic theme*: Ask-A-Question/Get-An-Answer. If you keep this in mind, you'll get along very well.

One more thought: The 48 is a *tool,* designed to be used in a certain way for certain things. It's a great general-purpose calculating tool, but it's not the best tool for every job. When it's easier to use pencil and paper —or a larger computer—do it! Always choose the right tool for the job.

What Is This Book?

This book is *not* a reference manual (HP already did their usual great job on that). It's *not* an intensely in-depth treatment of programming, equation-solving, or *any* of the many things you can do "in-depth" on the 48. There are simply not enough pages in one book to do all that.

This book *is* a tutorial *introductory* course on the 48—a step-by-step, self-pacing course to orient you and get you "up-to-speed" on most features of the machine—*so that you can then use the HP manuals more profitably as you continue to practice with your 48.*

The [ON] Key

From the looks of the keyboard, there's a lot to learn about this machine; each key has several meanings. So although the [ON] key may seem a trivial a place to start…

Do This: Turn on your 48 by pressing the [ON] key at the lower left. Now turn it off, by pressing [→][OFF]. Notice the different function names printed on or around the [ON] key. The functions are related to one another, but the one you get depends on whether you press one of the shift keys first. This is the case with most keys on the machine.

Adjusting the Display

Next, make sure that you can read the display comfortably.

Do This: With the machine turned on, press *and hold down* the [ON] key, then press either the [+] or [−] key until the display adjusts to a comfortable viewing angle.

You can do this at any time. And—like most of its modes and settings—the calculator will remember and use this viewing angle until you change it.

Setting the Machine for this Course

There's one other thing to do before beginning with the actual Course. You may not yet know what this is all about—but don't worry: This is the one time when it's all right simply to press buttons without trying to understand what you're doing. This procedure is just to be sure that *your* machine has the settings this Course assumes....

Do This: Type: [↱][CLR] [MTH] [↰][{ }][↱][#][0][↱][#][0] [ENTER]. Again, notice how you must press the orange [↰] or the blue [↱] to activate a keyboard function of that color.

Then [α][α][S][T][O][F][ENTER][1][6][+/−][SPC][α][S][α][F][↱][HOME] [↱] [POLAR] (the alphabetic characters are printed in white at the lower right of the keys). Now your display should look like this:*

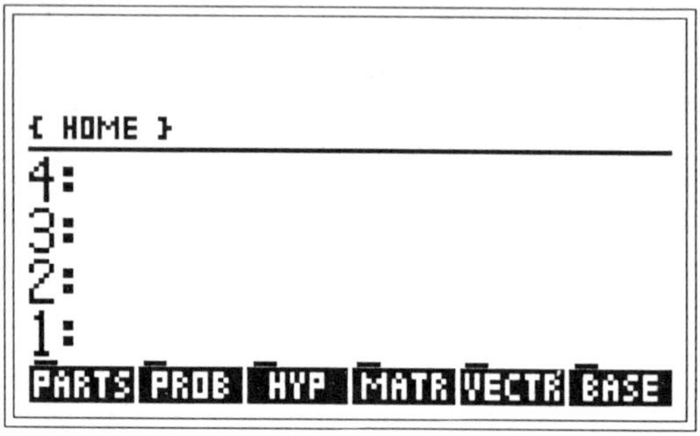

That's it—you're finished with the preparations. Now, on with the Course....

*If your display looks different, just repeat this entire procedure.

1 Your 48 Workshop

Calculating with Tools and Objects

Once upon a time, working with a calculator meant just using numbers and doing math. You could calculate lengths and angles in geometry, and distances, areas, rates, logarithms and roots—to 10-digit accuracy.

But that's not enough anymore. Now engineers, scientists and technicians from all sorts of disciplines expect a calculator to deal with complex numbers, vectors, matrices, tables of data, etc. And nearly everybody uses some kind of electronic note pad or text storage nowadays.

So, *wouldn't it be nice* to have a calculator that worked with these more sophisticated data types *in the same way* that your old calculator worked with numbers? (...yep—you guessed it....)

How the 48 Does It

One unifying idea now emerging in computers is that data are simply "things"—*objects* on which you perform work. And functions or programs are the *tools* with which you do this work. In the expression $2+3$, for example, the numbers 2 and 3 are simply objects that you combine to form a new object (5), using the + tool—just as you combine two blocks of wood to form a new object, using a hammer.

And now this idea of a *tool* (+) can apply to more than just real numbers. It works the same, whether you're adding real numbers, complex numbers or vectors. The results are different, because you start with different "materials," but the tool you use is the same—*so the 48 lets you use the same simple keystroke* ([+]) in each case.

The Big Picture: A Workshop

The 48 is a collection of *materials* (objects) and the *tools* to use on them (operations, etc.). So it's really a calculations *workshop:*

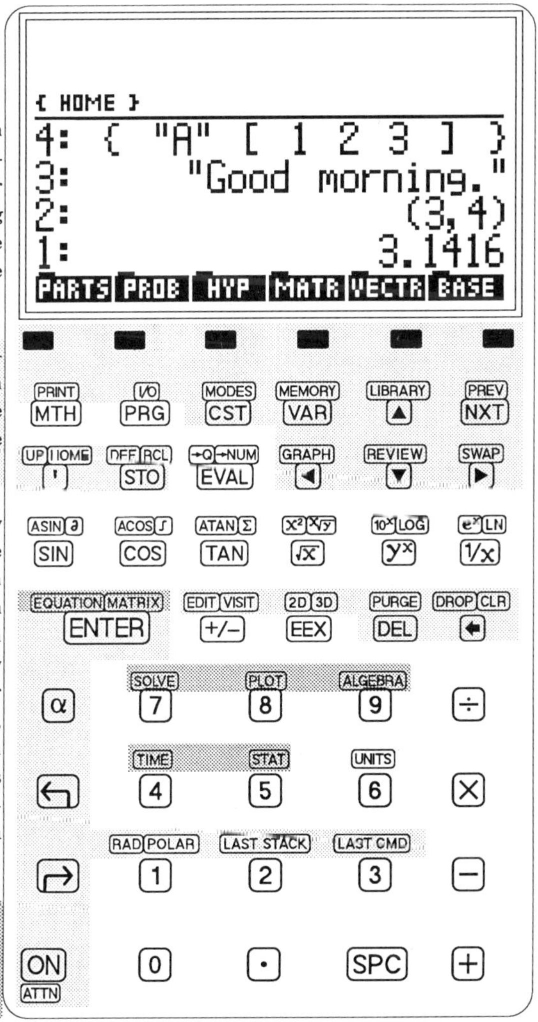

The Stack is the "workbench" in your workshop—where you literally "stack up" objects to use or combine. Most of this combining happens at the *bottom* of the Stack, so those bottom Levels are generally shown in the display.

Some keys simply help you control, move around and operate in the workshop—store and retrieve objects, get tools, rearrange the workbench, set modes, etc.

The rest of the keys are mostly "hand tools." That is, they are functions, within your easy reach at the workbench, that perform simple operations on objects on the Stack. The most commonly used hand tools (along with their inverses) have their own keys, but many others are gathered in "toolboxes"—*collections* of items you use via *menus* in the display—like the MaTH menu you see in the display here.

The "power tools" are smart, specialized tools that help you build, view or "crunch" sophisticated objects more conveniently.

As you work in the workshop, *you create your own storage compartments* for the objects you build (the objects shown below are just examples—these are not stored in your machine). The storage compartments are *directories.*

You can create directories *even within other* directories. And each directory has a *path* from the **HOME** (uppermost) directory—the route you must take to reach it. The path of the *current* directory (i.e. "where you are" right now) shows at the top of the display within **{ }**.

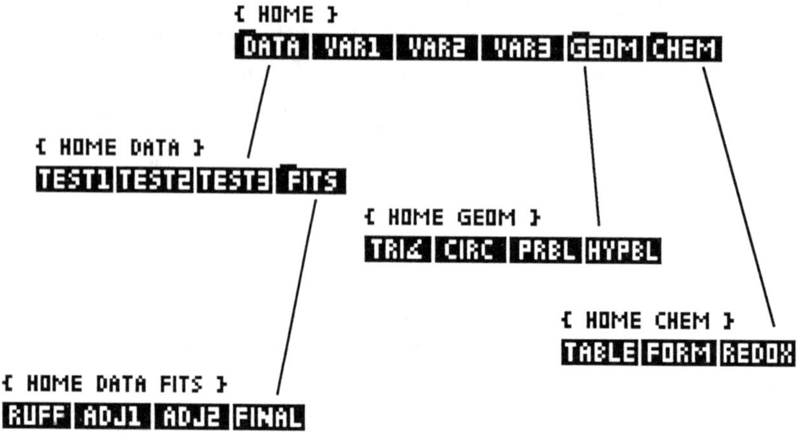

The VAR key shows you the menu of all the objects ("VARiables") you have stored in the current directory.

The Display: Your Window into the Workshop

To see into your workshop, turn on your 48 and look at the display....

The Stack

Look at the space *between* the horizontal line near the top of the display and the row of boxes at the very bottom (if you don't see these things, press [ATTN]—the [ON] key). This is the Stack—the actual "workbench" where you place the materials you're using. It's called a Stack because that's how objects "sit" on the workbench: The object *nearest to you* is at the *bottom* of the Stack (Level 1); and the next nearest object is at Level 2, etc. You may not see many more objects stacked up above that (in fact you'll never see more than the closest four objects), *but there can be hundreds more up there.* They reappear as you remove lower objects.

The Command Line

The Command Line is a *temporary space* created to let you gather your materials *before* putting them onto the Stack—your work bench.

Do This: Type a number—say, 14 (press [1][4]).... See how the Stack lines move up to make room for what you type? That 14 is *not* on the Stack—it's on the Command Line—until you specifically put it onto the Stack, by pressing [ENTER], or throw it away by pressing [ATTN] ([ON]). Throw it away now: [ATTN].

The Menu Line

At the very bottom of the display is the Menu Line. A menu is simply a convenient *collection* of related tools—a "toolbox", if you will. For although the crowded 48 keyboard already offers many tools "within your immediate reach," there are hundreds more stored in menus—even in menus *within* menus.

So, in making a selection from a menu, you are selecting a tool or opening another toolbox (menu). And it's easy: To make a selection from a menu, you just press the white key directly beneath it.

The Status Area

Now look at the display above the horizontal line. Here sits a set of warning lights and messages above your work bench—signs that light up to announce events or warn you of problems.

In a real workshop you might see "Power On" lights and "Saw Jammed" signs. On the 48, you'll see warning messages telling you, in effect: "You just tried to use a tool on the empty benchtop!" or "You can't use that tool on that object." And you'll see "indicator lights" that tell you when certain tools will operate differently because you've turned on an optional *mode*.

So be sure to watch the Status Area! Mode indicators stay on as long as the mode is active, but warning signs appear only temporarily; they turn off the next time you press a key.*

*Therefore, to further attract your attention to these warnings, the 48 usually beeps at you, too.

The Keyboard: Access to Your Workshop

The keyboard is how you make things happen in your workshop—putting objects on the workbench, using tools, moving around, etc.

The Shift Keys

The colored keys, [⬅] ("left-shift") and [➡] ("right-shift"),* indeed shift the meanings of keys to the colored functions printed above them.

Also, a *mode indicator* appears in the Status Area when a "shift" is in effect). Notice that shift keys are *toggle keys:* If a "shift" is on, pressing that shift key turns it *off*—and vice versa.

The Numeric Keys

Often the objects on your workbench are numbers, so the numeric keys and [+], [−], [×], [÷], [ENTER], [+/−], and [EEX] are all grouped together for your "calculating convenience."

The Alphabetic Keys

The [α] key is really another shift key: Press it prior to another key to obtain that key's *alphabetic* function (printed in *white* to the lower right). Again, notice how a mode indicator appears up in the Status Area.

*Astrophysicists: Please refrain from calling them "red-shift" and "blue-shift." Thank you.

Notice that you can *lock* this alpha mode on by pressing [α] a second time; the third time turns it off, so [α] is a *three*-way toggle key.

Also, note that you can use [←] and [→] *within* alpha mode (try it). Each key can have three *primary* meanings, and three *alpha* meanings.

The Menu Keys

The six blank white keys directly under the display are the menu keys. Menus appear in the display, and you make selections with these keys.

Try It: Press [←][MODES] and see the MODES menu in the display. This is the menu where you can set many of the machine's modes (options). As with most menus, there are more than six selections here, though. To move to other "pages," use the [NXT] key (to see the NeXT page) or [←][PREV] (the PREVious page). Try these now.... The MODES menu has four pages.

Now, move to the menu page that looks like this:

DEG▪ RAD GRAD XYZ▪ R∠Z R∠∠

The little boxes in the DEG▪ and XYZ▪ selections tell you what modes are currently in effect (DEGree angle mode and rectangular vector mode). But press the menu key under RAD.... The menu and the Status Area tell you the machine is now in RADians angle mode. Try other items on this menu page if you wish (but when you're finished, please leave the modes as you found them) and press [MTH].

The Control Keys

Finally, focus for a moment on the keys that help you direct the calculator's "movements," editing and attention.

The menu keys, [NXT] and [←][PREV] often act as control keys when they lead to other menus. But there are other control keys, too: [ATTN], [ENTER], [←], [DEL], [◄], [►], [▲], and [▼], to name a few. As you'll see, these keys help you "get to" and use many of the tools in the workshop.

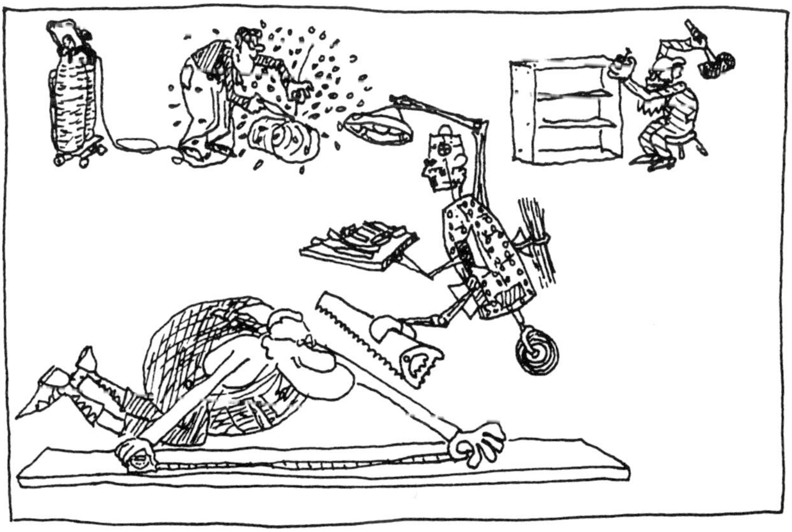

The Tools in Your Workshop

Hand Tools

Usually with the 48 , you create a simple object and select a simple, one-step tool to use on it—like putting a board onto the workbench and using a hammer to drive a nail into it. The drawers and toolboxes (*menus*) in your 48 workshop are full of such simple, one-step tools. You must simply learn when to use them—and how.

Power Tools

Sometimes simple tools aren't enough. To build, use, or make major changes to a sophisticated object (and be guided through the process) you need *power tools*—instruments and analyzers that perform more complex manipulations. For example, to create a table of numbers (an array)—4 rows of 5 columns, you *could* type the whole thing into the Command Line; or, you could use the MATRIX editor power tool, which presents you with a template that you can fill and edit more easily.

Other power tools let you build, solve or plot equations, manage time, do statistics, etc. These are all *smart* tools; they know something about the materials you're using and thus can eliminate much of the simple-minded work. So instead of a tool that "nails this piece to that," you have a tool that "makes a chair," or "designs a beam to support a 1-ton load." In this way, power tools actually augment your knowledge, by *automatically performing sophisticated operations* whose details would otherwise cost you time to learn or recall, and then execute one-by-one.

The Raw Materials in Your Workshop

With all the hundreds of *tools* in your 48 workshop, you have just a few basic types of *materials* (objects) with which to build. *Each type looks different* so that you can distinguish it from the others:

Real Numbers

On the 48, real numbers look and act like what you normally think of as numbers: `3` `15` `10000` `-0.9` `-50.2` `3.14`

Units

Units are real numbers with *dimensions.* That is, you can use real numbers to represent physical quantities (i.e., feet, pounds, psi, liters, etc.), by assigning them units—and these units will be used correctly throughout any calculations you perform. Here are some numbers with units: `1_ft` `17.3_kPa` `9.81_m/s^2`.
Note the *underscore* (_) that connects the number to its units.

Complex Numbers

A complex number is a vector—an ordered pair—in the complex plane. The 48 represents a *rectangular* complex number as two real numbers (real, imaginary), like this: `(3, 4)`. Or, that same number can also appear in *polar* form, with a magnitude and an angle: `(5, ∠53.13)`. The angle may be in degrees, radians or grads.

Arrays

An array is a group of numbers (either real or complex numbers), with no set limit on the size of the group, as long as it's arranged in a *table* of rows and columns—which can then be used mathematically as a *matrix*. The 48 represents arrays *within brackets*:

`[[ 1 2 ]` ` [ 3 4 ]]`	`[[ 1 2 3 ]]`	`[[ 1 ]` ` [ 2 ]]`
2x2 array	1-row array (row-vector)	1-column array (column-vector)

Flags

Flags are the simplest object type of all—*bits*—objects with only two possible values: 1 or 0 (on or off, set or clear—whatever)—usually to signal a mode or condition. Flags don't appear individually on the Stack, but you can set or test them individually or as groups.

Binary Integers

Binary integers are just that—integers made up of binary digits—bits (i.e. flags). You can do binary arithmetic on them and use them to represent *groups* of flags. The 48 displays binary integers on the Stack, not only in binary form (base 2) but also in number bases 8, 10 and 16. For example, 1011_2 appears as `# 1011b` 307_8 appears as `# 307o`

43_{10} appears as `# 43d` $A7F_{16}$ appears as `# A7Fh`

The `#` indicates a binary integer; the `b`, `o`, `d`, or `h` suffix tells you the base (`b`inary, `o`ctal, `d`ecimal, `h`exadecimal).

Character Strings

On the 48, you build character *strings*—sets of characters linked together to form objects—words or sentences of verbal information, *denoted by quotation marks:* "Hi!" "Phone home." "1+1=2"

Tags

Tags are temporary labels for objects on the workbench (the Stack)—like masking tape. A tag labels an object with an *identifier and a colon to its left:* Answer: 17 Altitude: 29000 RANGE: 10

Names

Names are words that identify things. On the 48, you use names to identify storage locations. The name is the *label* you tape onto the *storage location* to identify what's in it (you don't name an object itself). A 48 name is *a single word within apostrophes:* 'HUBERT' 'Wrench'

Algebraic Objects

Algebraic objects look and behave like algebraic expressions and equations. On the 48, you type them *between apostrophes*—just like names, except that algebraic objects contain mathematical operations and functions not allowed in names:

'A+B=C' 'SIN(x)' 'pi*RADIUS^2'

Programs

A program is a *custom-built* tool—a series of instructions (objects and tools) strung together, to be executed at a later time. You create a program, then name it (i.e., store it in a named toolbox). And then you have a new tool to use—just as you would use any other tool in the workshop. 48 programs are enclosed in « », like this:

```
« 1 2 + »          « "Hi" BEEP CLEAR »
```

Lists

Lists are *collections* of objects, the wire and glue of your workshop that binds together objects of *any types*—even other lists—within *braces:*

```
{ 1 2 3 }    { "Hi" 7 (3,4) "Bye" }
```

Directories

Directories are the *storage areas* you create for your objects. They appear as menu items with small "index tabs" :

```
DATA  GEOM  CHEM  FITS
```

There are other, more obscure object types on the 48, but those are the basic raw materials you'll be working with most often.

Look Again at the Workshop

Holding your place here, look back again at the Big Picture of your 48 workshop (page 14)....

Gradually, now, the maze of names and keys on your machine should be emerging into some kind of coherent picture of what you're working with here:

- You have a very sophisticated calculator—one that lets you *operate on* (build, edit, combine) not only numbers but many other types of objects.

- When performing these operations, you generally place these objects on your workbench—the Stack.

- You perform the operations themselves with commands that are available on keys or via menus. Most of these commands do simple things; they are "hand tools." A certain few are smarter and more complex—the "power tools."

- You name and store your created objects in directories that you create.

Conceptually, it's pretty simple, no? Be sure to keep this "Big Picture" in mind as you start to learn the details. Test yourself now....

Quiz on the "Big Picture"

At the end of every chapter this Course gives you a quiz, to make sure you're "digesting" what you read. These quizzes aren't trivial—they're a big part of your learning process—so don't breeze over them; think and apply your knowledge! The solutions immediately follow the questions, so study them and re-read parts of the chapter, as necessary.

1. What sorts of problems do you expect to solve with the 48?

2. Why use a workshop analogy when describing the 48?

3. How many keys would the 48 need if it didn't have the [α], [↰] and [↱] keys?

4. What's a menu? Why does the 48 use menus? What kinds of items may appear on its menus?

5. What's a real number (as represented on the 48)?

6. What's an array (as represented on the 48)?

7. What's a power tool (on the 48)? Name three of them.

Quiz Answers

1. You can expect to solve most kinds of number-crunching and data-intensive problems. Some may be intricate and require special programming, but for most you will key in some values, press a function key, and get an answer. The 48 has a vast supply of functions—and the flexibility to allow you to create your own.

2. The workshop analogy is good because the 48 uses *tools* (functions and operations) on *raw materials* (data objects—things like real numbers, arrays, lists, etc.). The Stack acts much like a workbench, too; it's where most of the building and crunching happens.

3. It would need about six times as many as it has now. The [α], [←] and [→] keys allow most keys to "mean" six different things.

4. The 48 uses menus to avoid the need for even more keys: A menu is a selection of items that appears in the display. To make a selection from a menu, you press the blank white key directly beneath that selection. Menu items may be tools for object manipulation, control operations—for moving around in your workshop—or keys that lead to other menus.

5. On the 48, real numbers are what you usually think of as real numbers: `1   15   -1000   0.3   -50   3.1416`

6. On the 48, arrays are groups of numbers—either real or complex number—arranged in rows and columns and represented *within brackets*:

2×2 array	1-row array (row-vector)	1-column array (column-vector)
[[1 2] [3 4]]	[[1 2 3]]	[[1] [2]]

7. A power tool is a smart, specialized tool that helps you build, view or "crunch" sophisticated objects more conveniently. Where your simpler "hand tools" are like saws and hammers, your power tools are more like lathes and drill presses. They are ⬅ EQUATION, ➡ MATRIX, ⬅ SOLVE, ⬅ PLOT, ⬅ ALGEBRA, ⬅ TIME, and ⬅ STAT.

2 The Stack and Command Line: Your Workbench

Typing and the Command Line

It's time to start learning how to work at your workbench....

To Begin: Press the digit keys (0 through 9) in sequence and look at the display. You should see something like this:*

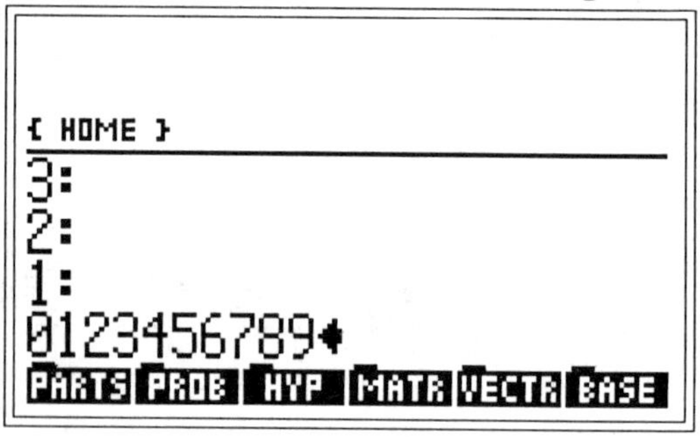

A space opens up between the workbench itself (the Stack) and the Menu Line. And what you just typed has been placed in this space, which is the *Command Line.*

The number you've typed is *not yet* on the workbench; it's still an *unfinished* command. To finish it—and to officially place the object onto the workbench—you must press ENTER. Do that now....

See? The Command Line disappears and the object, as the 48 has interpreted it, is placed on Level 1—that's the *bottom,* the nearest Level to you—on your workbench.

---

*If your display isn't exactly like this, don't worry too much. At this point you're most concerned with that number you just typed in.

So that's how to type in a real number and put it onto the workbench. Now, what about something that's not a number?

Do This: Press [α]....

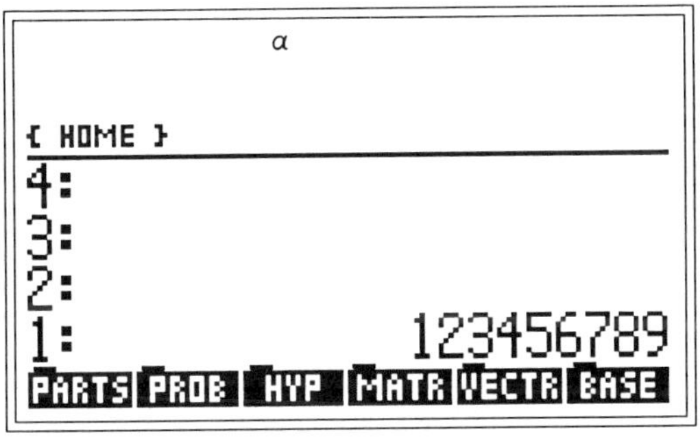

Notice the α that appears now in the Status Area, telling you that the next key you press will return its alphabetic character; you are in *alpha mode*.

Continue: Press [A][α][B][α][C]. ABC◆ appears on the Command Line—and notice that you had to press [α] before *every* letter.

Now press [ATTN] (that's the [ON] key).

What happened?

The ABC that you had typed on the Command Line was not put onto the workbench. It was *thrown away*.

That's what [ATTN] ("ATTentioN") does: it tells the calculator to drop whatever it's doing and give you its full attention.

Now try typing something a little more complicated.

Press: [α][α][W][H][A][T][SPC][Y][O][U][SPC][S][E][E][SPC][I][S][SPC][W][H][A][T] [SPC][Y][O][U][SPC][G][E][T][•][α]

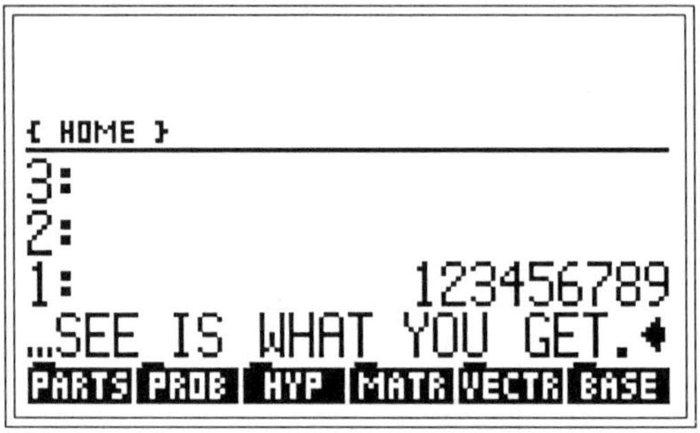

See how you can save a lot of keystrokes by using "alpha-lock" (pressing [α] twice in a row), so that the alpha annunciator stays on?

Notice also that the first part of what you typed is now pushed off the left-hand side of the display. The ... on the left tells you that the Command Line extends off that side of the display. To see what's missing, press [◄] repeatedly (or press it and hold it) until the 48 beeps to tell you "there ain't no more."

Notice that you couldn't do this if you hadn't switched back out of alpha mode with the final [α], above. In alpha mode, the [◄] key is something entirely different—the [P] key. So you can see that it's important to know what mode you're working in—watch your Status Area!

Inserting and Deleting Characters

Next question: How do you correct mistakes and make amendments to your typing on the Command Line?

Do This: Using [◀] and [▶], move the cursor so that it's on top of the S in SEE. Then type [α][α][C][A][N][SPC][α].

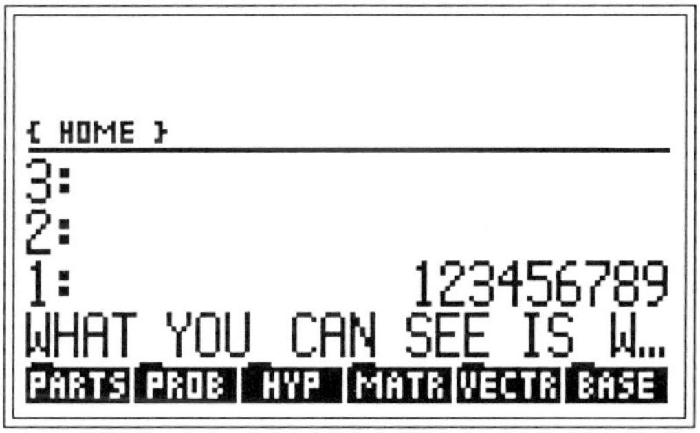

The new characters are *inserted*; this is how you add to what's already in the Command Line.

And it's just as easy to *remove* characters. For example, to remove the CAN that you just inserted...

Do This: Press [◆][◆][◆][◆]. Notice how [◆] deletes the character *before* the cursor.

You could have used the [DEL] (delete) key, also—but it deletes the character *under* the cursor (not to its left), so you would have had to move the cursor. Press [DEL] once now, to delete the S in SEE.

Lower-Case Letters

Up to now, you've typed only upper-case letters, but...

Try This: Type: [ATTN][α][α][H][←][I][SPC][←][T][←][H][←][E][←][R][←][E][•][α]. Nothing to it—you get lower-case by using [←] before each letter! But that's a lot of extra typing, so...

Notice: [ATTN][α][α][H][←][α][I][SPC][T][H][E][R][E][•][α]. Pressing [←][α] *when you're already in alpha mode* will *lock* the 48 into lower-case mode. And it will stay in effect until you leave the Command Line or press [←][α] again.

Special Characters

There are lots of *non-alphabetic* characters (things other than A–z) available to you on the 48. Most are *right-shifted* ([→]) alphabet keys, but the keys aren't labeled with these characters (no room), so there's a table of them on the back of HP's quick reference card.

Certain characters—called *delimiters*—have special significance to the 48 (you don't even need to go into alpha mode to use them), because they denote certain object types. For example, when you press ['] (not in alpha mode), you see ' ' (and the ♦ points between them)—because you'll usually want to *enclose* the object you're typing with these apostrophes. The other delimiter characters that come in pairs are on the shifted arithmetic keys [←][()], [←][[ ]], [←][« »], [→][" "], [←][{ }], and [→][::].

The [→][↵] (NEWLINE) Key

The Command Line is actually a space—not a line. It can be broken up into more than one line by using [→][↵] (right-shifted [•])—the NEWLINE key.

Try This: Type [ATTN][α][α][M][O][R][E][→][↵][T][H][A][N][→][↵][O][N][E][→][↵][L][I][N][E][→][↵][←][!] (that's [←][DEL]) [α].

You now have *five* lines in the Command "Line." The first line has scrolled off the top of the display, but it's still there.

Notice also that when you have more than one line like this, [▲] and [▼] move the cursor from line to line up and down—just as [◄] and [►] move you around to edit a single-line Command Line.

Not only that, [→][◄] and [→][►] will move you to the first and last characters of a line, and [→][▲] and [→][▼] will move you to the first and last lines.

Spend a little time now and play with this....

Then, without leaving your current Command "Line" (that multi-line thing), read on....

The EDIT Toolbox

Not all your Command Line editing tools are available on their own keys. With so many tools, the 48 has most of them stored in toolboxes (menus)—including a set of tools for editing the Command Line. You can open that toolbox with the [←][EDIT] key.

Try It: Press [←][EDIT] to see this menu of the items in that toolbox:

←SKIP | SKIP→ | ←DEL | DEL→ | INS ■ | ↑STK

←SKIP and SKIP→ move the cursor in the indicated directions (similar to [◄] and [►]), but they move until they encounter a space (or NEWLINE) and then stop at the next character. Try ←SKIP and SKIP→ now and watch how the cursor moves.

←DEL and DEL→ work the same way as ←SKIP and SKIP→, except that instead of *skipping over* those characters, they *delete* them.

INS ■ is a *mode* key (remember the RAD ■ key on the MODES menu?) The INS ■ key *changes the form of cursor* in the Command Line: When the ■ appears to the right of INS, the calculator is in *insert* mode; the cursor is ✦, and newly typed characters are *inserted* to its left.

But press INS ■ now.... Notice that it becomes INS , and that the ✦ becomes a ▮. The 48 is now in *replace* mode; a newly typed character will *replace* the character under the cursor.

Now press [ATTN] to throw away the current Command Line.

Next: Press [5][ENTER][4][3][ENTER]. You should now see this:

Then: Begin a new Command Line. Type: [α][α][I][SPC][A][M][SPC][SPC] [Y][E][A][R][S][SPC][O][L][D][•][α]. Next, use ←SKIP ←SKIP [◄] to move the insert cursor here: AM ◆YEARS, then press ↑STK:

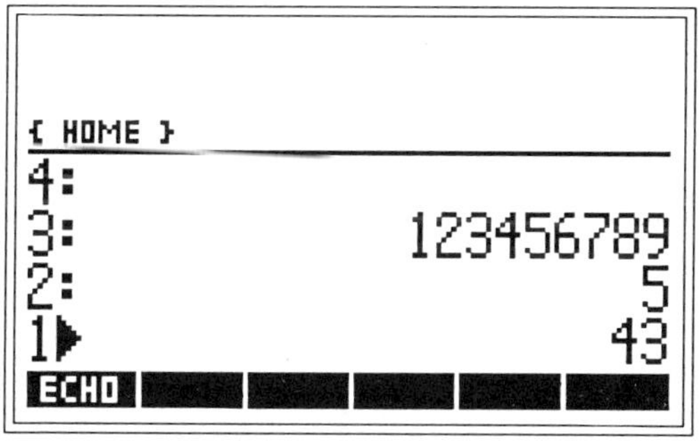

Now *ECHO* (i.e. copy) an object (the 5) from the Stack to the Command Line: Press [▲] once to move the pointer up a Level. Then press ECHO once, then [ENTER] to return to the Command Line.... See how ECHO works? A *copy* of the 5 is now inserted where the insert cursor was pointing (the replace cursor would have replaced existing characters, starting with the character under it).

A Command Line Summary

Review what you now know about the Command Line:

- You know how to type in a wide assortment of things—numbers and alphabetic characters, including lowercase letters, special symbols, and the NEWLINE character.
- You know how to use [◀], [▶], [▲], [▼], [DEL], and [⬅] to move around and edit the Command Line.
- You know that if you need even more tools—such as ←SKIP, DEL→, INS ■ and ↑STK—you can also open the EDIT toolbox: [←][EDIT].

But, *did you know?...*When you're *not* already working on something in the Command Line, [←][EDIT] lets you edit the object at Stack Level 1, by making a "working copy" of it for you on the Command Line!

Try It: Press [ATTN] to clear the current Command Line. Then press [←][EDIT].... The 43 has been *copied* into the Command Line, ready to be modified. Press [2][ENTER]. As usual, [ENTER] takes the object from the Command Line and put it onto the Stack. But in this case, it *replaces* the original 43 with the new version of that object in the Command Line: 243.

Now try another: [←][EDIT][DEL][·][ATTN]. The [ATTN] trashes only the edited version (.43) in the Command Line; it leaves the original 243 *intact* at Level 1 of the Stack.

Simple Materials: Real Numbers

All right, it's time to look at what happens once you've succeeded in putting an object on the Stack—after you've finished typing on the Command Line and pressed ENTER to put the object at Level 1.

Real numbers are the most intuitive objects to start with, since you're somewhat familiar with them already: As you know, real numbers include the positive and negative integers (1, 2, −3, −5, etc.), the positive and negative rational numbers (4.56, −2.3, etc.), the positive and negative irrational numbers ($\sqrt{2}$, π, e, etc.), and zero (0).

Well, your 48 "sees" real numbers in much the same way that you do. They're easy to represent—just a set of digits—as in any calculator. But what about extremely large or small numbers—so awkward to deal with because their decimal representations use lots of placeholding zeroes (e.g. 00000001 and 1,000,000,000)?

That's why there's *scientific notation.** Thus:

$5{,}280 = 5.28 \times 10^3$ $0.00023 = 2.3 \times 10^{-4}$ $1 = 1 \times 10^0$

The *mantissa* shows the number's *precision*. It is then multiplied by a power of 10 (the "exponent"), to show the number's *magnitude.*

Actually, the 48 uses a slightly compacted version of this notation—to avoid the need for superscripts in its line-oriented display:

5,280 = 5.28E3 0.00023 = 2.3E-4 1 = 1E0

*Not that it's any more "scientific" than other notations, but science is one discipline where you commonly encounter very large or very small numbers. It could as easily have been called "national debt notation," for example.

Real Number Limitations on the 48

As you would expect, the 48 uses this scientific notation to achieve a huge range in real-number calculations. But it's still a finite machine with a few reasonable limitations that you need to understand.

12-Digit Accuracy: Some real numbers simply have infinite decimal representations. For example, ⅓ is really 0.333.... But of course, it's impossible to use all of those 3's during arithmetic. Naturally, you round it, shortening it to a value that is both convenient and accurate enough for your purposes. Though the rounded number is *not* the same as the original, the difference is usually negligible in practice.

So, when dealing with infinite or extremely long decimal representations, the 48 rounds them, keeping a 12-digit mantissa of each number. The inaccuracy that results is *rounding error,* and—as you would expect—multiplying two rounded numbers will multiply this error.

So, how great an error is this?

Suppose you're the pilot of a plane flying from Los Angeles to New York. And it's a lovely day, and once airborne, your navigator lets it slip that he's been using his 48 to do fuel calculations—so his computations of miles per pound of fuel are accurate only to .000000000001 miles (uh-oh).... How big an error is this over 3,000 miles?

About *one two-hundredth of a millimeter.* If you'd flown clear to the *moon* and back, the error would be about 0.8 mm. And in a round trip to the sun, you'd be off by about a foot. Not a lot, really.

So the 48's 12-digit accuracy is slightly more than barely adequate.

Magnitude: Another limitation of the 48 is the *magnitude* of a real numbers (i.e., the value, not the number of digits) it can represent: You simply cannot expect it to represent arbitrarily large or small numbers. Everyone has a limit; you do—and so does your machine.

The largest real-number value representable on the 48 is a number called MAXR: 9.99999999999E499 $(9.99999999999 \times 10^{499})$

And the smallest value, called MINR, is 1E-499 (1×10^{-499})

These numbers are fantastically large and small. It is difficult—if not truly impossible—to contemplate these quantities.*

*"It's a tough job—but someone's gotta do it:" Compare MAXR and MINR with some of the largest and smallest things in the known universe....

The effective radius of an electron is about 2.817938×10^{-15} m(eters) or about 2.978626×10^{-31} light years (a light year is the distance that light travels through free space in one year's time). So the *volume* of an electron (assuming it's a sphere) is about 9.373093×10^{-44} cubic meters, or about 1.106972×10^{-91} cubic light years. Now, the radius of the sphere of the known universe is about 10^{10} light years—so its volume is about 10^{30} cubic light years. And so, if you were to pack the known universe absolutely solidly with electrons (no wasted space), you'd need about 10^{121} electrons.

Now that's a lot—more than anybody can really envision. But MAXR on the 48 is *so much larger* than *this*, that if you really had a collection of MAXR electrons, you'd have enough electrons to fill 10,000,
000,000,000,000,000,000,000,000,000,000,000,000,000,000,000,000,000,000,000,000,000,000,000,000,000
000,000,000,000,000,000,000,000,000,000,000,000,000,000,000,000,000,000,000,000,000,000,000,000,000
000,000,000,000,000,000,000,000,000,000,000,000,000,000,000,000,000,000,000,000,000,000,000,000,000
000,000,000,000,000,000,000,000,000,000,000,000,000,000,000,000,000,000,000,000,000,000,000,000,000
000,000,000,000,000,000,000,000,000,000,000,000,000,000,000,000,000,000,000,000,000,000,000,000,000
known universes.

On the small end of things, picture in your mind the colossal gob of electrons numbered above. Then picture yourself picking out just ten of those electrons. That ten—in relation to the whole—is the fraction you're talking about when you use the smallest 48 real value, MINR.

Suffice it to say that the magnitude limits of the 48 aren't all that restrictive.

Indeed, you may have heard of human cultures whose numbering systems went something like:

"1...2...3...more-than-3..."

...and that was all the higher they described numerical magnitude.

Well, so it is in every society. In this modern-day, technical world, for example, the numbering goes beyond 3, but at some point, it runs out of names and meanings too:

"...millions ... billions ... trillions ... quadrillions ..."

...and so on, up to about "nonillions"—about 10^{30}. But what do you call numbers on the order of 10^{100}, or 10^{400}?*

Truly, there is a limit to your practical needs to describe numbers. Yours may simply be a little higher than another's—but not by much.

*The authors recommend the term "several gadzillion."

Changing Signs and Entering Exponents

All right—enough worrying about the limitations of real numbers. It's time to see how they work as objects you manipulate on your workbench—the Stack. Try putting some real numbers on the bench-top....

Do This: Press [ATTN] [↱][CLR] [MTH] [5][2][8][0] [ENTER] [3][6][5][•][2][5] [ENTER] [6][•][0][2][2][α][E][2][3] [ENTER]. You should see:

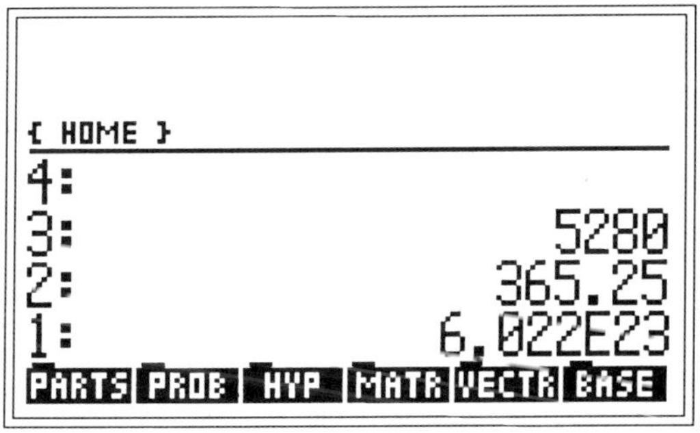

Notice that when you keyed in 6.022E23, you used [α][E] to key in the exponent—but you could have used [EEX] (Enter EXponent) instead.

For keying in exponents like this, [EEX] works much the same as [α][E] except for one case: Press [EEX] now....

See what happens? If there's no mantissa already on the Command Line, [EEX] gives you one: 1.

(Press [ATTN] now to clear the Command Line.)

Now, how about negative numbers? Try these...

Examples: Press [1] [ENTER] [+/–] [+/–]....The [+/–] key simply changes positive object values to negative—and vice versa.

Now put –1.3, 4.5×10^{-24}, -7.8×10^{3} and -9×10^{-54} onto the workbench. Press:

[1] [•] [3] [+/–] [ENTER]
[4] [•] [5] [EEX] [2] [4] [+/–] [ENTER]
[7] [+/–] [•] [8] [EEX] [3] [ENTER]
[9] [+/–] [EEX] [+/–] [5] [4] [ENTER].

You'll see this:

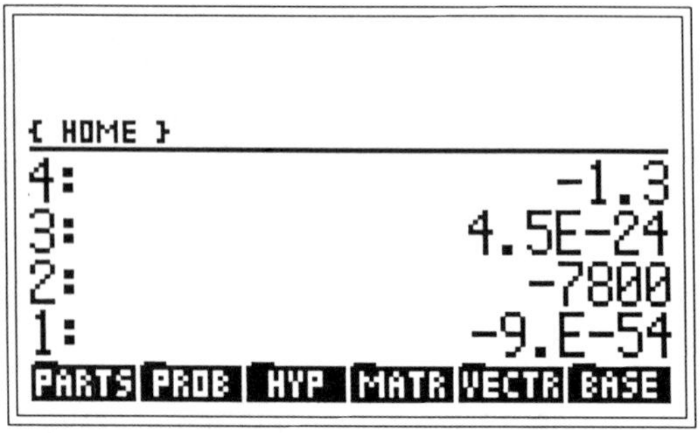

So there are two ways to get a negative number: You can put the positive number on the workbench in the usual way, then press [+/–]. Or, you can change the sign of either the mantissa or the exponent at any time while you're typing in that portion of the number.

Display Formats

You'll notice that the real numbers on the Stack have varying numbers of decimal places showing. What's going on?

Try This: Press ⬑ MODES 4 **FIX**. You should see:

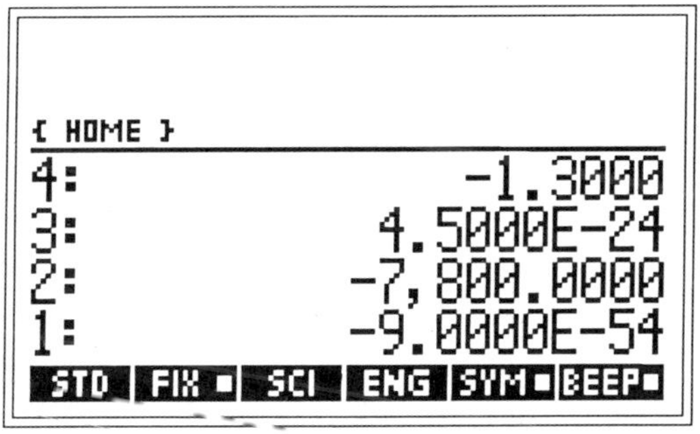

You just told the 48 to change the *format* of real numbers in the display. Their *values* haven't changed—just the way you see them.

4 **FIX** tells the 48 to show a FIX'ed number of digits—four in this case—to the right of the decimal point.

Notice how the ▪ has appeared on the **FIX** mode key to tell you that FIX mode is currently in effect.

Now press 0 **FIX ▪**.... See? Now there are zero digits to the right of the decimal point. Again, the numbers haven't changed in value—only in appearance.

Do This: Press [1] [1] **SCI**.

```
{ HOME }
4:    -1.30000000000E0
3:   4.50000000000E-24
2:    -7.80000000000E3
1:  -9.00000000000E-54
 STD | FIX | SCI ■| ENG | SYM ■|BEEP■
```

Notice: In the previous examples some numbers were displayed in scientific notation even though the requested display mode was FIX. But that was only because it was impossible to display them any other way—using the 12 available digits. Any number greater than 999,999,999,999 or smaller than .000000000001 *must* be displayed in scientific notation, since its magnitude exceeds the ability of the display to show it as an explicit, one-part number.

But now, with SCI mode, you are *forcing* the display to use scientific notation for *every* number, regardless whether that number could otherwise be correctly represented in the display.

Finally—before going on—press **STD**. This is STandarD display format, where all significant digits are displayed and where scientific notation is used only when the number's value is outside of the display's magnitude limits.

Postfix Notation

"...Scientific notation, real-number representation limits, display formatting...when am I going to start *doing* things—like arithmetic—with real numbers?"

Right now:

Remember that what you're seeing in the display is quite literally a Stack of objects. Everything you've created so far has been "stacked up" on this "workbench."

Remember, too, that you put the latest additions on the *bottom* here; that's "upside-down" from your notion of a stack of lumber or pancakes. But it *is* a stack, nevertheless—because it's a *last-in-first-out* type of arrangement: the *last* thing you put onto the Stack is the *first* thing you take off.

With that in mind, here's the one simple rule to know as you begin working with the 48's Stack:

Whenever you use some *tool* to work on an *object*—say, to change the sign of a real number, for example—*the tool assumes that the object is already on the bench-top (i.e. on the Stack) when you start to use the tool.*

This means that you must first put onto the Stack any number(s) that you want to manipulate and *then* perform the operation. This way of doing things is called "postfix" (from *post-affix:* literally, "to add after") because the operation itself comes *after* the operands.

Real Number Tools

Try this *postfix* pattern of operation with some real-number tools.

Do It: Press [7][ENTER]. Now press [1/x].... What happens? The 7 is replaced by .142857142857, which is $1/7$ (rounded to 12 digits). The [1/x] tool inverts the number in Stack Level 1.

Press [1/x] again. You get 7.00000000001 That's $\frac{1}{1/7}$.

Try another: Press [4][•][3][√x]....You get 2.07364413533—the square root of the 4.3 that was at Level 1. *But how did that 4.3 get to Level 1?* You never pressed [ENTER] to send it there from the Command Line—you just pressed [√x]!

Answer: When you're working in the Command Line, most tools automatically put the contents of that Command Line onto the Stack (i.e. "press [ENTER]" for you) before they start working—just to save you a step.

Notice: The *inverse* of a tool is often located on the same key as the tools itself. For example, press [⬅][X²] now.... You will get 4.29999999999, which is $(\sqrt{4.3})^2$ to 12 digits.

But there are far more tools than keys, so—as usual—when you want more tools, look in a toolbox....

Like So: Press [MTH] to open the MaTH toolbox. From the menu that appears, you can see that this toolbox has six "drawers" in it. You can tell that they're drawers and not tools because they each have a "folder tab" on their top, left-hand corner.

Select the **PARTS** drawer.... You now see six tools in this PARTS menu, but remember that there may be more than these six tools in this drawer—and you can see more by pressing [NXT] or [⬅][PREV].

So "rummage" around in this toolbox now, until you find the **IP** (Integer Portion) tool. Try it—press **IP**....

The result is 4—the Integer Portion of the 4.29999999999 that was at Level 1 of the Stack.

Again, the point is, whether you use tools from the keyboard or from some toolbox, they all make the same *postfix* assumption: the object to be "worked on" is *already on the Stack.*

Two-Number Tools

The tools you've seen so far have worked on one object on the Stack—at Level 1—the closest object to you. But many tools are designed to combine *two* objects to form another—as in "plain old arithmetic...."

Do Some: Add two real numbers on the Stack: Press [1][ENTER][2][+]. The result is no big surprise, right?

Try [3][ENTER][4][×]. Also no surprise.

Now, addition and multiplication are *commutative* operations (that is, $1+2=2+1$ and $3\times4=4\times3$). But that's not true for subtraction and division—so which number do you put onto the Stack first?

Just put the two numbers onto the bench-top in the order that you would say them. Thus $8-2$ would be [8][ENTER][2][−]; and $6\div4$ is [6][ENTER][4][÷]. Try those....

Notice also that several of the keyboard tools use *x* and *y* in their names. This is to help you remember where in the Stack the operand(s) should be to correctly use these tools:

The number at Level 1 is *x*; the number at Level 2 is *y*.

So, [5][ENTER][3][y^x] calculates 5^3; and [8][1][ENTER][4][→][$\sqrt[x]{y}$] finds $\sqrt[4]{81}$.

There are other one- and two-number math tools in the MTH PARTS, MTH PROB, and MTH HYP toolboxes. Check them out if you want.

Stack Manipulations

So that's the basic idea: You put objects on your 48's postfix Stack workbench and then use tools on them.

Of course, you've seen this only with real numbers so far—and there are plenty of other objects and tools to learn. But first you ought to know how to organize, arrange and rearrange your workbench—the Stack. As you might expect, there are tools to help you do this....

The first and most basic of these is [→][CLR] (CLeaR). As its name implies, it clears the Stack, throwing away every object on it.

Do It Now: [→][CLR]

Another commonly used command is [←][DROP]. It throws away the object on Level 1 object from the Stack and drops all remaining objects down one Level.

Try This: Press [1][ENTER][2][ENTER][3][ENTER] [←][DROP][←][DROP][←][DROP].

Or This: [1][ENTER][2][ENTER][3][ENTER][◆][◆][◆].

As long as the Command Line is *not* active, [◆] is DROP (but of course, if you *are* typing in the Command Line, then [◆] is backspace).

Now, what if you want to duplicate the object at Level 1? (You'll want to do this a lot, as you'll soon see.)

Guess what? [ENTER] serves that purpose. Remember that when the Command Line is active, [ENTER] places its contents on the Stack. But when the Command Line is *not* active, [ENTER] makes a copy of the level 1 object and pushes it onto the Stack.

Example: Press [6] [ENTER] [ENTER] [ENTER]....

The first [ENTER] puts the 6 on the Stack at Level 1. The second [ENTER] copies this 6, pushing the original up a Level; you now have two 6's. The third [ENTER] again copies the bottom 6 and pushes the fresh copy onto Level 1, again pushing the existing objects up a Level; you now have three 6's. Press [↱] [CLR] now to throw them all away.

The last of the common bench-top organizers is [↰] [SWAP]. It simply swaps Stack Levels 1 and 2, which is useful when working with order-sensitive tools such as subtraction and division. Similar to [↰] [DROP], when the Command Line is not active, you needn't press [↰] to use [SWAP].

Try It: Press [1] [ENTER] [2] [ENTER] [3] [ENTER] [↰] [SWAP] (or just [SWAP]—that's the [▶] key). See? The 2 and 3 are swapped. Play around with this, and then press [↱] [CLR] to go on....

The Interactive Stack

The workbench can become pretty crowded with projects and raw materials in various stages of completion. Organizing, throwing away or bringing down selected items can be a real chore. But—how'd you guess?—there's a tool to help you.

Watch: First, put some "stuff" on the bench-top to play with. Press:
[↱][CLR][1][ENTER][2][ENTER][3][ENTER][4][ENTER][5][ENTER][6][ENTER]
[7][ENTER][8][ENTER][9][ENTER][1][0][ENTER]

Now, press [▲] and see this:

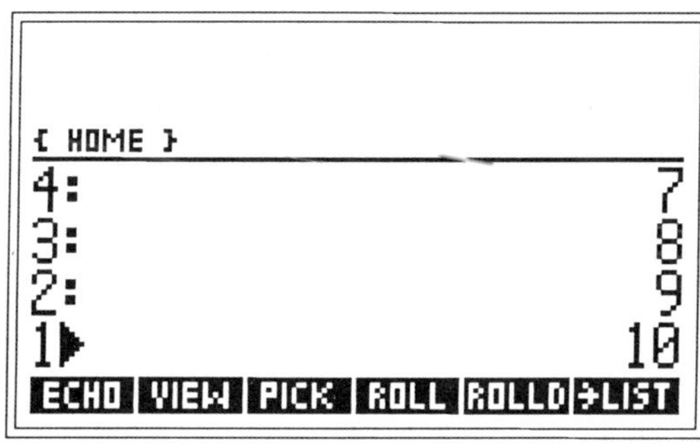

This is the *Interactive Stack*. It is designed to give you a quick and easy way to look at, edit and use an object at *any* Level in the Stack.

Remember the **↑STK** tool in the EDIT toolbox (page 38)? Well, the Interactive Stack's arrow keys work in the same way: [▲] and [▼] move the pointer up and down the Stack. And [↱][▲] and [↱][▼] jump all the way to the extreme top and bottom of the Stack, respectively.

Do This: Move to Level 1 now if you're not there (i.e., press [→][▼]).

ECHO should look familiar, too. It works like EDIT's **ECHO** except that it *opens* the Command Line (because there isn't one already) and echoes into it the object at the pointer Level. Try it—press **ECHO**....

Nothing *seems* to happen, except for the changed menu, but the Command Line *is* open—with 10 in it. But before showing it to you, the machine is giving you a chance to move around the Stack and echo other Levels, too.

Press [▲][▲] **ECHO** [ENTER]. *Now* the Command Line appears—and it contains the 10 *and* the 8 that you've echoed from the Stack. And if you were to press [ENTER] now, those numbers would go onto the Stack—just as they would if you had *typed* this Command Line instead. But press [ATTN] to discard them. And notice that you've left the Interactive Stack; press [▲] to reactivate it.

Notice also the next item in the Interactive Stack menu: **VIEW**. It works just like [←][EDIT] except that it edits the *object being pointed-to*—creating a working copy on the Command Line so that [ENTER] and [ATTN] can either accept or reject the changes you made.

Again, the idea of the Interactive Stack is to let you move around the Stack and work with any object as you normally do with the bottom-most object.

Continue across the Interactive Stack's menu items:

PICK makes a copy of the pointed-to object and pushes this copy onto the Stack at Level 1, moving everything else up a Level.

Try It Now: Make copies of Levels 3 and 11. Press: [↱][▼][▲][▲] **PICK** [↱][▲] **PICK** [↱][▼] and see:

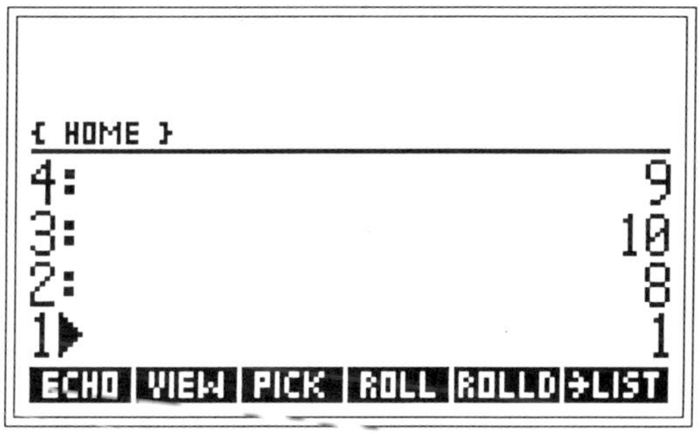

Then Notice: **ROLL** and **ROLLD** "roll" the contents of the Stack between Level 1 and the pointer's Level. **ROLL** rolls up; **ROLLD** rolls down.

Move the pointer to Level 4 ([▲][▲][▲]) and press **ROLL** several times to see the effect. Each time, the four numbers are "rolled up," with the Level-4 number coming down to replace the Level-1 number.

And **ROLLD** rolls the other direction. So roll Levels 1 through 4 around until you've had enough, then put them back in their original order: `9 10 8 1`.

Now turn to the next page of the Interactive Stack menu (press NXT) to see more tools.... These tools use the Level number of the pointer as a kind of counter—telling the machine how many Levels to *duplicate*, *drop* or *keep*.

Examples: Move the pointer to Level 2 and press **DUPN**. You see:

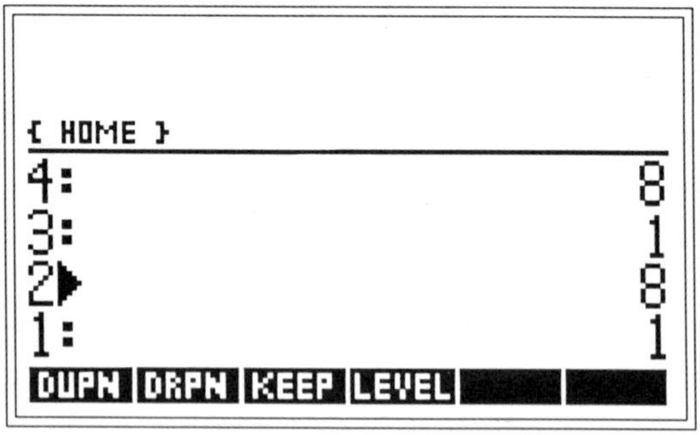

You now have two copies of the contents of Levels 1 and 2. The duplicate set was pushed onto the bottom of the Stack—bumping the originals up to Levels 3 and 4.

DRPN drops (discards) the pointed-to level *and everything below it.* Press **DRPN** now to drop levels 1 and 2. Conversely, **KEEP** *keeps* the pointed-to Level and everything below it—but discards everything above it. Press **KEEP** now....See? Only Levels 1 and 2 remain.

LEVEL simply pushes the *Level number* of the pointer onto the Stack. Press **LEVEL** now, while pointing to Level 2, and watch as the 48 pushes a 2 onto the Stack.

Finally, there's one other Interactive Stack tool that's not in the toolbox (the menu)—because it's on the keyboard: [◆]

As you may remember from page 52, when there's no Command Line, [◆] acts as a DROP (identical to [↰][DROP]), dropping (discarding) the Level-1 object.

Well, in the Interactive Stack, [◆] drops the *pointed-to* object....

Prove It: Press [◆] to drop the 1 at Level 2. Press [◆] again to drop the 8.

Press [◆] once more to drop the 2. Notice how the pointer won't ever go any higher than the highest filled Level of the Stack.

Notice also that dropping the last object on the Stack terminates Interactive Stack—you're back to the menu you were looking at before that—probably somewhere in the MaTH menu.

You can see that the 48 is designed to be as convenient as possible: Maybe you went into the Interactive Stack to do some vast (or half-vast) Stack manipulations, object building, copying—who knows? But the *reason* for it all might be that you need to use something in this MaTH menu on the resulting object(s). So the 48 remembers which menu you were in and treats the Interactive Stack excursion as just a temporary "side-trip"—a "time-out" for preparations.

Learning By Doing

By now, you're surely reeling with all the tools at your disposal—just to "mess around" in the Stack. Look how much you've seen:

- You know how to type on the Command Line, and how to use the [α] key (one [α] per character or [α][α] to "lock" it on);
- You know how to use lowercase letters, NEWLINE and other special characters;
- You know how to edit the Command Line with, [DEL], [←] and the EDIT toolbox, which (among other things) lets you choose between the insert (◆) and the overwrite (█) cursors and ECHO objects from the Stack into the Command Line
- You know various and sundry other things, too.

Of course, there's no way you're going to memorize all the various Stack and Command Line manipulation tools just through brief introductions like these—so don't panic if a lot of this has blurred together by now.

But *now is the time* to drive it home to yourself: The best way to become familiar with the tools and concepts presented in this chapter is to *use* them. So there's a quiz on the following pages—mainly real-number math and Stack problems. You may not be able to work every problem correctly the first time. If you get stuck, look at the answer! See how it's done. Then work the problem again until you understand the solution. After you've done all these problems, think up some of your own. Play with the Stack—get used to it. Master it.

Workbench Quiz

1. Find $1+2+3+4$

Find $1+2+3\times4$ Then find $(1+2+3)\times4$

Find $1+2\div3$ Then find $(1+2)\div3$

2. Find $\dfrac{1}{2+3}$

3. Find $\dfrac{2\ln(7)}{45}$

4. Find $\dfrac{-12+\sqrt{12^2-4(3)(-5)}}{2(3)}$

5. Find $173e^{\left[\frac{-16+43(.004)}{32-16.3}\right]}$

6. Find $1+.5+\dfrac{.5^2}{2!}+\dfrac{.5^3}{3!}+\dfrac{.5^4}{4!}$

7. Find both answers: $\dfrac{16\pm\sqrt{(-16)^2-4(20)(-48)}}{2(20)}$

8. Find $\sin 45°$, $\cos 134\text{grad}$, and $\arcsin 0.5$, in radians.

9. For $\theta = 75°$, show that: $\sin 3\theta = 2\sin\theta\cos^2\theta + (1 - 2\sin^2\theta)\sin\theta$

10. What are the differences in rounding error for $\sin\pi$ radians if you round π to 4 decimal places? 11 places? What if you *truncate* at 4 decimal places? 11 places?

11. With 26 refrigerator magnets, one of each letter in the alphabet, how many different six-letter "words" can you make? What if no two "words" may use the same six magnets?

12. By what percentage must you decrease $\frac{\sqrt{5}+1}{2}$ to get $\frac{\sqrt{5}-1}{2}$?

13. Put the numbers 12, 34, 56, 78, and 90 onto the Stack. Now reverse their order (without typing them in again).

14. Without typing any digits, form the least possible positive integer from the digits of the five numbers in the previous problem.

Workbench Solutions*

1. [1][ENTER][2][+][3][+][4][+] Answer: 10

[1][ENTER][2][+][3][ENTER][4][×][+] Answer: 15

[1][ENTER][2][+][3][+][4][×] Answer: 24

[1][ENTER][2][ENTER][3][÷][+] Answer: 1.66666666667

[1][ENTER][2][+][3][÷] Answer: 1

Remember: In the absence of parentheses, do multiplication before addition. When construing a written arithmetic problem to solve on the Stack, work from the highest operator priority to the lowest—and from the innermost parentheses outward.

2. [2][ENTER][3][+][1/x] Answer: .2

3. [7][→][LN][2][×][4][5][÷] Answer: 8.64848955138E-2

4. [1][2][←][x²][4][ENTER][3][×][5][+/−][×][−][√x][1][2][+/−][+]
[2][ENTER][3][×][÷] Answer: .38047614285

5. [4][3][ENTER][•][0][0][4][×][1][6][+/−][+][3][2][ENTER][1][6][•][3][−][÷]
[←][e^x][1][7][3][×] Answer: 63.1263787068

*Keep in mind that there are many ways to solve arithmetic problems on the Stack. The solutions shown here are among the most straightforward and easiest to understand. But there are certainly other solutions—some of which use fewer keystrokes—so use whatever methods make sense to you. Unless otherwise noted, the answers assume STD display notation.

6. [1][ENTER][•][5][+][•][5][←][x²][2][MTH] **PROB** **!** [÷][+]
[•][5][ENTER][3][yˣ][3] **!** [÷][+]
[•][5][ENTER][4][yˣ][4] **!** [÷][+] Answer: 1.6484375

As you can see, the PROB toolbox in your MTH menu has the factorial function, to help you "crunch" this Taylor expansion by brute force; later you'll see another function to make this easier.

7. [1][6][ENTER][2][ENTER][2][0][×][÷]
[1][6][+/-][←][x²][4][ENTER][2][0][×][4][8][+/-][×][−][√x][2][ENTER][2][0][×][÷]
[▲][▲][NXT] **DUPN** [ATTN] [+] Answer: 2
[◆][−] Answer: -1.2

Keep in mind your Interactive Stack.

8. [←][MODES][NXT][NXT] **DEG** (if necessary) [4][5][SIN]
Answer: .707106781187
GRAD [1][3][4][COS] Answer: -.50904141575
RAD [•][5][←][ASIN] Answer: .523598775598

You've seen the MODES menu before. Here you use it to set the *angle mode*—degrees, radians or grads.

9. [←][MODES][NXT][NXT] **DEG** [7][5][ENTER][3][×][SIN][7][5][SIN][ENTER][ENTER]
[←][x²][2][×][1][−][+/-][×][▶][2][×][7][5][COS][←][x²][×][+]
Answers: -.707106781187 and -.707106781181

That's close enough, allowing for rounding error (see prob. **10**).

10. π is 3.14159265358979323846.... But no machine represents it (or any irrational value) exactly; any numerical computation *must* approximate. As for all values, the 48 uses a 12-digit representation of π (11 decimal places), then *rounds* for best accuracy:

3.1415926535<u>8979323846...</u> ----> 3.14159265359

To *truncate* would decrease the accuracy:
3.14159265358|979323846... ----> 3.14159265358

The same argument is true at the fourth decimal place:
3.141<u>59265358979323846...</u> ----> 3.1416
3.1415|9265358979323846... ----> 3.1415

The sine function is sensitive* to such approximations of π: Since $\sin \pi \equiv 0$, any approximation greater than π gives a *negative* sine; any "under-approximation" gives a *positive* sine:

⬑MODES NXT NXT **RAD** 3 • 1 4 1 5 9 2 6 5 3 5 9 ENTER
ENTER ENTER ENTER SIN — Answer: -2.06761537357E-13
⬅ EEX +/- 1 1 − SIN — Answer: 9.79323846264E-12
⬅ MTH **PARTS** ⬑PREV 4 **RND** SIN
Answer: -7.3464102067E-6
⬅ 4 **TRNC** SIN — Answer: 9.26535896607E-5

The RND and TRNC functions round or truncate to the number of decimal places you specify (4 here). A *negative* specifier requests that many *significant digits* (rather than decimal places).

*This isn't true for all angles. For example, sin 1.5707963268 (sin "π/2") is 1.00000000000—to 11 decimal places—but only because the rounding happens to works out, not because the 48 treats π somehow specially in its numeric calculations. It *never uses* π itself and can never give answers other than those produced by the digits it does use. This is true for any irrational number: Take $\sqrt{2}$ on the 48 and then square the 12-digit answer. You do *not* (and *should* not) get 2.00000000000 (do the arithmetic by hand, to prove this, if you wish: 1.41421356237 × 1.41421356237). Any calculator that gives you 2.00000000000 for that answer (or 0.00000000000 for sin 3.14159265359) is doing "funny math"—and you should feel free to be outraged.

11. This is a probability problem—so go to the PROB tool box: [MTH] **PROB**. The question is, how many *permutations* (the order matters) can you make of 26 objects, taking 6 at a time?
[2][6][ENTER][6] **PERM** <u>Answer</u>: 165765600

If the order doesn't matter, then it's *combinations* of 26, taking 6 at a time: [2][6][ENTER][6] **COMB** <u>Answer</u>: 230230

12. [5][√x][1][+][2][÷] (<u>Result</u>: 1.61803398875)
[5][√x][1][−][2][÷] (<u>Result</u>: .61803398875)
Now, the percentage calculations are kept in the PARTS toolbox, so [MTH] **PARTS** [NXT] **%CH** <u>Answer</u>: -61.803398875

That's a 61.80...% decrease (it's a *negative* change).

13. Press [1][2][ENTER][3][4][ENTER][5][6][ENTER][7][8][ENTER][9][0][ENTER]. Of course, there are many solutions to the reversal problem. here's one with the Interactive Stack: [▲][▲] **ROLL** [▲] **ROLL** [▲] **ROLL** [▲] **ROLL** [ENTER].

14. The key here is to use the Interactive Stack to ECHO items from the Stack onto your Command Line: [▲] **ECHO** [▲] **ECHO** [▲] **ECHO** [▲] **ECHO** [▲] **ECHO** [ENTER]. That sends you to the Command Line, where all you need to do is delete the space delimiters*: [←] **EDIT** [←] **←SKIP** [←] **←SKIP** [←] **←SKIP** [←] **←SKIP** [←] [ENTER].

*Technically, the smallest positive integer possible is 0123456789, which, when [ENTER]'ed, would be 123456789, so you could argue that it's "legal" to delete the 0 character here too. ("OK, *fine*.")

3 Objects: Your Raw Materials

The Fundamental Idea

This chapter is an introduction to the basic raw materials—"objects"—in your 48 workshop. You may not use all of these objects, but read this chapter completely, anyway—so that at least you'll know what options you have for solving problems. Many solutions on the 48 use more than one type of object, so take the time now to understand the basics of each type—even if you don't see what good it is right away.

Besides, this will give you a better understanding of the 48's way of doing things—its Fundamental Idea: *You can generalize the problem-solving process.* Once you know the keystrokes and strategies for problem-solving with one type of object, you can use other objects similarly—without learning entire new sets of commands and rules.

Real Numbers

You've already seen real numbers in action on the 48—to show you how postfix arithmetic works on the Stack. The only point to reiterate here is this:

Just as you combine real numbers on the Stack via real-number math functions, so you combine other objects via math functions, often using the same function keys (e.g. [+] [−] [×] [÷]*, etc.).*

So now it's time to look at how these other object types work. Of course, to use them, you must know how to build and recognize them, too....

Units

In a sense, real numbers aren't so real. When you add 1 to 2, what does that mean? 1 *what?* 2 *whats?* 3 *whats?*

In the real *world,* you generally talk about real numbers as indicating quantities of *something.* When you drive 100 miles one day and 75 the next, you speak of distances; the basic unit of measure is the mile. When you fill your gasoline tank by adding 7.4 gallons to your 15 gallon tank, you're talking about volume, with a basic unit of a gallon.

The point is, you wouldn't need to specify such units if everybody measured things the same way; if that were the case, you *could* simply use real numbers. But it's not. You can add 1 foot to 1 yard and get 4 feet or 1.3333 yards. And just how many teaspoons of liquid are there in a liter? And how many square feet in an acre? Sometimes, doing the unit conversions and checking your units for consistency are the most difficult parts of doing a calculation.

How does the 48 represent them?

The 48 allows you to *associate* units with real numbers—much as you do now. When you associate values and units on paper, you write the unit after the value: 14 ft 26.3 in 142 acre

The 48 does it very similarly, simply using an underscore (_) to link the real number with its unit:

```
14_ft        26.3_in        142_acre
```

How do you build a unit object?

The easiest way to create a unit object is to use the UNITS toolbox....

Do This: Press [→][CLR], then open the UNITS toolbox to explore it.

Like So: Press [←][UNITS].... Notice that each of the resulting menu items is a drawer with an "tab"—telling you that each leads to yet another menu—a sub-menu with more selections (use [NXT] to see all 16 submenus available): LENGth, AREA, VOLume, TIME, SPEED, MASS, FORCE, ENeRGy, POWeR, PRESSure, TEMPerature, ELECtricity ANGle, LIGHT, RADiation and VISCosity.

On the first page of the menu, select the LENGth sub-menu: LENG. Looking through this menu, you'll find 22 different units of length.

To build a unit object, simply key in the real number value and press the corresponding unit key. For example, to build the unit object 14_ft, press [1][4] FT (do this now)....* By pressing the FT key, you created a single unit, 1_ft, and then *multiplied* this by the real number, 14, to form the unit object, 14_ft.

That's true in general: Pressing any unit key forms a value of 1 of that unit, then *multiplies* that by the object already at Level 1 of the Stack.

---

*The menu keys show all letters in upper case, but the unit name itself often uses lower case.

How do you use a unit object?

The beauty of unit objects is that *you use them just as you would real numbers—and the 48 will keep track of the units automatically.*

Example: Calculate how many feet of 10-inch-wide lumber planks you'll need to build a 7-level (backless) shelf unit that is 2 meters tall, 1 yard wide and 10 inches deep.

Solution: You need seven 1-yard pieces and two 2-meter pieces, each 10 inches wide. So press: ⮫CLR 1 YD 7 × 2 M 2 × + ⮪ FT. Answer*: 34.12_ft

---

Things to notice:

- 1_yd x 7 = 7_yd. And 2 x 2_m = 4_m.
  Multiplying a unit object by a real number (scalar) gives you another unit object with the same units.

- 7_yd + 4_m = 10.40_m.
  Adding (or subtracting) two compatible unit objects gives you an object with units the same as that of the previous *Level-1* object.

- To convert a unit object to other compatible units, simply press ⮪ before pressing the desired unit's key. Any of the LENGth units are compatible with each other; any of the AREA units are compatible with one another, etc.

*Until further notice, all answers will assume a display mode of FIX 2 (so press ⮪MODES 2 FIX, then return to your UNITS LENGth menu with the handy shortcut key, ⮫LAST MENU).

Now: You've just calculated the length of 10-inch planking you'll need. How many square feet of lumber is this?

Easy: Simply multiply this length by 10 inches: [1][0] [IN] [×].
Result: 341.23_ft*in *Notice* that the units of a product ([×] or [÷]) is *not* forced into the units of either of the previous values. Instead it forms a *combination* of those previous units. This is different than with a sum ([+] or [−]).

So you now have a correct area—but in rather uninformative "mixed" units—ft*in. To convert it to something more meaningful, simply move to the AREA menu ([←][UNITS] [AREA]), and convert it to square feet: [←] [FT^2].
Answer: 28.44_ft^2

Notice that the 48 uses ^ to indicate raising to a power. That is, ft^2 represents ft^2.

Question: What happens if you ask the 48 to add *incompatible units?*

Try It: Move back to the LENGth menu (press [←][UNITS] [LENG]) and try to add 1_ft to the square feet from the above answer (press [1] [FT] [+]).... No go, right? The 48 says:

```
+ Error:
Inconsistent Units
```

The 48 saves you from these common—but deadly—unit errors.

Press [ATTN] to clear that error message, and practice some more....

Problem: It's roughly 700 km by road from Calgary to Saskatoon, and you've just filled up in Calgary with 50 liters of fuel. You know that your car gets about 35 miles per U.S. gallon in the kind of driving conditions you expect. Can you make it all the way to Saskatoon without refueling?

Solution: As with most problems, there are several ways to do this. One way is to convert your car's mpg rating into kilometers per liter: At the LENGth menu, press [NXT] [3] [5] [MI] [◄] [UNITS] [VOL] [NXT] [►] [GAL] (the [►] key is other variation available on each unit key: just as the unshifted [GAL] key *multiplies* `1_gal` by the Level-1 object, so [►] [GAL] *divides*).

There's your known mpg. Now build your desired units: 1 [►] [L], then [►] [LAST MENU] [0] [KM] [×]....

Why *zero* `km/l`? Because then you can convert your answer to `km/l` simply by *adding* this zero harmlessly to your `35_mi/gal` (recall what addition does with units)! Do it: [+] Result: `14.88_km/l`

This is your car's fuel usage rate in local units. Now, to see your car's probable range, just multiply your rate by your fuel supply: [◄] [UNITS] [VOL] [NXT] [5] [0] [L] [×].... Result: `744.00_km`

Yep—barring unforeseen problems—you should make it to Saskatoon.

That's one way to attack this kind of units conversion problem—using the 48's ability to convert between compatible units during addition. But there's a more direct way....

Recalculate: When you reached Saskatoon and refueled, your 50-liter tank took 48.4 liters, and your trip-meter odometer showed 712.8 km. What was your actual mileage (miles per gallon) for the trip?

Solution: First, find your fuel usage in km/l: [→][CLR] [←][UNITS] **LENG** [NXT] [7] [1] [2] [•] [8] **KM** [←][UNITS] **VOL** [NXT] [4] [8] [•] [4] **L** [÷].... Result: 14.73_km/l

Now build your desired units:
[1] [→] **GAL** [→][LAST MENU] **MI**.

Now here's the point where you can do things differently: Press [→][UNITS] (the *other* shift key).... This small menu has units *commands* on them—specific things you can do with unit objects.

That first item is the one you'll probably use the most: CONVert simply converts the object in Stack Level 2 to the *units* of the object in Level 1 (the *number* in Level 1 doesn't matter). Try it now—press **CONV**....
Result: 34.64_mi/gal

So just remember that you can convert between units either through addition/subtraction or with the CONVert command (you'll explore the other items on the [→][UNITS] menu later).

Lists

Before you go on to explore the other object types available to you in the 48, consider this: A unit object is an *ordered collection* of two simpler "things"—a real number and a unit, in that order. The new object arises from this specifically ordered collection of otherwise distinct parts. This is a general pattern within the 48: More sophisticated "things" are often created from *collections* of simpler "things."

So what makes a collection an object? Simply gathering together an ordered collection of "things" doesn't mean anything by itself. `14_ft` is an ordered collection of two "things"—but it means nothing *until* those numerals, underscore and letters are given *rules* governing their significance and use: "The numerals stand for a real number and may be mathematically treated as such; the underscore links the number with an associated (multiplied) unit."

The point is, only with such specific governing rules for manipulating and interpreting a collection does it become a distinct form—an *object*. Each object *type* is distinguished by a different set of these rules.

So what's a list?

A list is simply the object type with the most general—*least restrictive*—rules for manipulating and interpreting its collection of elements: It's just an ordered collection of objects of any type, listed together in a sequence. That's why it's called simply a *list*: there's no more specific mathematical or physical interpretation of it.

How does the 48 represent a list?

The telltale characteristic of a list is its enclosing set of `{ }`. Here are examples of lists:

```
{ 1 2 3 4 5 6 7 "Hi there" 14_feet }
{ "Yo, dude!" (3,4) { 1 2 } 98.6_F }
{ [ 1 2 ] (5,∠53.1) { } }
```

A list can contain any number of any type of object* in any mixture—including other lists—or even no objects at all.

*Some of the object types in these sample lists may be new to you yet. Don't sweat their details—just realize that they, too, may be elements of lists.

How do you build a list?

There are several ways to put a list onto your Stack workbench. Naturally, you can type it in directly from the Command Line....

Do This: Press [→][CLR][←][{ }][1][SPC][2][ENTER]....
You've just built the list `{ 1.00 2.00 }`

Easy, right? And did you notice the **PRG** sign in the Status Area while you were keying in the list? (Do the above exercise again, if you wish). This mode activates when you start the list, so that keystrokes that would normally execute immediately will instead just *record* their names as items in your list.

So use the [←][{ }] key to start a list. Then you can key in any objects—even executable commands—as elements in that list.

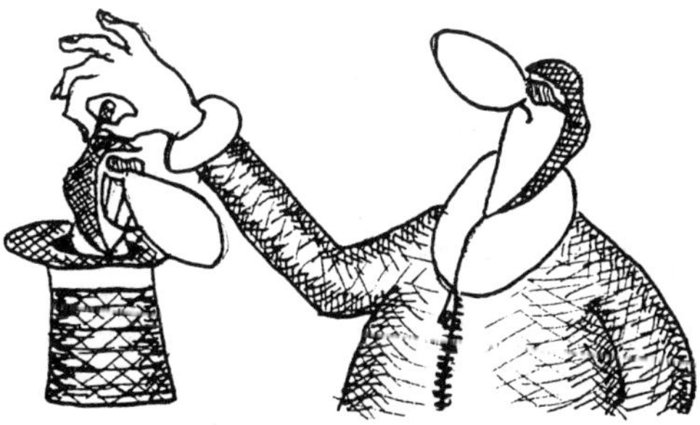

Now, what about making lists from objects already on the Stack?

To start with, consider this: What happens when you add different (but compatible) *unit objects* on the Stack? The result takes the units of the previous Level-1 object, right? All right, then what do you think might happen when you try to add different object *types* together?

Find Out: Key in the objects `5` and `14_feet` (press [→][CLR][5][ENTER] [←][UNITS] **LENG** [1][4] **FT**), and then add them together ([+])....No can do, right? Nor does the order matter: Try the above addition again, reversing the order of the two objects: [ATTN] (to clear the error message), then [1][4] **FT** [5][+]....nope. But you knew this from page 71, right?

Ah, but what if at least one of the objects is a *list*? Press [ATTN][←][{ }][5][ENTER].... Result: `{ 5.00 }`

Now, try adding another object type to it. Press [2][+]....

How about *that*? Make a copy ([ENTER]), and then try another object type: [1][4] **FT** [+]....

And what about adding *another list*? Press [+]....

Notice how the order matters: Try [1][ENTER][SWAP][+]....

Moral of the story: *You can add unlike object types if at least one of them is a list.* If the non-list object is in Level 2, it will be appended to the *front* of the list; if at Level 1, it goes onto the *end* of the list.

The other question: How do create a list out of existing Stack objects where *none* of them are necessarily lists?

Try This: (→)(CLR)(1)(ENTER)(2)(ENTER)(3)(ENTER)(PRG) **OBJ** (3) **→LIST**
Result: `{ 1.00 2.00 3.00 }`

You can put any number of Stack objects into a list simply by specifying that number and invoking **→LIST**.

Try another: (←)(UNITS) **LENG** (1)(4) **FT** (5)(ENTER) (←)({ })(ENTER)(PRG) **OBJ** (4) **→LIST** Result:
`{ { 1.00 2.00 3.00 } 14_ft 5.00 { } }`

Notice the order of list formation: First onto the Stack goes first into the list.

Notice also the list "length specifier"—the number that goes onto the Stack last, before you invoke **→LIST**. This is the *argument* of the **→LIST** command. With its postfix notation, the 48 assumes that all information necessary for the execution of any command is already on the Stack* when you invoke a command name; it won't stop and prompt you for anything more once you invoke the command.

You've already seen at least one argument in action: remember how you set the display to FIX 2 decimal places (page 70)? *First* you entered the 2—your argument—*then* you selected the command (**FIX**).

*or in the Command Line—remember that most executable commands come with a "built-in ENTER" that effectively put the current Command Line on the Stack before proceeding.

One other key point about arguments on the Stack: The 48 reads each argument *and then discards* (DROPs) *it before proceeding with a command.* It never includes the argument(s) as part of the Stack when actually carrying out the command's actions. This is why, for example, you got `{ 1.00 2.00 3.00 }` instead of `{ 2.00 3.00 3.00 }` in the first exercise on the opposite page: the bottommost `3.00` was the *argument* of →LIST and was therefore read and dropped before →LIST was actually performed.*

So that's how to *build* a list from objects on the Stack. Now, can you take it apart again?

No Sweat: Press OBJ→.... See what happens?

OBJ→ is the 48's General Purpose Object Decomposer. That is, it breaks down virtually any compound object into its list of components, stacking up these components in order in the Stack. And for objects such as lists—that don't necessarily have a fixed number of components OBJ→ also leaves the element count at Level 1—so that you can *re*-compose with a single command (→LIST, in this case—try it)!

---

*To practice more with arguments, you might want to play with some of the commands in the STK toolbox. This Course covered some of the basics of Stack manipulations in Chapter 2, mainly with the Interactive Stack. But if you stop and think about it for a moment, you'll realize that the pointer you moved around in the Interactive Stack is just a visual way of providing the 48 with an argument for those Stack commands that require it. When you're *not* in the interactive Stack, you can still use all those same Stack manipulation functions, but you must *key in* the necessary argument—just as you did here with →LIST. In fact, you'll notice that →LIST appears also on that STK menu, because forming lists out of objects on the Stack is something you'll do quite a bit.

Complex Numbers

Time to move on now, to learn about the next object type.

Mathematically, a *complex number* is a vector in the complex plane, an ordered pair of numbers representing the vector's coordinates. The coordinates are usually expressed in either rectangular form ($a+bi$) or in polar form ($Z\measuredangle\theta$).

How does the 48 represent a complex number?

On the 48, a complex number is also an ordered pair of (i.e. a *list* of two) real numbers, which are *vector coordinates* expressed in either rectangular form `(3.00, 4.00)` or polar form `(5.00, ∡53.13)`. The pair is surrounded by parentheses and separated by `,` and possibly `∡`. Of course, you can use this pair to represent anything you want, but it is indeed a mathematically complex number—to be added, multiplied, etc.

Try One: [→][CLR][←][()][3][SPC][4][ENTER]. Result: `(3.00, 4.00)` This is the complex number $3+4i$. Now press [ENTER][ENTER][ENTER] to make some copies, then [+].... Complex addition is as easy as real addition. Press [×].... Also easy, no? Now [DROP] that result (leaving the last `(3.00, 4.00)` at Stack Level 1).

Question: When does the 48 display a complex number in rectangular form, and when in polar form?

Answer: It depends on the current *vector display mode*. Go to the third page of the MODES menu (press ⬅ MODES NXT NXT) and find these three items XYZ ■, R∠Z and R∠∠ (the ■ means that XYZ mode is currently in effect): XYZ ■ displays complex numbers in *rectangular* mode; either R∠Z ■ or R∠∠ ■ displays them in polar mode.

Try changing the mode and watch the complex number at Level 1 change its format (notice the annunciators in the Status Area, too). But keep in mind that the number retains its same (rectangular) complex value (3+4*i*); only its display *formatting* is being altered—for your eyes. This is true in general: Once you've keyed in a complex number, the machine "remembers" it internally in rectangular form, but it presents the number to you according to the current mode settings.

Question: How does the 48 know when to represent a complex number's vector *angle* in degrees, radians or grads?

Answer: It judges by the current *angular mode*. You can switch this mode—and thus the *polar* formats of the number—by pressing RAD or GRAD (try these now, but leave things in DEG ■ and XYZ ■ modes when you finish).

How do you build a complex number?

You have several ways to put a complex number onto the work bench—and you've already seen the most rudimentary way to do it.

Again: Type it in directly from the Command Line: Press [⬑][()][1] [SPC][2][ENTER]. This gives `(1.00, 2.00)`, a complex number *in rectangular form.* (You could use either [↱][,] or [SPC]. Both act as *delimiters* to separate the two parts of the number.)

Now change the mode to polar form (press [↱][POLAR]—a handy keyboard modes toggle). Of course, you won't get `(1.00, ∡2.00)`, which is (1.00∠2.00°). Rather, you get the polar *representation* of 1+2*i*—about (2.24∠63.43°). Remember, you don't change the existing vector *value* by changing its *displayed format.*

To actually key in a complex number *value* in polar form, you must precede the second value with a ∡—because using a `,` or a [SPC] always means rectangular complex input to the 48. Try it: [⬑][()][1][↱][∡][2][ENTER]. *Now* the 48 will take the second value to be an angle—in the current angle mode. *This* is the value (1.00∠2.00°)—or about 1.00+.03*i*, as you can verify now by returning to rectangular mode ([↱][POLAR]).

So that's the basic idea when *keying in* complex-numbers—either in rectangular or polar format. But to build complex numbers from other values *already on the Stack,* the 48 has some tools to help you....

Example: Put the numbers 5 and 10 on the Stack (5 ENTER 1 0 ENTER). Now use these two real numbers to form the rectangular complex number (5.00, 10.00).

Like This: Press the PRG key, and then from the resulting menu, select the OBJ toolbox. This is a menu of operations you can perform on various object types. On the second page (press NXT), you'll find R→C ("Real to Complex"). Try it now.... As you see, R→C takes two real numbers from the Stack, using the Level-2 number as the real portion and Level 1 as the imaginary portion of the new complex number.

And the C→R ("Complex to Real") goes the other way—taking apart the complex number and leaving two real numbers on the Stack. Try it now: C→R

The 48 is full of tools like these—designed to build or take apart a given type of object. And remember that there's one very "smart" operation that can dismantle virtually *any* object into its components....

Watch: Press R→C to rebuild the (5.00, 10.00). Then ← PREV OBJ→. Same effect as C→R, right? So here's a reminder: OBJ→ is the *general-purpose object decomposition* tool.

But you can also extract the two parts of a complex number *mathematically*—with some specialized tools in the MaTH tool collection....

Challenge: Extract the two components of (3.00, 4.00)—both in rectangular and polar forms.

Solution: Key in the number ([←][()][3][SPC][4]) and make four copies of it ([ENTER][ENTER][ENTER][ENTER]). Then press the [MTH] key and select the **PARTS** toolbox. Here are some commands made to order "for all your extraction needs:"

RE extracts the REal portion: 3.00 ([DROP] that);

IM extracts the IMaginary portion: 4.00 ([DROP] it);

ABS extracts the ABSolute value of the complex number, which is simply the magnitude of its *polar* representation: 5.00 (now [DROP] that);

ARG extracts the angle (in the current angle mode) of the complex value in its polar form: 53.13

Complex Number Math

Complex numbers have mathematical properties similar to those of real numbers, so many of the 48's real-number operations also work for complex numbers. You've already seen complex arithmetic, but trigonometric and logarithmic functions work, too. And remember that you can use mixtures of complex and real numbers in complex math.

So practice some more now. As you do these, concentrate on your number entry format—and the 48's interpretation of it. Which *vector display mode* and which *angle display mode* is it using?

Challenge: Find $\frac{2}{3+i}$ and $\frac{3+i}{2}$ in rectangular format.

Solution: [2][ENTER][⬑][()][3][SPC][1][÷].... Result: (0.60,-0.20)
[1/x].... Result: (1.50,0.50)

The 48 converts the real number 2.00 into the complex number (2.00,0.00) before doing the division. Then just invert the first answer to get the second.

Another: Find $\ln(5\angle 1.618)$, in polar format.

Solution: Change the angle and vector modes: [⬑][RAD][⮣][POLAR].
Then: [⬑][()][5][⮣][∡][1][·][6][1][8][⮣][LN]....
Result: (2.28,∡0.79)

Another: Find $\sin\sqrt{7+10i}$ rad in rectangular format.

Solution: [⮣][POLAR] (back to rectangular mode), then [⬑][()][7][SPC][1][0]. Now take the square root ([√x]), then the sine ([SIN]).
Result: (0.11,-2.41)

Another: Find $\frac{\ln 2 + i\sqrt{2}}{\sin 45° \times (1 + i\sqrt{3})}$ in rectangular format.

Solution: [2][⮣][LN][2][+/-][√x][+]
[⬑][RAD][4][5][SIN][1][ENTER][3][+/-][√x][+][×][÷]....
Result: (1.11,0.08)

Vectors

A complex number is one special kind of vector. But in general, a vector is an ordered list of numbers—usually representing dimensions (directions) in some physical sense. The typical vectors you use most often are therefore two-and three-dimensional ("2D" and "3D") quantities:

2D

rectangular notation

$x\mathbf{i}+y\mathbf{j}$ or (x,y)

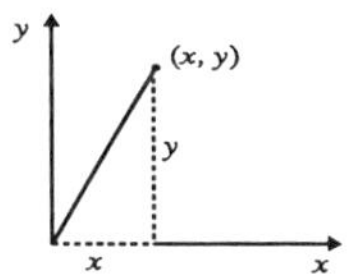

polar notation

(r,θ)

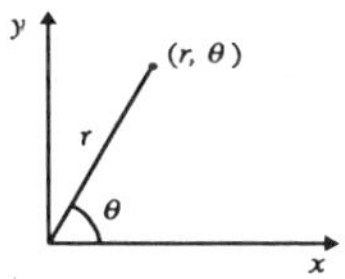

3D

rectangular notation

$x\mathbf{i}+y\mathbf{j}+z\mathbf{k}$ or (x,y,z)

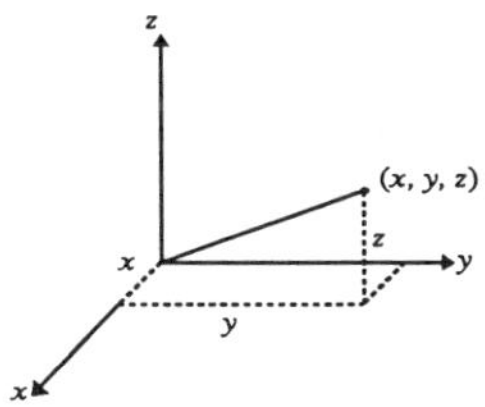

cylindrical notation

(r,θ,z)

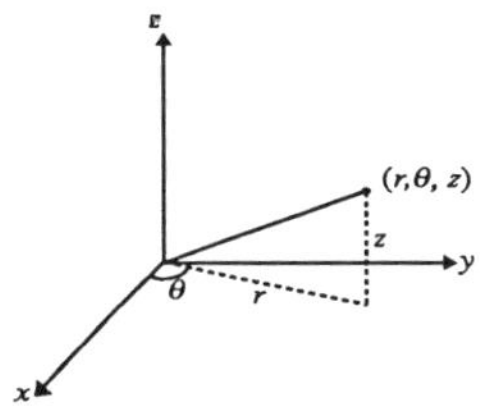

spherical notation

(ρ,θ,ϕ)

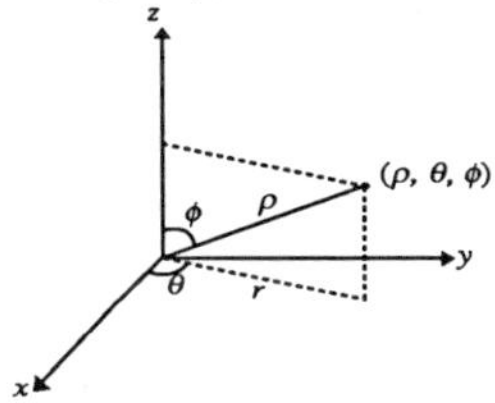

Vectors are more generally defined mathematically as *single-column matrices**—often encountered, for example, in linear systems:

$$\begin{bmatrix} a_{11} & a_{12} & a_{13} & a_{14} \\ a_{21} & a_{22} & a_{23} & a_{24} \\ a_{31} & a_{32} & a_{33} & a_{34} \\ a_{41} & a_{42} & a_{43} & a_{44} \end{bmatrix} \begin{bmatrix} x_1 \\ x_2 \\ x_3 \\ x_4 \end{bmatrix} = \begin{bmatrix} b_1 \\ b_2 \\ b_3 \\ b_4 \end{bmatrix}$$

In this capacity, of course, vectors are not limited to everyday physical interpretations; they may be *n*-dimensional ("*n*-**D**"). And their format is then only rectangular notation: *(a,b,c,d,e...)*

How does the 48 represent vectors?

Though you can use vector objects to represent anything you want, the 48 can also treat them as mathematical vectors. But since `( )` are used for complex numbers, vectors are bracketted within `[ ]`. *Notice* that a vector's elements may be real *or* complex—but not both:

2D	**3D**
`[ 1 2 ]`	`[ 1 -2 3 ]`
`[ 3 ∡-30 ]`	`[ 6 ∡45 -19 ]`
	`[ 93 ∡121 ∡23.5 ]`

n-**D**

```
[ (1,2) (-1,4) ]
[ (5,∡37) (13.5,∡-155.9) (0,∡0) ]
[ 2 34 19 -44 64 110 -25 37.5 9.09 ]
```

*The 48's display represents vectors *horizontally;* nevertheless, the machine uses them mathematically as *vertical* (single-*column*) matrices. Don't let the visual difference throw you.

How do you build a vector?

As usual, the most straightforward way to build a vector is to type it in directly from the Command Line. Try a few examples (these assume that your vector display and angle modes are as you left them in the last problem—rectangular and degrees, respectively):

Examples: Press [↱][CLR], then [↰][[ ]][1][SPC][2][SPC][3][SPC][4][ENTER].... Here's what you get: `[ 1.00 2.00 3.00 4.00 ]`

Press [↰][[ ]][1][↱][∡][2][ENTER]....You get:
`[ 1.00 0.03 ]`
Of course, to see this in the polar form you had intended, just press [↱][POLAR].... `[ 1.00 ∡2.00 ]`

Press [↰][[ ]][1][1][↱][∡][1][•][9][+/-][SPC][7][ENTER]....You get:
`[ 11.00 ∡-1.90 7.00 ]`
To see this in rectangular form, just press [↱][POLAR]....
`[ 10.99 -0.36 7.00 ]`

As you can see, the rules for separating components in vectors are the same as for complex numbers: You separate rectangular components with [SPC] (or **,**); you precede angular components with ∡. And keep in mind that the ∡ is meaningful only in the second and third components of **2D** and **3D** vectors. You won't be allowed to key it in anywhere else; and any vector larger than **3D** doesn't change from rectangular format when you change the vector display modes, anyway.

Speaking of vector display modes,...

Do This: Press [MTH] **VECTR**....Did you know that those mode keys were available here—as well as in the MODES menu? As you see, HP has put some often-used commands in several places so you needn't jump around as much to use them.

Something else to notice: At the moment, when you press [↱][POLAR] on the keyboard, it alternates (toggles) between rectangular and *cylindrical* (R∡Z) modes. But if you press **R∡∡**, then [↱][POLAR] will toggle between rectangular and *spherical* (R∡∡) modes...(try it—and then leave the mode at rectangular and the toggle to cylindrical).

Now This: Press [NXT] to move to the next page of the VECTR menu. Now put two values on the Stack, [1][2][ENTER][1][5][ENTER], and press **→V2** *to build a* ***2D*** *vector from these values.* Easy, no? And the "loading" order of the vector's components is like those of complex numbers and lists: The higher in the Stack, the farther forward in the object.

Try a **3D** case: [2][9][ENTER][4][5][ENTER][1][1] **→V3**. Voilá. And **→V2** and **→V3** are *sensitive to the vector display mode.* To see this, press [↱][POLAR] to change to polar/cylindrical mode, then repeat the above keystrokes.... See the difference? The resulting vectors took the corresponding values to be angular. This is how to key in angular components without using the [↱][∡] key.

What goes up must come down: How do you tear apart vectors?

Easy: Just press **V→**—try it.... Thus, with either **→V2** or **→V3** and **V→**, you can go back and forth between the vector itself and its Stack of individual components.

Not only that: *Notice* the ⬅2D and ➡3D keys on the keyboard (shifted versions of the key). Try them now.... See? They're *keyboard* versions of **→V2** / **V→** and **→V3** / **V→**, respectively—vector building/decomposing toggle keys!

Question: The commands in the VECTR menu are all good and fine for **2D** and **3D** vectors, but what about an *n*-**D** vector—of any arbitrary size? How do you build that?

Answer: Use an *argument*, just as for a list of arbitrary size. Go to the general *object-building* menu: PRG **OBJ**. Now key in your *n*-**D** vector's values: 1 ENTER 4 ENTER 9 ENTER 1 6 ENTER 2 5 ENTER. Now press 5 **→ARR**....
Result: [1.00 4.00 9.00 16.00 25.00]

Your vector-size argument (5.00 here) is just like the list-length argument you use to build a list—except that you use **→ARR**, instead of **→LIST**, to do the building.*

---

*There's no command called **→VEC**; you use **→ARR** because an *n*-**D** vector is actually a one-column *array* (matrix)—and the 48 treats it as such, mathematically. In fact, to break down an *n*-**D** vector into its components once again, you use **OBJ→** (the All-Purpose, Whole-wheat, Recyclable, Biodegradable, Universal Decomposer Tool), and it leaves the vector length argument as a *list* (the argument form used by arrays), rather than the *real number* argument you used to build the vector.

Vector Math

Now that you know how to build them and tear them apart, there's not much more to say about vectors in the 48 ex:ept "use them!"

Find: $|(3+4i,7+11i)|$

Press: (in rectangular mode—[→][POLAR], if necessary), then [←][[ ]] [←][( )][3][SPC][4][▶][←][( )][7][SPC][1][1][ENTER][MTH] PARTS ABS.

Result: `13.96` A vector may be complex-valued, but ABS finds its *magnitude* ("length")—always a real value.

Find: $10(-1,-2,-3)+\frac{(4,5,6)}{2}$

Press: [1][0][ENTER][1][ENTER][2][ENTER][3][→][3D][+/–][×][4][ENTER][5][ENTER] [6][→][3D][2][÷][+] Result: `[ -8.00 -17.50 -27.00 ]`

You can *add* vectors of the same dimensions; and you can *multiply* any vector by any scalar (including `-1`, via [+/–]).

Find: $(1,2)\cdot(3,4)$ and $(3,\angle 45°,10)\times(9,\angle 60°,2)$

Press: [1][ENTER][2][←][2D][3][ENTER][4][←][2D]

[MTH] VECTR DOT Result: `11.00`

The dot product of two same-dimension vectors is a scalar.

Then: [→][POLAR][3][ENTER][4][5][ENTER][1][0][→][3D][9][ENTER][6][0] [ENTER][2][→][3D] CROSS

Result: `[ 84.22 ∠151.06 6.99 ]`

The cross product of two **3D** vectors is another **3D** vector. And notice how easy it is to key in these cylindrical formats.

Arrays

In the most general sense, arrays are simply tables of "things" (dots, sticks, numbers—anything), arranged in rectangular formations of rows and columns:

$$\begin{array}{cccc} \bullet & \bullet & \bullet & \bullet \\ \bullet & \bullet & \bullet & \bullet \\ \bullet & \bullet & \bullet & \bullet \\ \bullet & \bullet & \bullet & \bullet \end{array} \qquad \begin{array}{cc} \nabla & \nabla \\ \nabla & \nabla \\ \nabla & \nabla \end{array} \qquad \begin{array}{cc} a_{11} & a_{12} \\ a_{21} & a_{22} \end{array}$$

$$\begin{array}{ccccc} \perp & \perp & \perp & \perp & \perp \\ \perp & \perp & \perp & \perp & \perp \\ \perp & \perp & \perp & \perp & \perp \\ \perp & \perp & \perp & \perp & \perp \end{array} \qquad \begin{array}{ccc} \propto & \propto & \propto \end{array} \qquad \begin{array}{ccc} a_{11}+b_{11}i & a_{12}+b_{12}i & a_{13}+b_{13}i \\ a_{21}+b_{21}i & a_{22}+b_{22}i & a_{23}+b_{23}i \\ a_{31}+b_{31}i & a_{32}+b_{32}i & a_{33}+b_{33}i \end{array}$$

When you arrange *numbers* (either real or complex) in this way, you can, of course, use them for anything you wish, but one of the most common uses is as a *matrix*—an array with mathematical rules and properties:

$$\begin{bmatrix} a_{11} & a_{12} & a_{13} & a_{14} \\ a_{21} & a_{22} & a_{23} & a_{24} \\ a_{31} & a_{32} & a_{33} & a_{34} \\ a_{41} & a_{42} & a_{43} & a_{44} \end{bmatrix} \begin{bmatrix} x_1 \\ x_2 \\ x_3 \\ x_4 \end{bmatrix} = \begin{bmatrix} b_1 \\ b_2 \\ b_3 \\ b_4 \end{bmatrix}$$

Notice the numbering convention used in arrays: $element_{ij}$ is the element in the ith row, at the jth column. An $n \times m$ array is an array with n rows and m columns.

How does the 48 represent arrays?

The 48 can represent real-valued and complex-valued arrays—and do many matrix operations on them. But because it also does non-matrix operations, the object type is called by its more general name—*array.*

The 48 uses double brackets to delimit the array itself—and single brackets to delimit each row within the array:

```
[[ 1 1 ]]
```

1×2 real-valued array

```
[[ 1 2 3 ]
 [ 4 5 6 ]
 [ 7 8 9 ]]
```

3×3 real-valued array

```
[[ (1,2) (-13.5,24.1) (4,-3.2) ]]
```

1×3 complex-valued array

```
[[ -32.4 ]
 [ 15.6 ]
 [ 1.015 ]
 [ -19.623 ]]
```

4×1 real-valued array

```
[ -32.4 15.6 1.015 -19.623 ]
```

4-element vector

Notice that these last two examples are actually different object *types* (the array, with its `[[  ]]` notation on the left; the vector, with its simpler `[  ]` on the right). But mathematically, they are treated the same by the 48 in many of its array/matrix operations. That is, a vector is actually a *1-column array,* displayed on its side for ease of viewing.

How do you build an array?

As usual, start with the basics—keying in the object at the Command Line. You key in arrays by *row*—a sequence called *row-major* order. Practice by keying in the examples on the previous page....

Go: Clear your Stack and go to STD mode, then: [←][[ ]][←][[ ]][1][SPC][1][ENTER]. There's your **1×2** real-valued array.

Next: [←][[ ]][←][[ ]][1][SPC][2][SPC][3][▶][4][SPC][5][SPC][6][SPC][7][SPC][8][SPC][9][ENTER]. There's your **3×3** real-valued array.

Notice how you use [▶] to skip over the closing bracket at the end of the first row in the array. And that's the only time you need to key in the inner brackets—around the first row. After that, as long as you enter the elements in row-major order, the 48 can arrange the remaining elements correctly—because it knows that all rows must have the same number of elements.

Continue: Go to rectangular mode ([→][POLAR]), if necessary, then [←][[ ]][←][[ ]][←][( )][1][SPC][2][▶][←][( )][1][3][•][5][+/-][SPC][2][4][•][1][▶][←][( )][4][SPC][3][•][2][+/-][ENTER]. There's your **1×3** complex-valued array.

And: [←][[ ]][←][[ ]][3][2][•][4][▶][1][5][•][6][SPC][1][•][0][1][5][SPC][1][9][•][6][2][3][+/-][ENTER]. There's your **4×1** real-valued *array*;

Or: [←][[ ]][3][2][•][4][+/-][SPC][1][5][•][6][SPC][1][•][0][1][5][SPC][1][9][•][6][2][3][+/-][ENTER]. There's your 4-element real-valued *vector.*

The Next Step: Build these same arrays from elements that you put onto the Stack first....

OK: Press [→][CLR] to clean the slate, then: [1][ENTER][1][ENTER][←][{ }][1][SPC][2][ENTER][PRG] **OBJ** **→ARR**. There's your **1×2** real-valued array.

As you'll recall from your practice with building vectors, the **→ARR** command takes the argument from Stack Level 1 and uses this to build an array or vector of the proper dimensions. To build a vector—whose dimensions are always n×**1**—you use a real number argument (since only n needs to be specified). But to build an n×m array, you must specify both n and m in your argument—and you do this in a *list*.

Next: [1][SPC][2][SPC][3][SPC][4][SPC][5][SPC][6][SPC][7][SPC][8][SPC][9] [ENTER] (remember that you can line up several objects in the Command Line—separated by delimiting spaces like this—then [ENTER] them onto the Stack all at once). Now [←][{ }][3][SPC] [3][ENTER] **→ARR**. There's your **3×3** real-valued array.

Then: [←][( )][1][SPC][2][ENTER][←][( )][1][3][•][5][+/-][SPC][2][4][•][1] [ENTER][←][( )][4][SPC][3][•][2][+/-][ENTER][←][{ }][1][SPC][3][ENTER] **→ARR**. There's your **1×3** complex-valued array.

And: [3][2][•][4][+/-][SPC][1][5][•][6][SPC][1][•][0][1][5][SPC][1][9][•][6] [2][3][+/-][ENTER]. Then *either* [←][{ }][4][SPC][1][ENTER] **→ARR**—to build your **4×1** real-valued *array*; *or* [4] **→ARR** —to build your 4-element, real-valued *vector*. Try both. The *type* of argument (real or list) determines the type of object (vector or array).

No prizes for guessing what **OBJ→** does to arrays....

Try It: Press **OBJ→** and see that **4×1** array/vector decompose right before your eyes....Notice, however, that the machine always puts the argument onto the Stack as a *list*—even if it's decomposing a vector. But the fact that there's just a single dimension in the list tells the machine that this is meant to build a vector rather than an array. Try **→ARR** now and watch it reconstruct....

In this way you can toggle back and forth all day between **→ARR** and **OBJ→**. This is precisely the purpose of all of these object-building and decomposing functions: to let you quickly take an object apart, edit some or all of it, then rebuild the result with a minimum of hassle.

Feel free to (DROP) the **4×1** array off the Stack and observe **OBJ→** in action with some of the other arrays you still have hanging around up there....

The best thing about arrays is how easy it is to do matrix math....

To Wit: Let $A = \begin{bmatrix} 2 & 5 \\ 1 & 3 \end{bmatrix}$ and $C = \begin{bmatrix} 8 & 8 \\ 8 & 8 \end{bmatrix}$. If $2AB + C = \mathbf{0}$, find B.

What if $C = \begin{bmatrix} -2 & 0 \\ 0 & -2 \end{bmatrix}$?

Too Easy: Solving for B gives $B=(A^{-1})(-C/2)$. So first, press [→][CLR] [MTH] **MATR**. Here's where the matrix operations live. These and the arithmetic keys will do the job:

To build C, press [←][[ ]][←][[ ]][8][SPC][8][▶][8][SPC][8][ENTER] *or* [←][{ }][2][SPC][2][ENTER][8] **CON** (the quick way to build a matrix filled with a CONstant value). Next, [+/−] to negate C (i.e. all its elements), then divide it by 2 ([2][÷]). Now, the 48 knows that when you say $Y \div X$, what you really mean is $X^{-1}Y$. So *just divide by A*: [←][[ ]][←][[ ]][2][SPC][5] [▶][1][SPC][3][÷]   Result:

```
[[ 8 8 ]
 [ -4 -4 ]]
```

This is B.

Now, using C =

```
[[ -2 0 ]
 [ 0 -2 ]]
```

repeat the calculation.*

You should get B =

```
[[ 3 -5 ]
 [ -1 2 ]]
```

---

*And note that to build this value of C, you also have the **IDN** command, which creates a multiplicative *identity* matrix (a square matrix with 1's on the diagonal)—provided that you tell it the size of the matrix. So you *could* build C as follows: [2] **IDN** [2][+/−][×]

Flags

A flag is one of the simplest objects of all. It's just a single *bit*—a binary digit—that has just two possible values: 1 or 0. Using the 48's jargon, a flag is either *set* or *clear*. If you set a given flag, you turn that bit on (giving it a value of 1); if you clear it, you turn the bit off (giving it a value of 0).

How does the 48 represent flags?

Flags are indeed objects in the 48, but they're a little different than the other objects you've seen so far. First of all you don't *build* flags; they're already built. There are a fixed number of them—128—already identified by number and reserved in the machine (whereas, with other object types, you can build as many as you want).

Secondly, *some flags already have very specific meanings to the machine*—not so with the real numbers, vectors, lists you might use in your calculations. Those objects' values have no preconceived significance to the 48; the values may be meaningful to *you*, causing you to change *your* behavior (e.g. answer a tough test question, redesign a bridge, etc.)—but they don't cause the 48 to change *its* behavior (e.g. redefine the keyboard, change the display format, etc.). By contrast, fully half of the flags (numbered –1 to –64 and called *system flags*) are indeed dedicated to controlling parts of the 48 workshop itself—like operating lights on the wall that flip on/off as indicators of certain conditions (display modes, etc.). The other 64 flags (numbered 1 to 64 and called *user flags*) have no such prescribed meanings; they're left up to you to interpret—much like other object types.

The third big difference between flags and other objects is in their representation: they have none. That is, the 48 doesn't represent a flag "on the Stack." There's simply no delimiter (such as { } or [ ]) that means "this is a flag."

To "see" a flag, you must identify it by number and *inquire* as to its current value. The machine will then respond by putting either a 1 or 0 onto the Stack. But this response is just the machine's message to you—just a *real number* object—not the flag itself. You can change this response number however you want without affecting the flag; tearing up a sports page doesn't alter the outcome of the contests it reports.

Also, besides reporting the status of any flag you ask about, the 48 continually informs you of the states of certain flags—with annunciators in the Status Area. Several system flags are tied to the annunciators for angle mode and vector display mode. And, when set, *user* flags 1 through 5 display their numbers in the Status Area, too—just so you have a few flags of your own that you can monitor easily.

How do you control flags?

Of course, you can do more than just test flags (ask if they're set or clear); you can set or clear them yourself....

Watch: System flags –17 and –18 control the display's angle mode. When both these flags are *clear*, you're in degrees mode (as you should be now—press [←][RAD] if necessary). But if only flag –17 is set, this sets RADians mode. Press [→] (not [←]) [MODES] [NXT]. Here are your flag control functions.

As with all commands on the 48, you key in any necessary *argument* (in this case, that's the number of the flag) and then invoke the command. Thus, to use Set Flag (SF), you would press [1][7][+/–] **SF**.... See? The RAD annunciator appears in the Status Area.

Now test flag –17 (ask "is it set?"): [NXT][1][7][+/–] **FS?**.... The answer is 1 ("yes"). But ask a different question: "Is the flag *clear*?" [1][7][+/–] **FC?**.... And of course, this answer is 0 ("no")—it's not clear. Now return to degrees mode: [←][PREV] [1][7][+/–] **CF**.

You can set, clear and test *any* of the 128 flags. Try setting and clearing some user flags (if you're using just a few user flags, it's usually handiest to use the first five, because the Status Area informs you when these are set): [1] **SF** [2] **SF** [3] **SF** [4] **SF** [5] **SF**.... You get the idea (now clear those five flags—in any order you wish).

Flags aren't particularly useful from the keyboard. You'll use them most often within programs—to inquire of the current system states and to remember previous decisions and inputs—as you'll see later.

Here are some questions to consider, though:

Question: You know you can test or change the value of any single flag. Can you test or change the values of a *group* of flags?

Answer: Yes, you can test or adjust the values of all 128 flags or the 64 system flags—all at once (see p. 105).

Question: If you ask for the states of all 128 flags, what kind of response value could possibly represent this?

Answer: Since a flag is just a single bit, you'd need a value that contained multiple bits—a *binary integer*. That's the object type you're going to study next. The results of your multiple flag test (via a command called RCLF—"ReCalL Flags") will be such a binary integer. And the argument you give to simultaneously *alter* the values of a group of flags (via a command called STOF—"STOre Flags") will also be a binary integer.

Now, if you stop and think about it, you'll realize that RCLF and STOF lets you preserve *in a different object type*—a binary integer—exact "blueprints" of all the flag settings at *any* given time. So although you can have only 128 flag states at once, *there's no limit to the number of such "blueprints" you can save and later transplant as necessary.*

Binary Integers

All right—now for binary integers. A binary integer is an ordered collection of flags, or *bits*. And, like other object types, the binary integer object has its own set of rules for manipulating and interpreting this collection.

First of all, the reason it's called an integer is that its list of bits is most commonly used to *represent integer values*. The integer may vary length from 1 to 64 bits. For example, here's an 8-bit binary integer:

0 0 1 0 1 1 0 0

The integer value these bits form is commonly expressed in any of four convenient number *bases:*

00101100_2 (base 2 or *binary* format)

54_8 (base 8 or *octal* format)

44_{10} (base 10 or *decimal* format—which you know and love)

$2C_{16}$ (base 16 or *hexadecimal* format)

How does the 48 represent binary integers?

The 48 can express binary integer values in any of those four bases, but its display doesn't accommodate subscripts very well, so it represents a binary integer on the Stack beginning with a pound sign, # (to signal that it's a binary integer) and ending with either b, o, d or h—to indicate which *base* it's using to *format* the value:

101100b   # 54o   # 44d   # 2Ch

Do This: Build a binary integer with the above value (there's only one value represented there), and then view it in each of those four formats.

Like So: Press MTH, then BASE, and notice the first four items on that menu. *The base currently in use will be the interpretation the 48 puts on any value you key in with a #.* For example, press OCT, then ⮣ # 5 4 ENTER....

Nothing to it, right? And now you can view this value in any of the other three base formats also: Press BIN...; press HEX...; press DEC.... Simple.

These four format keys are in the MODES menu, too—on the last page of that menu.

All right, now how do you change the number of bits in a binary integer? As you read, you can have anywhere from 1 to 64 bits.

Simple: Change the current *word size*—the maximum number of bits allowed in the integer. For instance, to change the word size to 8, you would press [8] (there's the *argument* of the command), then **STWS** (there's the command). And you can check the current word size any time you want, too—with **RCWS** (try it now).... The 48 answers your question with the appropriate real number.

The largest value you can represent in 8 bits would be # 11111111b, which is # 255d. So, what if you try to key in a value larger than this, say, # 256d?

Press **DEC** [→][#][2][5][6][ENTER]....Hmm...You get: # 0d Why? Because # 256d is # 100000000b, which takes nine bits to represent. But you've told the 48—via the word size—that you want to use only the first (*rightmost*) eight bits (00000000), which form the value # 0d.

Good news: That ninth bit is actually still there. Press [9] **STWS** and "thar she blows"—the complete number (go back to an 8-bit word size and do this change while watching in binary format, too).

Want to see how the flags look when you use RCLF to put their aggregate values onto the Stack as binary integers?

OK: Change the current word size to 64 (press [6][4] **STWS**). And to make the values easier to comprehend, use decimal formatting (press **DEC**, if necessary). Now, execute the RCLF command: [α][α][R][C][L][F][ENTER].... You should* get this list:

`{ # 316659348800496 # 0d }`

The first number is the aggregate binary-integer value of all 64 system flags; the second is the aggregate binary-integer value of your 64 user flags. These two values represent the entire "blueprint" of the machine's status and your own flag settings.

Now, holding your place here, look back at page 11. That preparatory exercise you performed before starting the Course was simply a setting of all flags to their *clear* states—so both the two desired values were given as `# 0`. You did this mass flag adjustment with the STOF command—do it again now:

[←][{ }][#][0][SPC][#][0][ENTER][α][α][S][T][O][F][ENTER]

If you give STOF a single binary integer value (not a list), this will adjust only the 64 *system* flags: [#][0][α][α][S][T][O][F][ENTER]

---

*If you don't get these values, don't worry. It just means one of the your display settings or angle modes or something like that is set differently than assumed here. No problem—you're going to reset them here anyway.

Math and logic with binary integers

The principal reason you have binary integers is so that you can do digital math and logic operations—the stuff so near and dear to the hearts of computer scientists. Don't worry—you're not going to explore all the bit manipulations and logical operations the BASE menu offers (if you need them, then you already know what they're good for, and you don't need an Easy Course to tell you).

But it's good for everybody to see a little bit of integer arithmetic in action—just so you understand some of the 48's rules.

Example: What's $125_{10} + ABC_{16}$ expressed in 64-bit decimal?

Solution: Press [6][4] **STWS** [1][2][5][ENTER] **HEX** [↱][#][α][α][A][B][C][α] [+] **DEC** .... Answer: # 2873d As you can see, you can combine a real number with a binary integer. The result is a binary integer in the same base. To make this possible, the machine transforms the real number into a binary integer first—with the **R→B** command ("Real-to-Binary", which you'll find, with its counterpart, **B→R**, on another page of the BASE menu). Of course, you can also use **R→B** "manually" on a real number, but the 48 is smart enough to do it for you here. Be aware that **R→B** *rounds* fractional portions of the real number, and it takes negative numbers to be 0. And any value requiring a binary representation larger than the current word size is silently truncated.

Example: What's $125_{10} - ABC_{16}$ expressed in 64-bit decimal?

Solution: Press [1][2][5][ENTER] [→][#] [α][α][A][B][C][←][H][α][−]....
Answer: # 18446744073709548993d

Notice that you can key in the base identifier (h here) directly—without switching to that display mode.

Why this huge answer? Why not # -2623d ?
Because instead of subtracting a binary integer, the 48 adds its *2's-complement*.*

Example: What are $258_{10} \times 3_{10}$ and $258_{10} \div 3_{10}$ computed in 8-bit decimal?

Solutions: [8] **STWS** [→][#][2][5][8][ENTER][3][×] Answer: # 6d
[→][#][2][5][8][ENTER][3][÷] Answer: # 0d

The 48 actually *truncates* (to the current word size) any value you use in arithmetic. Thus the above multiplication was actually $2_{10} \times 3_{10}$. And the division was actually $2_{10} \div 3_{10}$ (binary division remainders are dropped).

That's different than if you did the division with reals and then limited the word size in the result. And you can do just that with the **R→B** (Real-to-Binary) command in the BASE menu: [2][5][8][ENTER][3][÷][NXT] **R→B**.

---

*Complementing is the computer scientist's method for carrying and borrowing and negation during arithmetic with binary integers. If you don't already know how complementing works, you probably don't need to worry about it.

Character Strings

Character strings are just that—strings of characters (letters, numbers, symbols—basically, anything you can type):

ABCDEF_XYZ   12345   #~$@&(%)?!   3.1416+pi=oops

Within such strings, characters have no numeric or other quantitative or special significance; they're just characters. A string may have many characters, one character, or even none at all.

How does the 48 represent character strings?

Often called simply *strings*, character strings on the 48 appear within quotation marks, `"  "`, as if to say that the enclosed characters are to be taken literally, with no further interpretation:

```
"ABCDEF_XYZ"        "12345"

"#~$@&(%)?!"        "3.1416+pi=oops"
```

The main purpose of strings is to let you store and manipulate verbal information. For example, you can use strings to put together results such as `"The answer is no."` and `"The AREA is 2.5_ft"`, thus making your calculations more meaningful and complete than just unadorned numeric results. And then there's textual information—the kind of "stuff" that can be represented only by character strings: names and addresses, etc.

How do you build a string?

Begin as usual....

Type It: Try building the four strings on the opposite page.

Like So: [↱][CLR][↱][""][α][α][A][B][C][D][E][F][↱][_][X][Y][Z][ENTER], and [↱][""] [1][2][3][4][5][ENTER]; then [↱][""][α][α][↱][#][↱][V][↰][4][↱][ENTER] [↰][ENTER][↰][()][↱][U][α][▶][α][α][↰][◆][↰][DEL][ENTER]; then [↱][""][3][•][1][4][1][6][α][α][+][↰][α][P][I][↰][=][O][O][P][S][ENTER];

No big mysteries, right?* But remember: no matter what *numerals* you see within strings (as with the "12345"), they're *not* numbers.

Then: Guess how you can build strings from other Stack values?

Hmm: Press [+]....Two strings "add" (append) to one another just like two lists do (recall page 77). Press [DROP], then [6][7][+].... When you "add" other object types** to a string, the machine converts those objects to their *string representations**** and then *appends* these to the existing string. Try [↰][[ ]][1][SPC][2] [ENTER][SWAP][+].... The order matters—again, just as with lists.

---

*Though it was a bit of a refresher in Command Line typing. Do you remember how to find non-letter characters and type in lowercase, etc.? If not, look back at pages 31-39.

**except lists—you can't [+] them to strings (you'll add the string to the list instead).

***The string representations of some objects are slightly different than the objects themselves.

Of course, you can also convert objects to strings "manually"—instead of letting the machine do it—during a concatenation (appending).

Try It: Press PRG **OBJ**. Here, in the object building/decomposing menu is where to find the string-manipulation commands. Key in, say, a vector: ⬅ [ ] 2 SPC 2 7 SPC 5 ENTER. Now convert this into a string, by pressing **→STR** (it simply wraps this object in quotes, thus transforming its type into a string.... Now concatenate this to the string above it: +.

As you might suspect from all this object conversion, a string is only slightly less "general" an object type than a list. So it's almost as important to know how to take strings apart as to build them....

Do This: Remember the All-Purpose Object Dissector? Try it now (press **OBJ→**)....See what happens?

When a string contains representations of other objects, the machine will extract them, one by one (from left to right), and put them onto the Stack—just as if they had been ENTER'ed from the Command Line without quotation marks. But remember, too, that a string can contain anything else too—*besides* syntactically correct object representations. Therefore **OBJ→** can often give you errors as the machine tries to make an object out of characters in the string that were never meant for such.

Then: Press (ENTER) to make a copy of the vector now at Level 1. Then **→STR** (ENTER) and (NXT)(NXT), to move through the OBJ menu.

Here's where you'll find commands for editing and manipulating strings (and some work on other objects, too).

Example: Press **SIZE**. The number you get, 10, tells you how many characters were in "[2 27 5]". Now (←), (▶), and use **SIZE** on the *vector* [2 27 5] instead. The result is { 3 }, right? There are three elements in the vector, so its SIZE appears in this single-element *list*—just as it would have if you had used **OBJ→** to break it down into its components (recall page 90). Now press (←).

Question: The 48 can display 256 different characters, but not all are available on keys. How do you put them into strings?

Answer: Each character has an associated number—a character code, so you convert between the character and its code. **NUM** returns the character code of the *first character* of a given string. Try **NUM** now and see 91, which is the code for the [character. Then use **CHR** to confirm this—converting from the code back to the character.

Of course, there's certainly a lot more you can do with strings—just as with all the other objects—but at least you get the idea here.

Tags

Just as real numbers are linked together to build complex numbers and arrays—and just as bits form flags or binary integers—so too can strings be the simpler building blocks of other, "hybrid" object types. One simple one is a tag.

A tag is a pairing of a string with another object (any type) on the Stack so that the string forms a *temporary label.* Your workbench can get pretty "Stacked" up with objects, and so it's difficult to keep track of them all and remember what meant what. Tags are a harmless, temporary way to help you do this.

How does the 48 represent tags?

You don't build a tag by itself. As the name implies, you attach it to some other object—so it's more meaningful to ask "How does the 48 represent tagged objects?"

On the Stack, they might look, for example, like these:

```
Root: -1            Extrm: (0,-1)

Zero: 0             Unit: [ 0.27 0.53 0.80 ]
```

The tag itself is everything to the left of (and including) the colon. To the right of the colon is the object being tagged

How do you build a tag?

First—as always—you can simply type it in.

Thus: [→][::][α][α][R][←][α][O][O][T][α][▶][1][+/−][ENTER].

Notice that the displayed version of a tag has one colon—to save space in the display. But you must *enclose* the tag (*both* sides) with colons when you type it in, so use [▶] to skip over the second : before typing the object—just as you do when starting a new row of elements in an array.

That's how to build a tag when you key in an object, but most of the time you'll want to tag an object that's already on the Stack.

Well, you can't put a tag by itself on the Stack. A tag is just a string until it is attached to another object. Fortunately the tag-attachment tool, **→TAG**, is right there on the first page of the PRG OBJ menu.

Try This: Press [→][CLR], then put -1 onto the Stack: [1][+/-][ENTER]. Suppose that's the result of some calculation, and now, afterwards, you want to label it with a tag. Just key in the tag, as a string: [→]["'"][α][α][R][←][α][O][O][T][ENTER]. Then use **→TAG**. The result is the same as before.

And Also: You can use real numbers as tags. Suppose you're a land surveyor who deals with coordinates all day long. Each point in a survey might have an identifying number—a tag—attached to the vector coordinate pair itself:

Press [1][5][0][•][2][3][ENTER][6][5][•][7][9][←][2D]... There are your coordinates. Now label it with some identifying number: [1][2] **→TAG**. The 48 actually converts the real number to a string and then uses this as the tag.

As Usual: You can break up a tagged object into its object and its tag string, by using the General Purpose Object Decomposer, **OBJ→**. Try it now....
Now **→TAG** to rebuild the tagged object.

How do you use tags?

Tags are indeed *temporary* labels. If you do any operation on a tagged object, the 48 will remove and discard the tag. After all, the result of the operation isn't generally the same object as before.

Watch: Try adding another vector to the tagged vector now sitting at Level 1: ⬅ [ ] 1 0 SPC 2 0 + ... See what happens? The vector addition works just fine, but the tag on the previous object goes away.

Try another: multiply the `Root: -1` by this result vector: × .... Again, the math works fine, but the tag doesn't stick to the result.

As you saw with that surveyor's scenario, you can use real numbers as tags to index multiple results of the same kind (e.g. the points in the surveyor example). Or—more commonly—you use a string to give it some kind of temporary label of characters.

No matter what, a tag is the most fragile of objects—as you can see from above. Any meaningful operation of the object will "rip the tag off." A tag is for your benefit only; it doesn't mean anything to the machine. So the best use for tags is at the end of programs or other calculations, when you can attach them and display finished results.

Names

By contrast to tags, a name in the 48 is a much more "solid" kind of label. Names are very important, because they identify *places* where objects are stored. Names are like *labelled boxes* in your workshop. When you want to "use an object," you simply *invoke* (type) its name.

That goes for all the built-in objects, too. Every command (every key and menu item) is an object of some type, and when you press its key, this actually *invokes* ("types") the object's *built-in* name. For example, when you press the [SIN] key, you are invoking the *name*, SIN, which is the built-in (permanently labelled) box containing the sine program.

Well, building your own names is simply the act of creating new storage boxes with your own labels on them. Once you've done that, the names exist; you can put them onto the Stack, move them around, etc.—just like other objects—even when they're empty. But, of course, they're usually more useful when you do store objects in them. So here's where you start learning how to do that—how to save the objects you build....

How does the 48 represent names?

A name is simply a character string with special restrictions on the characters allowed. Examples:

'A' 'EX1' 'Tuesday' 'ΣDAT' 'PPAR'

'Whatchamacallit' 'SINx'

How do you build a name?

Build the first couple of names you see above.

Easy: Press ['][α][A][ENTER]; press ['][α][E][α][X][1][ENTER]; and so on—you get the idea. The ' ' delimiters appear in pairs—just like so many others you've seen by now.

As you can see, names are always enclosed in *apostrophes* (' ') rather than quotes (" ")—to distinguish them from normal character strings. Also, names have these special restrictions:

- You cannot use any *delimiter* in a name: #, ', ", _, :, ( ), [ ], { }, « », ∡, , , <space> and <newline> are all off limits.
- Numerals (0-9) and decimal points are OK, *except* as the first character: You can use 'A1' and 'Hi.', but not '1A' or '.WP'.
- No arithmetic symbols or operators! Names like 'A+B' are out.
- You can't create a name that's already used by a *built-in* command: 'SIN' is the *built-in name* for the sine function; 'SINx' is not.

How do you use a name?

To put something into a named box, you use [STO] (STOre).

Watch: Press [1][ENTER]['][α][A][STO]....

You just stored the real number 1 into the name 'A'.

Notice the order of the objects: First you put the *object to be stored* onto the workbench. Then you put the *name* (that labelled storage box). Then the STO command puts the object into the box, takes the filled box off the Stack and puts it into storage.

Question: *"...into storage"*—where's that?

Answer: It's in your own personal toolbox—the VAR menu. To get to it, simply press [VAR] (do this now)....

This is the menu of all the names that you've filled with objects (i.e. STOred objects into). As you can see, [A] is now the left-most box because it's the most recently filled; anything else you've stored (if anything) is bumped farther to the right in the menu.

It's called the VARiable menu because a *variable* is exactly that—a name labelling and containing some value, which can be changed (i.e. it can *vary*).

Once you've named an object, to use it you simply refer to it by name.

Look: Type [α][A][ENTER]....
Result: You get the *value* in 'A', which is the real number, 1.

This is the general rule: Whenever you type the name of an object you are *invoking* that name. The machine will *evaluate* the object for you—*exactly as if you had typed the object itself from the Command Line* (i.e. as if you had typed [1][ENTER] here).

And: Press the [A] item on the VAR menu.... Same thing, right? Again—as you read earlier—pressing a VARiable key is just a shortcut for *typing that name.*

But: Type ['][α][A][ENTER] (or ['][A][ENTER])....
Result: You don't get the *value* in 'A'—only its *name.*

This is just what you saw when creating names (page 117): The ' means that you simply want to put the name onto the Stack. Maybe you're building a new name; maybe you want to STOre a new value into an existing name—whatever.

It's a very important point—worth "harping on" once more:

- To put just the *name* onto the Stack, enclose it in ' marks.
- To *invoke* the name—i.e. to get the *value* it contains—use it *without* ' marks.

Question: What if you have a name on the Stack and *then* you decide that you want to evaluate it?

No Sweat: To *evaluate* a name already on the Stack, simply press [EVAL].... See? It EVALuates the name 'A'.

By the way, notice this: Evaluating a name always gets you a *copy* of its object's value. Thus, you can evaluate the name over and over again—using and consuming the resulting values on the Stack—but the original object stays safely in its labelled box.

Clean Up: Press [→][CLR]['] [A] (a menu key is just a shortcut for typing, right?). Now [←][PURGE].... [A] disappears from your VAR menu; you PURGE'd it from your toolbox (threw it away)—both the name and the object it contained.

Now: What will happen if you try to invoke the name A? Hmm—there's no such name, right? Try it: Press [α][A][ENTER]....

You get the name: 'A' How? And why?

Because whenever you *invoke* a name—any name—the 48 actually puts ' marks around it and puts the name onto the Stack first. *Then* it performs an EVAL on it. If the name contains any other object, then of course, you'll get that object's value. But if the name contains no other object, *it uses its own object value* (after all, a name is an object, too—right?).

Practice some more: Store some objects and evaluate some names....

Example: Store the vector [1 2 3] in the name 'Vector.1'

Solution: Press [→][CLR] to remove distractions. Then press [1][SPC] [2][SPC][3][→][3D]['][α][α][V][←][α][E][C][T][O][R][•][1][α][STO]. Now look in your VAR menu. The left-most box is VECTO. Did the 48 truncate (and capitalize) the name you keyed in—just to fit it into the display's menu box?

To find out, press [']VECTO.... Nope—the 48 knows and remembers the entire actual name; it simply needs to alter it for its menu boxes. So keep your names short and distinct! *Each menu box holds only up to 5 characters—and uppercase always.* So any similar (yet completely valid) names such as 'Vector.1' and 'Vector.2' or 'VECT' and 'Vect' will *appear* identical in the menu.

Question: Can you store a name within a name? It seems reasonable. After all, you can put one box containing an object into another box, right? Try it—store 1 in 'B' and 'B' in 'A': [ATTN][1]['][α][B][STO]['] B [ENTER]['][α][A][STO].

OK, But: *What will you get* now when you invoke (*evaluate*) the name A? Press A .... You get 1! So the EVALuation process *goes all the way:* If the value of one name is yet another name, the 48 then evaluates *that* name, and so on—down to the last "box within a box within a box...".

So evaluation is really a chain of evaluations—as long as necessary:* The 48 follows its nose through each name, evaluating its contents—until finally it finds the value of the "innermost" object.

Problem: What if you're interested in a name's actual contents only—the object immediately "inside" the name? That is, you don't want the 48 to evaluate *that* object any further—just put it on the Stack. How do you do this?

Solution: Use RCL to recall the contents of 'A': ['] [A] [→][RCL]... You get 'B'—the actual contents of 'A'. Because you *recalled* the contents of 'A' (rather than evaluating it), the 48 did *not* go on to evaluate those contents. And note that RCL is a *copying* process: the object in 'A' (the name 'B') is still in 'A' (try ['] [A] [→][RCL] again).

So [STO] and [→][RCL] form a kind of matched set:

- To STOre an object into a name, you put the object onto the Stack, then the name, then press [STO]. The STOrage process *consumes* both object and name—it's *not* a copying process (the object is taken as the original, and no duplicate is left on the Stack).
- To ReCalL the object, you put the name onto the Stack. Then you use [→][RCL] and you get (a *copy* of) the object back on the Stack.

*Up to the memory of the machine, of course. And beware of circular references: If you were to store 'A' into 'B' right now, then 'A' would contain 'B' and 'B' would contain 'A'. And M.C. Escher would love such a conundrum—but your 48 wouldn't. It would evaluate in a circle, and you'd need to press [ATTN] to interrupt this infinite goose-chase. The 48 can actually catch self-referencing names (i.e. storing 'A' into 'A') and give you a message, Error: Circular Reference.

In fact, STO and RCL are so useful that the VAR menu offers a shortcut:

This: Press [→][CLR], then [4][←][A]. Now press [→][A]....
You just did this: [→][CLR][4]['][A][STO]['][A][→][RCL].

Using a VAR menu key *by itself* will *evaluate* the name.
Using ['] first simply *types* the name onto the Command Line.
Using [←] first STOres the Level-1 object into that name.
Using [→] first ReCalLs a copy of the actual object in the name.

Of course, once you recall the contents of a name to the Stack, you might want to alter it. But how?

Easy: EDIT it! For example, to change the first value in Vector.1 to 10: [→][VECTO] (recall its current value), then [←][EDIT][▶][▶][▶][0][ENTER] (EDIT that object), and [←][VECTO] (store this new version back into the name 'Vector.1'). *Remember:* EDITing alters only a copy of the contents of a name on the Stack. It does *not* automatically STOre the EDITed version back into that name.

So: To recall, edit *and* restore a named object in one smooth motion, use VISIT instead of EDIT. Change that vector component back to 1: ['][VECTO][→][VISIT][▶][▶][▶][▶][◆][ENTER].... See? VISIT lets you skip the initial RCL and the final STO.*

---

*And in case of mistakes during "alterations," remember that, just as [ATTN] aborts an EDIT, leaving Level 1 unchanged, so it also aborts a VISIT and leaves the named object unchanged.

Algebraic Objects

Algebra is the branch of mathematics that manipulates expressions and equations involving *variables*—"unidentified numbers" that can nevertheless be manipulated as symbols because their numerical *properties* are known and predictable:

$$x^2 + y^2 = r^2 \qquad\qquad ax^2 + bx + c = 0$$

The beauty of algebra is that you can manipulate the symbols into the most advantageous arrangement—before ever worrying about the numerical values these symbols might represent.

$$y = \sqrt{r^2 - x^2} \qquad\qquad x = \frac{-b \pm \sqrt{b^2 - 4ac}}{2a}$$

Then you can "plug in" numerical values:

$$y = \sqrt{5^2 - 4^2} \qquad\qquad x = \frac{-10 \pm \sqrt{10^2 - 4(3)(3)}}{2(3)}$$

Well, it's no coincidence that your menu of named objects in the 48 is called a VARiable menu: *You can use names in the 48 literally as algebraic symbols,* to form algebraic expressions and equations (such as those above) that you manipulate and solve *symbolically.* And just like algebra on paper, you needn't worry about the actual, numerical values in those variables until you're ready to "plug them in!"

How does the 48 represent algebraic objects?

As you know, you can't use math operators (e.g. + − * ⁄) as characters in names. If you do, you'll form an algebraic object instead. *Names and algebraic objects use the same delimiter* (').

Examples: At your VAR menu, press ' A ENTER. That's a name. Press ' B ENTER. That's another name. But press ' A + B ENTER. That's an *algebraic object.* You built it by typing a mathematically meaningful *combination* of names and algebraic operations.

And of course, you can edit this object—just like any other: ← EDIT SKIP→ ◄ − α C ENTER. Result: 'A+B-C'

So you can always type in an algebraic object at the Command Line—using whatever combinations of VAR and alphabetic keys that are most convenient. But often it's easier to let the Stack's postfix operations actually help you build an algebraic object:

Watch: DROP the 'A+B-C', then press +.... See what happens? Just as + lets you combine lists or strings, so it combines names and algebraic objects into larger algebraic objects.

Try another: Key in the name 'C' (press ' α C ENTER), then −.... Voilá!

How do you use algebraic objects?

"Ah—how sweet it is!..."

Question: *What's going to happen* now if you EVALuate this algebraic object, 'A+B-C' ? Press EVAL.... Result: '5-C'. Why? Because *the machine evaluates everything in the expression that it can* (the variable names 'A' and 'B' have the values 4 and 1 stored in them); *but it leaves any undefined value as is—in symbolic form* (the name 'C' contains nothing—it's not on your VAR menu).*

Do This: Evaluate the algebraic object 'A+B'.
Press ' A + B ENTER (or ' A ENTER ' B ENTER + —your choice), then EVAL.... Result: 5
This result is *not* an algebraic object—it's a real number— because all the parts of 'A+B' are numerically evaluable; it has no undefined names (such as 'C').

One More: Evaluate 'A*Vector.1': ' A × VECTO ENTER (or ' A ENTER ' VECTO ENTER ×), then EVAL....
Result: [4 8 12]   Isn't this great?

---

*Notice that this exactly matches how the 48 EVALuates names: If a name has an object stored in it, the 48 evaluates that object; if not, *the name itself becomes the final object value.*

Question: How do you know this last answer is correct? That is, how can you verify the current values of your VARiables 'A' and 'Vector.1'?

Answer(s): An easy way is simply to *evaluate* 'A' and 'Vector.1', by pressing [A] and [VECTO]. You should get, respectively: 4 and [1 2 3].

Or, to review the values in *all* the names on the current page of your VAR menu, press [←][REVIEW]:

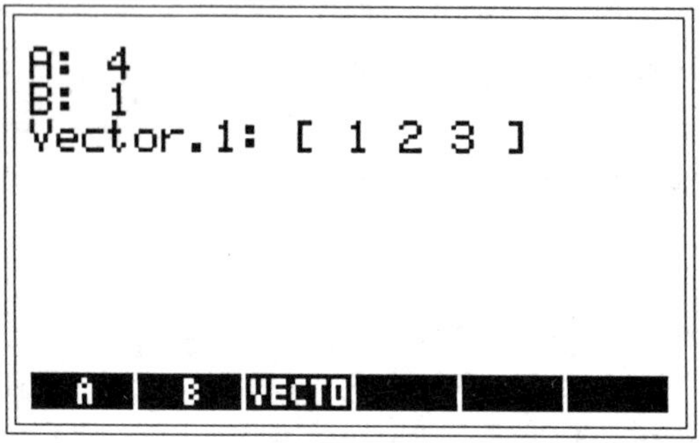

REVIEW is especially handy when you want to check a lot of values at once—but you don't want to mess up the Stack with name evaluations. Notice that the entire review is just a large message that appears temporarily over the normal Stack display (press [ATTN] to clear it).

For practice with a more complicated example, try using an algebraic object to build one of the general solutions to a quadratic equation:

$$x = \frac{-b \pm \sqrt{b^2 - 4ac}}{2a}$$

Go: First, press [→][CLR] to tidy up the workbench. Now start building:

Press ['][α][←][B][ENTER][+/-]. Result: '-b' So far, so good. Again, you're doing a mathematical operation on an algebraic object, and the object changes to reflect that operation.

Next, press [ENTER][+/-] (no sense keying 'b' in again from scratch; this is quicker). Then [2][yˣ]... Result: 'b^2' Because the 48 can't display superscripts in the Stack, it uses the circumflex (^) to indicate "raising to a power." *

Next, [4]['][α][←][A][ENTER][×]['][α][←][C][ENTER][×]....Result: '4*a*c' Notice that the result is *not* '4ac'. Such *implied* multiplication (i.e. omitting the multiplication signs between single-character variables—often used in written algebra) would confuse algebraic objects with *names* on the 48 Stack: 'xy', 'abc', etc.

Now [−], to form 'b^2-4*a*c' *Notice* how the 48's postfix subtraction rule ("Level 2 minus Level1") determines the order of the subtraction operation formed inside the algebraic object.**

*You could have typed [←][x²] instead of [2][yˣ], but the result, 'SQ(b)', isn't quite as readable. Either form is OK, though—they both evaluate the same way.

**Notice also that you don't need any parentheses here: Under conventional algebraic notation (which the 48 uses), exponentiation takes precedence over multiplication/division, which takes precedence over addition/subtraction.

Next step: [√x].... You get '√(b^2-4*a*c)'
Notice the parentheses. A one-line algebraic object can't draw the radical to include an entire expression under it. Instead, the square root is represented as a mathematical function (as in $f(x)$), and the parentheses enclose the argument of the function: √( )

Now press [+]. Result: '-b+√(b^2-4*a*c)'
No surprises, right?

Keep going: [2]['][α][←][A][ENTER][×].... Result: '2*a'
Nothing unusual here, either—but by now you may have noticed something that's worth a little discussion: Normally, when doing Stack arithmetic with something like real numbers, you could just press [2][ENTER][3][×]. Here, you need a second [ENTER], to put the 'a' onto the Stack before multiplying. This is because when you press ['], the 48 goes into algebraic entry mode (the **ALG** annunciator appears in the Status Area), so that operations such as [×] are *not executed immediately*. Instead, they're simply typed (*, +, etc.) onto the Command Line. Therefore, you could also key in the expression '2*a' as ['][2][×][α][←][A][ENTER], rather than build it via Stack operations.

Finally, press [÷].... Result: '(-b+√(b^2-4*a*c))/(2*a)'
Since algebraic objects are represented in a line on the Stack , the extra parentheses are needed to show what's being divided by what. Indeed, without them you'd have '-b+√(b^2-4*a*c)/2*a', which, according to the notational conventions, would be evaluated as

$$-b+\left(\frac{\sqrt{b^2-4ac}}{2}\right)a$$

Some observations:

When building expressions involving your variable names, you began each name with ' , to tell the machine that you were merely *spelling out* the name as part of this object, not *evaluating* it. But if you *know* that the names you're using are empty (i.e. they're not on your VAR list—either you've PURGEd them or never used them before), then you can get away *without* the ' —because evaluating an *empty* name just gives you that name anyway.

Of course, you could have typed in the entire object directly from the Command Line: ['] [⬅] [()] [+/-] [α] [⬅] [α] [α] [B] [+] [√x] [⬅] [()] [α] [B] [y^x] [2] [−] [4] [×] [α] [A] [×] [α] [C] [▶] [▶] [÷] [⬅] [()] [2] [×] [α] [A] [ENTER]

Admittedly, this saves some [ENTER]'s—and you can use lower-case lock ([⬅] [α] in alpha mode) to make it easier to type a, b, and c. But it also means you have to know where all the parentheses go *before you start*. And so you must know and follow the algebraic syntax and precedence conventions—instead of letting the 48 put it together for you "on the fly," as you simply specify the order of operations with the postfix Stack operations. So *you* decide—use the method easiest for you.

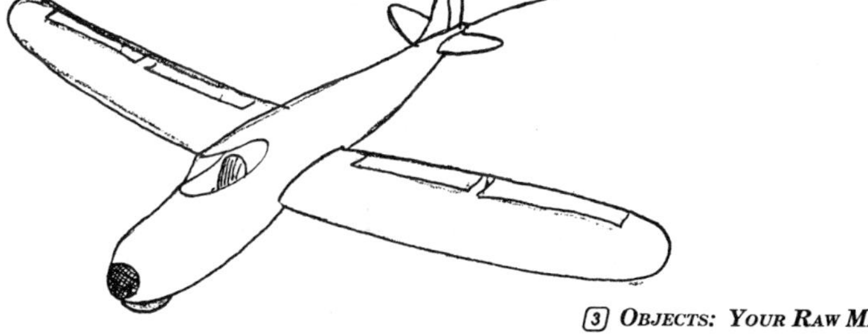

No matter how you've built it, now that you have such an impressive algebraic object all built, what do you do with it?

This: Put values into the variables and evaluate the expression:

[VAR] ['] [α] [E] [α] [Q] [STO]   [1] ['] [α] [←] [C] [STO]

[2] [+/−] ['] [α] [←] [B] [STO]   [1] ['] [α] [←] [A] [STO]   **EQ** [EVAL]

You've just stored your freshly-built algebraic object into the name 'EQ'. Then you stored 1 into 'a', −2 into 'b', and 1 into 'c' (in reverse order—to appear in order in the menu*).

Then you put the expression back on the Stack by pressing **EQ**, thus *evaluating* the name 'EQ'. Then you evaluated the expression, and you got the real result.

"Hmm...but why doesn't the EVALuation process 'go all the way,' and evaluate the algebraic object?"

It's an exception to the "EVALuate-all-the-way" rule: If a name contains an algebraic object, the 48 evaluates only to that object; you must press [EVAL] explicitly to evaluate the algebraic any more. So you did—and zap—the machine replaced all names with their values and did the math. And as with all evaluations, the result was left on the Stack: 1

Anyway, the ***beauty*** of such algebraic objects is this: Now you have your algebraic expression named, *you can easily reuse it.* For example: [2] [←] **A** [1] [5] [+/−] [←] **B** [4] [←] **C** **EQ** [EVAL]. Result: 7.22...

*Remember that they will appear in *uppercase* in the menu boxes—but you know they're the boxes farther to the *left* because they've been more recently created than the boxes for 'A' and 'B'.

Postfix Programs

When you say the word *program,* you probably think of some task or series of tasks that you "record" in a computer now and then "play back" later—at which time the machine *automatically* performs those tasks. The power of a program is that you can play the recording over and over with very little effort on your part every time—often the touch of a single key. *It can become a new tool in your workshop.*

Well, that's a fair way to think about a program. But then that means that *algebraic objects* are really *programs* of a sort. For look at how much work the machine does automatically when you press the [EVAL] key with an algebraic object: It evaluates all the names, then uses the math to combine them as you've specified—and it will do this over and over, for whatever values of variables you wish to give it.

You could make a similar argument for simply EVALuating a series of "names within names," too: That chain of evaluations can go on a long time—a very convenient series of tasks the machine does for you automatically. And, as you'll soon see, you can even get the 48 to sequentially evaluate the objects contained in a *list object* ({ })—again, simply by pressing that all-powerful [EVAL] key.

The point is, although there are several different types of objects that can act as programs, they have other roles as well. In fact, there's only one object type that was defined *strictly* for the purpose of acting as such a pre-recorded, ready-to-use series of commands. This is the object type called a *postfix program.*

How does the 48 represent postfix programs?

A postfix program (you can call it simply "program" for short), is indeed an object; you can put it onto the Stack, store (name) it, recall it and evaluate it. And, as with most other objects in your workshop, programs are bracketed by a pair of distinctive delimiters—in this case, guillemets: « »

Also true to the pattern of other objects is the program's underlying list-like structure: A program is an ordered collection of zero or more elements (objects and commands). When you evaluate the program, it sequentially evaluates its elements.

How do you build a postfix program?

Unlike most other objects, there is only one way to create a program, and that's to type it in from the Command Line.

Try One: Press [⬅][« »][1][SPC][2][+][ENTER]. Result: « 1 2 + »

Notice that *program entry mode* activates (i.e. the **PRG** annunciator appears in the Status Area) when you press [« »]—so that commands such as [+] simply type their names in the Command Line rather than executing immediately.

So there you have it—a three-step program.

Question: What does it do?

Answer: See for yourself: It's called a *postfix* program because *it handles objects and commands in the same manner as your 48's postfix Stack would handle them as you key them in on the Command Line.* So you can mimic this program's behavior at the Command Line: [1][SPC][2][+].*

Now [DROP] this "manual" result, then press [ENTER] once (to DUPlicate the program so you don't need to rebuild it later), and [EVAL]uate it.... Sure enough: 3

Of course, you can *name* the program, too—to save for later....

Do It: [DROP] the EVAL result, and then ['][α][E][α][X][1][STO].... Just like any other freshly-named object, the program, now called EX1, will appear on the left side of your growing VAR menu.

---

*You'll notice, however, that the program can delay the execution of +, whereas you can't at the normal Command Line. To mimic the program even more closely, you can activate program entry mode without using the [« »], by pressing [↱][ENTRY].

But this EX1 program doesn't do anything particularly valuable (you already know what 1+2 is). So you ought to change it.

OK: Suppose you want EX1 to add 1 to *whatever* object is at Stack Level 1.

How? You can't decompose a postfix program into its elements with OBJ→. In fact, the only way to change it (other than PURGE it and start over) is to edit it—easiest with VISIT: ['] EX1 [→][VISIT]. Now delete the 2: SKIP→ SKIP→ DEL→; and restore the program: [ENTER]. Now EX1 will simply put the number 1 onto the Stack and then perform a +.

Try It: [→][CLR], then [1] EX1 gives a result of 2; EX1 again: 3
[←][( )][3][2][SPC][4][4] EX1 gives (33, 44).
[PRG] OBJ [2] →LIST [VAR] EX1 gives { 3 (33, 44) 1 }.
[→][" "][α][H][α][←][I] EX1 gives "Hi1".
['][α][H][α][←][I][ENTER] EX1 gives 'Hi+1'.
[1][SPC][2][SPC][3][→][3D] EX1 gives *an error* (you can't add a scalar to a vector). This leaves the Stack *as it was at the time of the error* (the 1 put there by the program remains).

Don't worry—you'll get lots more sophisticated practice with programs (and most of the other objects later). The point here is this: Using a program—such as EX1—from your VAR menu is really *no different from using any built-in command*—such as [X^2]. Naming a program creates a new tool in your workshop, and it works like any built-in tool.

Directories

A directory—any directory (a phone book, a map, a kiosk in the mall, whatever)—is a reference tool to help you find what you need from among a given selection. And there are different directories for different selections. For example, it would be a hopeless mess to try to list all the telephone numbers in the country in one huge phone book, so the listings are broken down into different books. And each book is often divided even further—by city or suburb—into *subdirectories*.

The point is, a directory's very purpose is this dividing/subdividing effect. It offers you *only* a certain selection among "all possible items"—in order to simplify and narrow the field of your search (assuming, of course, that the selection uses some logical criterion—all the names in the phone book from the same city, etc.).

In the 48, you use directories in just that way: Your VAR menu—your toolbox for your own custom-built objects—is quite roomy, and you can put anything you want into it. You can divide it up into drawers, each with some more specific criterion for the named objects it contains. And you can even subdivide those drawers into still smaller compartments, then subcompartments, etc.

How does the 48 represent directories?

Directories are objects—just as arrays, strings and lists are objects—but because it's seldom useful to put a directory on your Stack workbench, there's no 48 delimiter reserved to denote a directory object. The best way to *see* one is to *build* one....

How do you build a directory?

To create a directory, just put a unique *name* into Level 1 of the Stack and invoke the CRDIR command....

Watch: Press [→] [CLR] ['] [α] [α] [D] [I] [R] [1] [α] [←] [MEMORY] **CRDIR** [VAR].... The new name, **DIR1**, is now in the VAR menu.

Notice the "file folder tab" on the top of the **DIR1** menu box. This is to help you distinguish directories from the other named objects.

How do you use a directory?

So you now have a new, empty directory called DIR1.

Question: Can you look into it—and store objects into it now?

Answer: Sure—but you need to *open* it first. Just *evaluate its name*—press **DIR1**. Your VAR menu becomes *empty*, because now it's showing you only the contents of the DIR1 directory. And the Status Area shows a list, telling you "where" you are: **{ HOME DIR1 }**
That is, you started in your **HOME** "toolbox," then opened the **DIR1** "drawer" within that toolbox.

Now, to put something into this drawer, you do exactly what you always do—just STOre into a name.

Like So: For example, [1][']⟨α⟩[A][STO] puts the named object 'A' into your opened DIR1 drawer. With this drawer open, whenever you evaluate, store or recall 'A', you'll be referring to this 'A'.

Question: Does this replace the 'A' in your HOME directory—the one that contained the value of 4 (recall pages 118-123)?

Find Out: Return to the HOME directory (i.e. *close* the DIR1 drawer), by pressing [↱][HOME].... The list in the Status Area now shows { HOME }, and the VAR menu should look familiar. All right, *now* evaluate the name 'A' (press [NXT] [A]*). You get 4. So the 'A' in DIR1 is *different* than the 'A' in the HOME directory—like two **John Smith**'s in two different phone books. *You can use identical names for different objects if they're in different directories.*

When evaluating a name, apparently, the 48 looks for that name only in the *current* directory (HOME, in this case). Test that theory: Go back to DIR1 ([NXT] [DIR1]) and evaluate 'A' (press [A]).... Yep—you get 1—the value of the 'A' stored in the DIR1 directory.

---

*Remember that there are two items that look like [A]—the one farther to the left is for 'a'; the other is for 'A' (but if you forget which is which, pressing ['] [A] would tell you).

But: PURGE the name 'A' from the DIR1 directory: ['] [A] [←][PURGE].

Now evaluate 'A': [α][A][ENTER].... You get 4 !

How can this be? The name 'A' *doesn't exist* in DIR1—you just PURGEd it. This is the value of the name 'A' *in the HOME directory*—and yet you obtained it by evaluating 'A' from the DIR1 directory!

This is because the 'A' in HOME is *in your current PATH.*

As you've read, the directories you create in the HOME directory are "drawers"—subdivisions of that HOME directory "toolbox." And directories you create from any such "drawer" are further subdivisions ("compartments") *within that drawer.* So, starting from HOME, to get to any particular directory, you sequentially open the correct drawer, the correct compartment within that drawer, etc. That is, you traverse an access PATH through your directory structure.

That list in the Status Area is your PATH list—the description of the PATH you took from HOME to get to where you are now. When you evaluate or recall a name, the 48 first looks in the *current* directory (the directory at the *end* of the PATH list). But if it can't find the specified name there, the 48 will methodically search *backward* through that PATH list until it either finds the name or exhausts all directories in that PATH list.

A little terminology clarification: Directories within other directories are commonly called *subdirectories*. So DIR1 is a subdirectory of HOME and HOME is the *parent* directory of DIR1.

A directory may contain many objects—and many subdirectories.

Watch: Create a subdirectory, 'DIR2', in the HOME directory.

Like So: [→][HOME]['] DIR1 [←][2][←][MEMORY] CRDIR [VAR].... Now DIR2 is DIR1's "sibling"—another drawer in the HOME toolbox.

Next, create another directory, 'DIR3', *inside* DIR2: First, open the empty DIR2 (press DIR2). Then: ['][α][α][D][I][R][3] [α][←][MEMORY] CRDIR [VAR].

You now have a directory (DIR3) within a directory (DIR2) within a directory (HOME). So HOME is DIR3's "grandparent," if you will. Since a family tree is such an obvious analogy for this directory structure, it is commonly referred to as a directory *tree*.

Practice moving through the tree:

Store 2 into 'D' in DIR3: DIR3 [2]['][α][D][STO].

Store 8 into 'C' in DIR2: [←][UP][8]['][α][C][STO]. The UP command moves you up to the current directory's *parent*.

Store 16 into 'B' in DIR1: [←][UP] DIR1 [1][6]['][α][B][STO].

Questions: From which directories can you now recall and evaluate 'A', 'B', 'C', and 'D'? Feel free to use your 48 to help.

Answers: 'A': HOME, DIR1, DIR2, DIR3
'B': DIR1
'C': DIR2, DIR3
'D': DIR3

Remember: You can recall or evaluate any name in the current directory's PATH. Since *all* PATHs contain the HOME directory, anything stored there is accessible from *any* subdirectory—no matter how many generations removed. By contrast, objects stored in the "leaves" of the tree (i.e. in directories with no children) are accessible *only* from that "leaf" directory.

Now: Time to clean up: There are two ways to PURGE a directory....

As with any other name, you may use the PURGE command on a directory name—but *only* if that directory is *empty* (so you can't easily destroy a lot of valuable information with PURGE).

Or, if you're *sure* that you want to destroy a directory *and* everything in it (objects, subdirectories, their contents—the whole shootin' match), use PGDIR (PurGe DIRectory). PGDIR assumes that you know what you're doing. It removes a directory *and its contents*—so use it with caution (go ahead and do this now): [→][HOME] ['] [DIR1] [ENTER] ['] [DIR2] [←][MEMORY] [NXT][NXT] [PGDIR] [PGDIR] [VAR].

Objects: A Summary

No sense kidding yourself: You've covered a lot in this long chapter. You've seen how to build and at least begin to use the basic object types available in the 48:

Real numbers	Units	Lists
Complex numbers	Vectors	Arrays
Flags	Binary integers	
Strings	Tags	
Names	Algebraic objects	
Postfix programs	Directories	

Yes, there are few other object types that you haven't seen yet—mainly because they're for special purposes—plotting, programming, backing up your data, etc.

Right now, hold your place here and look back at pages 14-15—"The Big Picture".... Surely the keyboard's organizational structure ought to seem more familiar now—and of course, the Stack is definitely "home turf" by now, right? But even that example directory tree structure on page 15 ought to be clearer, now that you know a little about subdirectories, parent directories and PATHs, no?

But just in case, here are a few more exercises to help you put it all together. These quiz problems will force you to *use and combine* what you know—and you'll even see a few new variations and features not covered before now—so heads up!—and enjoy....

Test Your Objectivity

1. Sum the first 10 positive integers. Now sum the first 1000 positive integers.

2. Silver (Ag) crystallizes in a face-centered cubic unit cell (4 atoms). The density of Ag is 10.5 g/cm^3. The atomic mass of silver is 107.868 g/mol. There are 6.022×10^{23} atoms/mole. Find the mass, volume and dimensions (in Ångstroms) of a silver unit cell.

3. In an elementary chemical reaction, $e^{\frac{-E_A}{RT}}$ is the fraction of collisions with enough energy to react. E_A is the activation energy; R is the ideal gas constant (8.314 J/K-mol); T is the absolute temperature (in Kelvins). Find the fraction of successful collisions for a reaction at 980° F with an activation energy of 2.14×10^4 J/mol.

4. What are the differences between `{ 1 2 3 4 }` and `[ 1 2 3 4 ]`? How would you convert between them?

5. You can add elements to a list using the [+] key, but how might you *delete*, say, the last element? The first element?

6. How would you change the value $1+2i$ into $2+i$ on the 48?

7. Fill in the table below to compare the costs and benefits of three strategies for replacing part of the current U.S. daily use of petroleum—now totalling about 15 million barrels:

Option	Costs (Savings)	Energy gain (bbl/d)	% of current use
80 nuclear reactors	**Total: $**__________	__________	____%
80 coal plants	**Total: $**__________	__________	____%
Simple efficiency measures	H_2O heat: __________	__________	____%
	Appliances: __________	__________	____%
	Lighting: __________	__________	____%
	Tire infl.: __________	__________	____%
	Total: $__________	__________	____%

Nuclear reactor (1000 MW):	Capital invest. (3-5-yr constr./testing):	$	1200/kW
	Fuel and maintenance (for 25-year life):		200/kW
	Disposal/cleanup (100-1,000 years):		50000/kW
Coal-fired plant (1000 MW):	Capital invest. (3-year constr./testing):	$	1000/kW
	Fuel and maintenance (for 50-year life):		100/kW
	Disposal/cleanup (10 years):		10000/kW

Efficiencies: 100 million U.S. households each use the energy equivalent average of 1253 gallons of oil per year—at a cost of about $1,200. 40% of this goes for space heating, 20% for water heating, 15% for major appliances, 10% for lighting, the rest for other uses. 140 million U.S. cars average 10,000 miles per year each, at 19 mpg. 1 barrel of oil has 5900 MJ of chemical energy and produces 16.4 gallons of gasoline. A unit of electrical energy requires 3 units of oil energy. Electric plants typically operate at 75% of rated capacity.

Low-flow heads on faucets and showers cost $40 per household and last at least 10 years. That plus using cold water rinse in the washer would save 20% on water heating. Lowering the H_2O heater to 130°F. and raising the freezer and refrigerator to 0° and 40° F. would save at least 5% on appliance usage. Using compact fluorescent light bulbs (20 per household) would cost $150 more to buy (for the same 5-yr. life) than incandescent bulbs but save 75% in electricity. Inflating car tires to correct pressures would save 3% in fuel consumption.

8. What's $\sin^{-1}(2)$? What are the units of the solution angle? What does this solution mean?

9. Find the angle, ϕ, between $-9\mathbf{i}+4\mathbf{j}-2\mathbf{k}$ and $(12, 1.39\,\text{rad}, 0.48\,\text{rad})$.

10. Find the volume of the parallelpiped defined by:

$$a = 3\mathbf{i} + 3\mathbf{j} + 5\mathbf{k} \qquad b = 7\mathbf{i} + \mathbf{j} -.2\mathbf{k} \qquad c = \mathbf{i} + 8\mathbf{j} - \mathbf{k}$$

11. If $A = (1,2,3)$, $\boldsymbol{B} = (-3\angle 25°, -.2)$, and $\boldsymbol{C} = (1/3\angle\sqrt{2}\,\text{rad}, -6\,\text{rad})$, find the unit vector that points in the same direction as of the *sum* of the real and imaginary portions of $14.5A - 0.2\boldsymbol{B} + (1+i)\boldsymbol{C}$

12. Within the vector `[ 2 4 6 8 10 ]`, how could you change the `8` to `19`? How could you change the `2` to `(1, 1)`?

13. Create the vector `[ 1 2 ]`. Now redimension it to a 5-element vector. Then change the third element to `5`. Then "dot" it with `[ 5 4 3 2 1 ]`.

Sources:

The 1990 Information Please Almanac, Houghton Mifflin Company, Boston, 1990.

50 Simple Things You Can Do To Save The Earth, The Earth Works Group, Earthworks Press, Berkeley, 1989 (book available through: NRDC, 40 West 20th St., New York, NY 10011).

Ecoscience: Population, Resources, Environment, Erlich, Erlich and Holdren, W.H. Freeman & Co., San Francisco, 1977.

14. Convert the vector `[ 1 2 3 4 5 6 7 8 9 ]` into a **3 x 3** array. Then change $element_{12}$ to `10`. Then convert the resulting array into an array with complex elements.

15. How might you extract individual rows from the result of problem **14**? Would these be vectors?

16. Legends still speak of that dark and fateful night, over a century ago, when a U.S. Mail Express locomotive became a runaway and collided with a long-haul Canadian grain engine at a remote prairie border junction. The crews may have bailed out in time, but they were never found. Your theory: The collision startled a large herd of bison nearby, whose ensuing stampede obliterated the entire scene. You've surmised that the wreckage itself landed somewhere out in a bison mud wallow, sinking well out of sight beneath the muck and chaos of the stampede. Vague stories of some such incident—pieced together from railroad memorabilia in both countries—have allowed you to estimate these speeds, compass headings and weights for each engine (including its coal tender) at the point of collision:

Engine	Speed	Heading	Weight
Squash Blossom Special	88 mph	44°19'	150 tons
Home, Wheat, Home	110 km/hr	256°32'	300,000 kg

Problem: Which government should have excavation jurisdiction over your proposed International Peace-Railroad Memorial Mud Wallow?

17. Find the total hours worked by each person and by all together:

	Andy	Beth	Carla	David
Mon.	8	8	5	7
Tues.	8	8	6	7
Wed.	4	7	5	7
Thurs.	8	7	4	8
Fri.	8	8	5	7

18. Test matrix multiplication commutativity with these:

$$\boldsymbol{A} = \begin{bmatrix} 1 & 2 \\ 3 & 4 \end{bmatrix} \qquad \text{and} \qquad \boldsymbol{B} = \begin{bmatrix} 16 & 9 \\ 4 & 1 \end{bmatrix}$$

19. Use [⬅][2D] to help you build *complex numbers*.

20. Set ENG display notation and polar/cylindrical vector mode—using only one page of one menu and the digit keys.

21. Find the 48's current binary wordsize without using RCWS.

22. What's the easiest way to *preserve* the system settings—such as those discussed in problems **19-21**—for quick restoration later?

23. Calculate $2_{10} \times (FFF_{16} \div 2_{10})$ in 16-bit integers.

24. Key in # 100d and duplicate it. Then convert one copy to a string. Then set binary mode....Why are the two results different?

25. Change "You understand?" to "You understand!"

26. Build the string "Vol.= 4.0 gal." without using the 4 key. Then, starting with such a string, extract the numeric value.

27. Format a number in scientific notation—such as 6.022E23—within a string, in this format: "6.022 * 10^(23)"
What will OBJ→ produce from this string?

28. Use PURGE to rename 'A' as 'x'. Then use this name to tag the solution to $x = \dfrac{-b \pm \sqrt{b^2 - 4ac}}{2a}$, for $a = 1$, $b = -8$, and $c = 15$.

29. Set flag –3 and try to build the solution to prob. **28** "from scratch."

30. Key in the names 'π', 'i' and 'e' and evaluate them. Now set flag –2 and repeat this exercise.

31. How can you PURGE more than one name at a time?

32. Evaluate the expression `'2*x+y'` for:

a. $x = -2y$ **c.** $x = t,\ y = t - 1$

b. $y = -2x$ **d.** $x = z - 3y, \quad y = y - 3z$

33. Write the solutions to problem **4** as two complementary programs, named `L→V` and `V→L`. Test them with these lists:

```
{ 0 }                    { 1 2 3 }
{ 1 0 (1,0) }            { }
```

34. Use `L→V` and `V→L` to write another program, called `LADD` ("List ADD"), that adds the corresponding elements of two lists, producing a list of the sums. Test `LADD` with these pairs of lists:

```
a.  { 1 2 3 4 }                { 5 6 7 8 }
b.  { (1,1) (-3,4) }           { -5.4 (4.3,-8.1) }
c.  { 9 6 8 }                  { 1 1 }
d.  { [ 1 2 ] [ 3 4 ] }  { [ -3 1 ] [ 6 9 ] }
```

35. When would evaluating a directory's name *not* send you to that directory? How could you give a directory two different names?

36. Suppose you want to build yourself a little phone book: Write a program that will open the correct one among 26 alphabetically named (`A` through `Z`) subdirectories—depending upon the first letter of the string you key in.

Objective Answers

1. Just a reminder of the options you have for keying in objects and doing arithmetic with them on the Stack. For example:
[1][ENTER][2][+][3][+][4][+][5][+][6][+][7][+][8][+][9][+][1][0][+], *or*
[1][SPC][2][SPC][3][SPC][4][SPC][5][SPC][6][SPC][7][SPC][8][SPC][9][SPC][1][0]
[+][+][+][+][+][+][+][+][+], etc. Answer: 55

Of course, no such method is good for adding a *thousand* numbers, but observe that

$$1+2+3\ldots+998+999+1000$$
$$=(1+1000)+(2+999)+(3+998)\ldots+(500+501)$$
$$=1001\times500.$$

So: [1][0][0][1][ENTER][5][0][0][×] Answer: 500500

2. [←][MODES][2] **SCI**. Then key in the atomic mass: [1][0][7][•][8][6][8] [←][UNITS] **MASS** **G** [NXT][NXT][→] **MOL**. Next, key in Avogadro's number: [6][•][0][2][2][EEX][2][3][ENTER][→] **MOL**. Notice that the item being counted (atoms) is implied—as with cycles in "cycles per second" (Hz) or any other discrete item. Now divide the two arguments: [÷] (that's grams per atom), then multiply by 4 (atoms per cell): [4][×].... Result: 7.16E-22_g (grams per cell)

Volume is mass divided by density. You have the mass already, so key in the density: [1][0][•][5][NXT] **G** [←][UNITS] **VOL** [→] **CM^3**. And divide: [÷] Result: 6.82E-23_cm^3

And, since the unit cell is a cube, just take the cube root of the volume to find the length of an edge: [3][→][ˣ√y]. Now just convert to Å: [←][UNITS] **LENG** [←][PREV][←] **Å**.... Result: 4.09E0_Å

3. [←][UNITS][NXT] **ENRG** [2][•][1][4][EEX][4] **J**
[←][UNITS] **MASS** [←][PREV][→] **MOL**
[→][LAST MENU][8][•][3][1][4] **J**
[←][UNITS][NXT] **TEMP** [→] **K**
[←][UNITS] **MASS** [←][PREV][→] **MOL** [÷]
[9][8][0][→][LAST MENU] **°F** [←] **K** [÷]
[+/−][←][e^x] Result: 4.00E-2 (4.00%)

4. One is a list; the other is a vector.

To convert between them, start with the list: [←][MODES] **STD**
[←][{ }][1][SPC][2][SPC][3][SPC][4][ENTER] (and [PRG] **OBJ**).

Then **OBJ→** **→ARR** is the easiest conversion; **OBJ→** leaves the Stack all ready for **→ARR**.

To convert back: **OBJ→** **OBJ→** [◄] **→LIST**. Since **→LIST** needs a real number for a length argument, you use **OBJ→** [◄] to *extract* that real number from the *list*-type length argument produced by decomposing the vector.

5. Use the list from problem 4: **OBJ→** [1][−] **→LIST** deletes the first element; **OBJ→** [SWAP][DROP][1][−] **→LIST** deletes the last element.

6. Start with 1+2*i*: [←][( )][1][SPC][2][ENTER] (and [NXT] at the OBJ menu). Then **C→R** [►] **R→C** does the job.

7. Do the **power plants** first: Calculate the barrels of oil saved by their typical daily generating level: [←][MODES][1] [ENG] (to reflect the level of certainty of the data). Then [1][0][0][0][→][_][α][M][α][W] [ENTER][7][5][MTH] [PARTS] [NXT] [%] [1][→][_][α][←][D][ENTER][×][3][×][0] [→][_][α][M][α][J][ENTER][+][5][9][0][0][→][_][α][M][α][J][ENTER][÷][8][0][×] (notice the unit *prefixes* here). Result: 2.6E6 The oil (barrels) that eighty 1000-MW power plants would save daily. The costs?...
[1][0][0][0][EEX][6][ENTER][EEX][3][÷][8][0][×][ENTER] (rated kW for 80 plants)
[1][2][0][0][ENTER][2][0][0][+][5][0][0][0][0][+][×][2][5][÷][3][6][5][÷]
Result: 450.E6 That's $450 million spent per *day* for 25 years for the 80 nuclear plants
[←][1][0][0][0][ENTER][1][0][0][+][1][0][0][0][0][+][×][5][0][÷][3][6][5][÷]
Result: 49.E6 That's $49 million spent per *day* for 50 years for the 80 coal-fired plants

The **efficiencies**. First, the daily oil savings in water heating:
[1][2][5][3][ENTER][3][6][5][÷][•][2][×][•][2][×][EEX][8][×][←][UNITS] [VOL] [NXT] [GAL] [NXT][NXT][←] [BBL] Result: 330.E3_bbl
The $avings: [4][0][+/–][ENTER][1][0][÷] (the plumbing ought to last at least 10 years) [1][2][0][0][ENTER][•][2][×][•][2][×][+][3][6][5][÷][EEX][8][×]
Result: 12.E6 That's $12 million saved per day.

Next, the daily oil savings in electrical appliance efficiency:
[1][2][5][3][ENTER][3][6][5][÷][•][1][5][×][•][0][5][×][EEX][8][×][NXT][NXT] [GAL] [NXT][NXT][←] [BBL] [3][×] Result: 180.E3_bbl
The $avings: [1][2][0][0][ENTER][3][6][5][÷][•][1][5][×][•][0][5][×][EEX][8][×]
Result: 2.5E6 That's $2.5 million saved per day.

Then there's the daily oil savings in electrical lighting efficiency:
[1][2][5][3][ENTER][3][6][5][÷][•][1][×][•][7][5][×][EEX][8][×][NXT][NXT] [GAL] [NXT][NXT][←] [BBL] [3][×] Result: 1.8E6_bbl

The $avings: [1][5][0][+/−][ENTER][5][÷][1][2][0][0][ENTER][•][1][×][•][7][5] [×][+][3][6][5][÷][EEX][8][×]

Result: 16.E6 That's $16 million saved per day.

Finally, the daily oil savings from proper tire inflation:

[1][0][0][0][0][ENTER][1][9][÷][1][4][0][EEX][6][×][•][0][3][×][3][6][5][÷][ENTER] [1][6][•][4][÷] Result: 370.E3

The $avings: [⬅][1][•][2][5][×] (cheap for a gallon of gas by now)

Result: 7.6E6 $7.6 million saved per day.

So here's the filled-in table (remember—these are *daily* figures):

Option	$Costs (Savings)		Energy gain (bbl/d)	% of current use
80 nuclear reactors	**Total:**	**$ 450 million**	**2.6 million**	**17%**
80 coal plants	**Total:**	**$ 49 million**	**2.6 million**	**17%**
Efficiency measures	H_2O heat:	($12 million)	0.33 million	2.2%
	Appls.:	(2.5 million)	0.18 million	1.2%
	Lighting:	(16 million)	1.8 million	12%
	Tire infl.:	(7.6 million)	0.37 million	2.5%
	Total:	**($39.1 million)**	**2.7 million**	**18%**

So, to add 17-18% to the nation's daily oil supply—without any change to your life-style—which would you rather do:

spend $50-450 million/day—and wait 3-5 years for results?
or save $40 million/day—with immediate results?

8. Press [2][⇦][ASIN]. Answer: (1.57079632679,-1.31695789692) (assumes XYZ and STD modes here). A complex trig argument doesn't carry the circular geometric interpretation ("units") that real arguments do. The general sine function is an infinite series sum: $\sin x = x - \frac{x^3}{3!} + \frac{x^5}{5!} - \frac{x^7}{7!} + \cdots$

9. The angle, ϕ, between any two vectors, *A* and *B*, is given by

$$\phi = \cos^{-1}\left(\frac{\mathbf{A} \bullet \mathbf{B}}{|\mathbf{A}||\mathbf{B}|}\right)$$

Be sure that you enter each vector in its proper mode:

[⇦][[ ]][9][+/-][SPC][4][SPC][2][+/-][ENTER]['][α][A][STO]; [MTH] **VECTR** **R∡∡** [⇦][RAD][1][2][SPC][1][·][3][9][SPC][·][4][8][⇨][3D] ['][α][B][STO]. Now calculate: [VAR] **A** [NXT] **B** [⇨][LAST MENU] **DOT** [VAR] **A** [⇨][LAST MENU] **ABS** [÷][VAR][NXT] **B** [⇨][LAST MENU] **ABS** [÷][⇦][ACOS]....Result: 1.64093275493 (rad)

10. The volume of a parallelpiped is the absolute value of its vectors' *triple scalar product*, defined as any of these variations:

a • (b x c)	**b • (a x c)**	**c • (a x b)**
a • (c x b)	**b • (c x a)**	**c • (b x a)**

So: [⇦][[ ]][7][SPC][1][SPC][·][2][+/-][ENTER][⇦][[ ]][1][SPC][8][SPC][1][+/-] [ENTER][⇦][[ ]][3][SPC][3][SPC][5][ENTER]. Then evaluate the function: [MTH] **VECTR** **CROSS** **DOT** Result: 297.2

11. First, build and name your three vectors: [⬅][MODES][NXT][NXT], then **XYZ** [1][SPC][2][SPC][3][➦][3D]['][α][A][STO]
R∡Z **DEG** [3][+/−][SPC][2][5][SPC][•][2][+/−][➦][3D]['][α][B][STO]
R∡∡ **RAD** [3][1/x][2][√x][6][+/−][➦][3D]['][α][C][STO]
Then: [VAR][NXT][1][4][•][5] **A** [×][•][2] **B** [×][−][NXT][⬅][( )][1][SPC]
[1] **C** [×][+][➦][LAST MENU] **XYZ**—to see the real and imaginary portions of the complex vector result.
Next, [PRG] **OBJ** [NXT] **C→R** (yes, **C→R** / **R→C** will split/build complex-valued *vectors*, too).
Then [+] adds the two real-valued vectors, and to find the corresponding *unit* vector, you divide the vector by its own magnitude: [MTH] **PARTS** [ENTER] **ABS** [÷].... Answer:
`[ .27312118384 .533411568534 .80054788582 ]`

12. First, build the vector: [2][SPC][4][SPC][6][SPC][8][SPC][1][0][SPC][5][PRG] **OBJ** **→ARR**. Now [NXT][NXT][NXT][4] [SPC][1][9] **PUT**. The first argument for PUT is the *position* of the target element in the vector (or array or list). The second argument is its new value. Of course, you can't put a complex value into a real-valued vector, so [⬅][( )][1][SPC][0][×] first, to convert the vector, then [1][SPC][⬅][( )] [1][SPC][1] **PUT** does the job.

13. Press [⬅][[ ]][1][SPC][2][ENTER], then [⬅][{ }][5][ENTER][MTH] **MATR** **RDM**. The ReDiMension command needs a list-type argument to tell it the desired new dimension of your vector (for an array, you would need *two* dimension numbers in this list). Now [3][SPC][5][PRG] **OBJ** [⬅][PREV] **PUT** changes the third element, and [⬅][[ ]] [5][SPC] [4][SPC][3][SPC][2][SPC][1][MTH] **VECTR** **DOT** finds the Answer: 28

14. Build the vector: ⬅[ ] 1 SPC 2 SPC 3 SPC 4 SPC 5 SPC 6 SPC 7 SPC 8 SPC 9 ENTER. Then ⬅{ } 3 SPC 3 ENTER MTH **MATR** **RDM** to redimension, and ⬅{ } 1 SPC 2 ENTER 1 0 PRG **OBJ** ⬅PREV **PUT** to change element$_{12}$. ⬅( ) 1 SPC 0 × makes it complex.

15. Simply *multiply* by the appropriate *row identity* matrices. For example, to extract the first row, multiply by `[[ 1 0 0 ]]` (⬅[ ] ⬅[ ] 1 SPC 0 SPC 0 ⬅SWAP ×). And for the second row, multiply by `[[ 0 1 0 ]]`, and so on. *Notice* that the order of your multiplication is important. Notice, too, that each result is an *array* (**1x3**), not a vector.

16. This is just a vector problem—with *momentum* (mass × velocity): ➡POLAR ⬅RAD (you want polar mode, angles in degrees), then ⬅MODES 1 **FIX** 1 5 0 ➡_ α α ⬅α T O N ENTER 8 8 ➡_ α α ⬅α M P H α ENTER × ➡UNITS **UBASE** **UVAL** 4 4 • 1 9 ⬅TIME ⬅PREV **HMS→** ⬅2D
(UBASE, UVAL and HMS→ are new here; notice how they work.)

That's the first train's momentum. Now the other one: 3 EEX 5 ➡_ α ⬅K α ⬅G ENTER 1 1 0 ➡_ α α ⬅α K P H α ENTER × ➡UNITS **UBASE** **UVAL** 2 5 6 • 3 2 ➡LAST MENU **HMS→** ⬅2D

Now, the big moment: + <u>Result</u>: `[ 5445411.1 ∡-71.9 ]`

But compass bearings proceed *clockwise from north* (not counterclockwise from "east," as in math conventions). The momentum heading of the wreckage (–71.9°) therefore indicates *north* of due west (–90°)—so it looks like Canada should hire the backhoe.

17. One possible strategy: Build a "five-day" vector for each person.

[⬅][MODES] **STD** [NXT][NXT] **XYZ**
[⬅][[ ]][8][SPC][8][SPC][4][SPC][8][SPC][8][ENTER]['][α][A][STO]
[⬅][[ ]][8][SPC][8][SPC][7][SPC][7][SPC][8][ENTER]['][α][B][STO]
[⬅][[ ]][5][SPC][6][SPC][5][SPC][4][SPC][5][ENTER]['][α][C][STO]
[⬅][[ ]][7][SPC][7][SPC][7][SPC][8][SPC][7][ENTER]['][α][D][STO]

Now [MTH] **MATR** [⬅][PREV] and use **CNRM** on each person's vector to sum his/her hours ([α][A][ENTER] **CNRM**, [α][B][ENTER]**CNRM**, etc.). Then you can either sum these results ([+][+][+])—*or* sum the vectors ([α][A][ENTER][α][B][+]...) and **CNRM**—to total all hours: 135

18. [⬅][[ ]][⬅][[ ]][1][SPC][2][▶][3][SPC][4][ENTER]['][α][A][STO], and
[⬅][[ ]][⬅][[ ]][1][6][SPC][9][▶][4][SPC][1][ENTER]['][α][B][STO].

Then [VAR][NXT] **A** **B** [×] and **B** **A** [×].... So matrix multiplication is *not* commutative.

19. To use [⬅][2D] to build complex numbers, just set system flag –19: [1][9][+/–][SPC][α][S][α][F][ENTER]. Now [1][ENTER][2][⬅][2D]...Your result is a complex number, right?

20. Use system flags: When flag –15 is *clear* ([1][5][+/–][➡][MODES][NXT] **CF**), and flag –16 is *set* ([1][6][+/–] **SF**), this activates polar/cylindrical mode. Similarly, the combination of [4][9][+/–] **SF** and [5][0][+/–] **SF** activates ENG mode. Clear all four of these flags before going on.

21. The 48's current binary wordsize is determined by the states of system flags –5 through –10. These six flags form their own six-bit binary integer whose value *plus 1* becomes the machine's wordsize (the wordsize ranges from 1 to 64; a six-bit binary word represents values from 0 to 63—hence the addition of 1).

To extract this number from the flag settings, test those six flags, line up the bits and read the value: [PRG] **TEST** [⬅][PREV], then

Key-strokes	[1][0][+/–] **FS?**	[9][+/–] **FS?**	[8][+/–] **FS?**	[7][+/–] **FS?**	[6][+/–] **FS?**	[5][+/–] **FS?**
Results:	0	0	0	1	1	1

Thus, the wordsize here is $000111_2 + 1$, or 8_{10}

Alternatively, you could do it with math: Start with the adjustment value, 1: [➡][CLR][1][ENTER]. Then test each flag and multiply the result by that flag's *place value* in the six bit integer:
[1][0][+/–] **FS?** [3][2][×][+][9][+/–] **FS?** [1][6][×][+]
[8][+/–] **FS?** [8][×][+][7][+/–] **FS?** [4][×][+][6][+/–] **FS?** [2][×][+]
[5][+/–] **FS?** [+] Result: 8

22. The easiest way to *preserve* the 48's system settings is to save the binary integers that represent the values of all the flags:

[α][α][R][C][L][F][ENTER]['][α][α][S][Y][S][1][α][STO]

Now all flag states are saved as the VARiable SYS1. And since you can have all the VARiables you want, this means you can save *any number* of different flag settings—both the 48's system flags and your own user flags!

23. Press [MTH] BASE [1][6] STWS HEX [→][#][α][α][F][F][F][ENTER] [2][÷][2][×]   Result: `# FFEh`

You *don't* get `# FFFh` back again, because binary division truncates any remainder: Since FFF_{16} is an odd number (4095_{10}), dividing by 2 resulted in 2047_{10} (not 2047.5), and so multiplying by 2 then gave 4094_{10}, or FFE_{16}.

24. Press DEC [→][#][1][0][0][ENTER][ENTER], then [PRG] OBJ →STR [→][LAST MENU] BIN .... The results differ because they're different objects. Only a binary integer object changes its displayed appearance in response to a change in the binary integer format. The string was created with the *characters* it encountered in the format of the binary integer *at the moment* you pressed →STR.

25. First, press [→][""][α][α][Y][←][α][O][U][SPC][U][N][D][E][R][S][T][A][N][D] [←][◆][ENTER] (remember the many characters on the shifted keys when in alpha mode—use your Quick Reference Guide to help you). Then [←][EDIT] SKIP→ SKIP→ [◀][◆][α][←][DEL][ENTER].

26. [→][""][α][α][V][←][α][O][L][·][←][=][SPC][ENTER] [1][ENTER][α][α][F][I][X] [ENTER][2][ENTER][ENTER][+] (gets `4.0` without the [4] key).
Then [+][→][""][SPC] [α][α][←][α] [G][A][L][·][ENTER] [+]. To *extract* the value, assume that you know only its surrounding characters in the string, and use some handy string dissecting commands: [ENTER][ENTER][→][""][α][SPC][ENTER][PRG] OBJ [NXT][NXT] POS [1][+] [▶] SIZE SUB [ENTER][→][""][SPC][ENTER] POS [1][−][1][←][▶] SUB [NXT][NXT] OBJ→   Result: `4.0`

27. [α][α][S][T][D][ENTER][6][•][0][2][2][EEX][2][3][ENTER][ENTER][MTH] PARTS [NXT][NXT] MANT [▶] XPON [↱][""][↰][()][◆][+] [↱][""][α][α][SPC][X][SPC] [1][0][α][↱][ENTRY][↱][ENTRY][y^x]. [↰][()][DEL][ENTER][▶][+][+] finishes it. OBJ→ will produce an `Invalid Syntax` error, because it tries to decompose a string into objects and put them onto the Stack in *postfix* notation. So if you want a string that separates the mantissa and exponent but still evaluates back to the number, you would need to use `"6.022 10 23 ^ *"`.

28. Press [VAR][NXT] A ['] A [↰][PURGE]['][α][↰][X][STO]. Then [1] [↰] A , [NXT][8][+/−][↰] B , and [1][5][↰] C . Then ['] EQ [↱][VISIT][▶][▶][▶][▶][▶][◆][−][ENTER] EQ [EVAL][NXT]['] X [PRG] OBJ →TAG.... Result: `x: 3`

29. [3][+/−][SPC][α][S][α][F][ENTER]. Then [VAR][NXT]['] B [ENTER][+/−]. This isn't how things went when you built the other quadratic solution (pages 128-129). The difference: When flag –3, the Numerical Results flag, is *set*, the 48 *evaluates* names during Stack operations. Your name `'b'` contains `-8`, so [+/−] on `'b'` gives `8`.

30. [3][+/−][SPC][α][C][α][F][ENTER][↰][π][EVAL] (result: `'π'`); [α][↰][I][EVAL] (result: `'i'`); and [α][↰][E][EVAL] (result: `'e'`). Then [2][+/−][SPC][α][S][α][F][ENTER] and repeat these keystrokes.... Numerical values, right? Flag –2 is the Symbolic Constants flag. Only when Flag -2 is *set* will these constants' names evaluate to their respective numerical values (unless flag –3 is set, which *overrides* a clear flag –2).

31. To PURGE more than one name at a time from your VAR menu, just form a *list* of the names you want to PURGE: [VAR] [←] [{ }] **X** **SYS1** **D** **C** **EX1** **A** [NXT] **B** **C** **B** **VECTO** [ENTER] [←] [PURGE] PURGEs all VARiables except EQ.

32. Build the expression: [2] [ENTER] ['] [α] [←] [X] [ENTER] [×] ['] [α] [←] [Y] [ENTER] [+] ['] [α] [α] [E] [X] [P] [R] [α] [STO]. Then

a. [2] [+/−] ['] [α] [←] [Y] [ENTER] [×] ['] [α] [←] [X] [STO] **EXPR** [EVAL]
Result: '2*-(2*y)+y'

b. [2] [+/−] ['] **X** [ENTER] [×] ['] [α] [←] [Y] [STO] ['] **X** [←] [PURGE] **EXPR** [EVAL]   Result: '2*x-2*x'

c. ['] [α] [←] [T] [ENTER] [ENTER] ['] [α] [←] [X] [STO] [1] [−] ['] **Y** [STO] **EXPR** [EVAL]   Result: '2*t+(t-1)'

d. ['] [α] [←] [Z] [ENTER] [ENTER] [3] ['] **Y** [ENTER] [×] [−] [←] **X** [3] [←] [SWAP] [×] ['] **Y** [ENTER] [SWAP] [−] [←] **Y** **EXPR** [EVAL]   Result: '2*(z-3*y)+(y-3*z)'

This is just substitution. But notice how the 48 doesn't automatically simplify an algebraic. Notice also the self-referencing name (y) in case **d**: press [EVAL] repeatedly to see its effect....

33. L→V: « OBJ→ →ARRY »
V→L: « OBJ→ OBJ→ DROP →LIST »
First, clean up: [←][{ }] **X** **Y** [ENTER][←][PURGE][→][CLR]. Then: [←][« »][PRG] **OBJ** **OBJ→** **→ARR** [ENTER]['][α][α][L][→][→][V][α][STO]; and [←][« »] **OBJ→** **OBJ→** [←][DROP] **→LIST** [ENTER]['][α][α][V][→][→][L][α][STO]
Notice that these simple programs are really nothing more than a recording of the keystrokes you use manually. Now test them:
[VAR][←][{ }][0][ENTER] **L→V** ... **V→L** ....looks good;
[←][{ }][1][SPC][2][SPC][3][ENTER] **L→V** ... **V→L** ....OK—but notice that the vector display mode will affect your results;
[←][{ }][1][SPC][0][SPC][←][( )][1][SPC][0][ENTER] **L→V** ... **V→L** ....
OK—but since a vector can't contain real and complex numbers at the same time (unlike a list), it makes everything complex;
[←][{ }][ENTER] **L→V** ...nope—an error. You haven't allowed for the possibility of an empty list (consider how might you do that).

34. LADD: « L→V SWAP L→V + V→L » So, press [←][« »] **L→V** [←][SWAP] **L→V** [+] **V→L** [ENTER]['][α][α][L][A][D][D][α][STO]. Then:

a. [←][{ }][1][SPC][2][SPC][3][SPC][4][ENTER][←][{ }][5][SPC][6][SPC][7][SPC][8][ENTER] **LADD**.... Result: { 6 8 10 12 }

b. [←][{ }][←][( )][1][SPC][1][▶][←][( )][3][+/−][SPC][4][ENTER][←][[ ]][5][•][4][+/−][SPC][←][( )][4][•][3][SPC][8][•][1][+/−][ENTER] **LADD**
Result: { (-4.4,1) (1.3,-4.1) }

c. [←][{ }][9][SPC][6][SPC][8][ENTER][←][{ }][1][SPC][1][ENTER] **LADD**....
Result: Error: Invalid Dimension
You can't add vectors of different dimensions.

d. [←][{ }][←][[ ]][1][SPC][2][▶][←][[ ]][3][SPC][4][ENTER][←][{ }][←][[ ]][3][+/−][SPC][1][▶][←][[ ]][6][SPC][9][ENTER] **LADD**.... Result: Error: Bad Argument type A vector can't have vector components.

35. Invoking a directory's name will *not* move you to that directory unless it's in the current PATH ("between you and HOME").

To give a directory named BILL a second name—say, DAVE—just [STO]re 'BILL' into 'DAVE'. That way, when you evaluate either BILL or DAVE, you'll be sent to BILL.

36. Here's one way to do it—call this program PHONES:

« DUP NUM CHR OBJ→ »

To key this in: [←][« »][←][ENTER][PRG] OBJ [NXT][NXT] NUM CHR [NXT][NXT] OBJ→ [ENTER]['][α][α][P][H][O][N][E][S][α][STO]

First, DUP makes another copy of the string—so that it's still on the Stack at the end of the program. Then NUM gets the character number of the first character of the string; CHR changes this number back to a one-character string. Then OBJ→ decomposes the string and evaluates its single component character, thus opening the appropriate directory.

To test PHONES, just create a couple of test directories (named with single letters of the alphabet—say, Q, R and S). Then feed PHONES some hypothetical "words" (say, "Quine", "Roberts" and "Simons") to see if it will open up the correct directories. Will it find the directories if you fail to capitalize the target word?

4 FUNCTIONS AND EXPRESSIONS

Functions and Arguments

In Chapter 3, you learned about the various *objects* the 48 uses. That is, you learned all about the machine's "nouns"—its lists, units, directories, arrays, flags, strings, etc. In this chapter, you'll start to focus on the "verbs" of the calculator. These are the *tools* in your workshop—the commands that produce the problem-solving, "number-crunching" *actions*.

Your Owner's Manual refers to three kinds of calculator actions.

- Any action that you can do on the 48 is an *operation.*
- Operations that you can record in programs are *commands.*
- Commands that you can use in algebraic objects are *functions.*

This chapter is all about this third group, *functions*—and the algebraic *expressions* you can build with them. Why a whole chapter? Because many problems whose solutions require programs on other machines can be solved in the 48 with these algebraic objects.

To build and use algebraics well, you must first know what functions you can put into them. Functions in the 48 are much like those in the conventional mathematical definition: A **function** transforms one or more **argument** objects into exactly one **result** object.

A function is made up of a *name* and *arguments.* The name is the tool—the active, calculating, "verb" part of the process. The arguments are objects—the "nouns." When you *evaluate* the function, you get a *result.*

Some Built-In Functions

First, look at some of the 48's built-in functions—and consider the basic characteristics of this kind of tool....

Preparing Your Arguments

A function accepts only certain object types as arguments—and only in a certain order. For example, the square root function has a name (SQRT) and one argument (the object in Stack Level 1)—simple. But the subtraction function has a name (-) and *two* arguments (in Stack Levels 1 and 2). And of course, you must use the two arguments *in the right order* to get the right answer....

Scalpel: Use a built-in function to truncate the real number 9.778629 to its integer part.

Slice: First, *find the right function.* If you haven't discovered this already, you'll start to see it now: Finding the right function—and knowing its requirements—is half the battle in the 48. The function you need here is IP (Integer Portion). Press MTH PARTS NXT NXT to find it.

Next, *prepare your argument(s).* IP requires just one argument—at Stack Level 1: 9 • 7 7 8 6 2 9 ENTER.

Now *evaluate the function:* press IP.
Result: 9 (in STD display mode)

Try Again: Using the same function, find the integer part of the complex number, 6+4*i*.

Oops: Put (6, 4) into Level 1 (⬅ ( ) 6 SPC 4 ENTER) and **IP**. Error, right? Bad Argument Type You must know the limitations of your function: IP doesn't accept a complex number object as an argument.

Now consider a function with *two* arguments....

More Slicing: Use the TRNC function to TRuNCate 9.77863 at two decimal places.

Hmm... TRNC needs two arguments—the number being truncated (that's 9.778629 here) and the number of decimal places (2 in this case). So which argument goes on Level 1 and which on Level 2?

The *Quick Reference Guide* supplied with your 48 can help you remember such things. In the alphabetical Command Reference section, look up TRNC....

It says that the value being truncated goes at Level 2 and the number of decimal places at Level 1. Thus:

9 . 7 7 8 6 3 ENTER 2 NXT **TRNC** Result: 9.77

Checking the Machine's Assumptions

Whenever a function doesn't behave the way you think it should, check these three possible problems:

1. Did you key in all argument *values* correctly?
2. Did you place these arguments in proper order on the Stack?
3. Is your calculator in the correct *mode*?

Your own keystroking accuracy is the only solution to problem **1**;
The *Quick Reference Guide* is a simple way to avoid problem **2**;
But for problem **3**, you need to be thinking and alert....

Example: Find sin 3.49

Think: If you simply key in `3.49` and press [SIN], you'll get an answer—but it may be a wrong answer, if the 48 is in DEGree mode instead of RADian mode (math convention: without an explicit °, the argument of a trig function is assumed to be in *radians*, not degrees).

So press [←][RAD], if necessary, to set RADians mode (announced by the `RAD` in the Status Area). *Now* do it: [3][•][4][9][SIN].... Result: `-.341401277877`

The 48 can't read your mind; it doesn't know what mode is correct for the problem! It can only warn you of some of its current assumptions—with Status Area annunciators:

Angles	`RAD`	`GRAD`
Vector displays	`R∡Z`	`R∡∡`

But *not every mode* is announced in the display...

Example: Find $\sin N\pi$, for N=1.5.

Like So: [1] [•] [5] [ENTER] ['] [α] [N] [STO] [VAR] ['] **N** [ENTER] [←] [π] [×] [SIN]

What do you get? *That depends on the current states of system flags –2 and –3*—modes that are not displayed in the Status Area.

With both of these flags *clear*, the 48 will not evaluate the function beyond its symbolic form: 'SIN(N*π)'. To *force* the 48 to produce a numerical value for the function, you must use [→] [→NUM].

By contrast, with flag –3 (the Numerical Results flag) *set*, you always get the numerical result automatically.

Or, with flag –3 *clear* but flag –2 (the Symbolic Constants flag) *set*, the machine will automatically evaluate only the symbolic constant ('π')—but leave your variable ('N') unevaluated.

Try the above function with each of these flag setting combinations. Use the flag commands on the last page of the [→] [MODES] menu (or use the [←] [MODES] menu to change flag –3 between numerical and symbolic results: [←] [MODES] **SYM▪**).

Keep all this in mind now—*arguments* and *modes*—as you explore some more of the machine's built-in functions....

Complex Numbers vs. Vectors

Complex numbers and two-dimensional vectors share a number of properties as arguments for functions....

Try: Find the *inner product* ("dot product") of (4, 5) and (-3, 8).

Uh: [←][()][4][SPC][5][ENTER] [←][()][3][+/-][SPC][8][ENTER] loads the arguments onto the Stack. Then [α][α][D][O][T][ENTER].... No go, right? Often, you *can* solve a problem with either complex numbers or ***2D*** vectors, but they *are* different object types—and some functions accept only one of those types. Dot product is defined only for vectors in the 48, so change the complex numbers to vectors: Press [1][9][+/-][ENTER][α][C][α][F][ENTER] (recall page 157, problem **19**). Then [←][2D][←][2D][▶][←][2D][←][2D] [▶] and [α][α][D][O][T] [ENTER].... Result: 28

Dates and Times

Suppose: Your property taxes are due in 37 days. That date is...?

Easy: Press [←][TIME] **SET**. Now key in today's date—formatted in MM.DDYYYY date format used by the 48: If today is September 17, 1990, press [9][·][1][7][1][9][9][0] **→DAT**. Now *add* 37 days to today's date: [←][TIME] [NXT] **DATE** [3][7] **DATE+**.... There's your tax deadline date.

When: What day of the week was June 6, 1944?

How: In time and date arithmetic functions, your arguments (the times and dates) must be given in the current time and date formats (controlled by flags –41 and –42, respectively). Thus, June 6, 1944 would be 6.061944.
Key this in: [6][•][0][6][1][9][4][4][ENTER].
Now key in any time that day (you're not interested in the time, but you must give some time as an argument)—say, noon: [1][2]. And now use the handy TSTR function: **TSTR**....
Result: "TUE 06/06/44 12:00:00P"

Another: Find the average time per mile for this relay team:

Runner	Miles	Time	Runner	Miles	Time
Paul	5.4	36:23	Mike	5.2	32:38
Christy	5.3	40:49	Shirley	5.5	42:09
Bob	5.9	45:23	Bill	6.0	37:26

Solution: Press [4][←][MODES] **FIX** [←][TIME][←][PREV] to prepare. Then *sum* all the times—in HH.MMSSs notation—with **HMS+**:
[•][3][6][2][3][ENTER][•][4][0][4][9] **HMS+** [•][4][5][2][3] **HMS+** [•][3][2][3][8] **HMS+** [•][4][2][0][9] **HMS+** [•][3][7][2][6] **HMS+**.

Now convert to hours and fractions: **HMS→**.... And total the distances and divide: [5][•][4][ENTER][5][•][3][+][5][•][9][+][5][•][2][+][5][•][5][+][6][+][÷]. Finally, convert the resulting average back to HMS form: **→HMS**....
Result: .0703 (that's 7:03/mile).

Fractions

Your 48 can convert from decimal representation of rational numbers to fractional representation of them (a ratio of integers). Set your display mode to STD ([⬅][MODES] **STD**) for these exercises....

Example: What fraction is approximately equal to 0.875968992248?

Answer: Press [.][8][7][5][9][6][8][9][9][2][2][4][8][⬅][→Q].
Result: '113/129'

Try This: What fraction is approximately equal to 3.4592385747?

Simple: Press [3][.][4][5][9][2][3][8][5][7][4][7][⬅][→Q]
Result: '1809884/523203' (Now *that's* a fraction.)

But: Press [2][SPC][α][α][F][I][X][ENTER] and repeat the problem.
Result: '38/11' *The display setting affects the precision with which the 48 searches for the fraction.* Press [EVAL][⬅][EDIT] to compare the two conversions.

Also: Convert 5.83438635667 to its closest fraction.

Solution: Set STD mode to get the most accurate conversion.
Then: [5][.][8][3][4][3][8][6][3][5][6][6][7][⬅][→Q]....
Result: '2665031/456780'

"But maybe π is involved somehow." To find out, press [5][.][8][3][4][3][8][6][3][5][6][6][7][⬅][ALGEBRA][NXT] **→Qπ**
Result: '13/7*π' (Aha!)

One More: Use →Qπ to convert 6.85972486853 to a fraction.

Solution: Press 6 • 8 5 9 7 2 4 8 6 8 5 3 →Qπ.
Result: '1800129/262420' With →Qπ, you get the best of everything: First it searches for multiples of π, but if it doesn't find any, it does a ← →Q conversion!

Probabilities

Another very useful group of functions are in the PROBability menu....

Try Some: There are 100 senators in the U.S. Senate. How many different 7-member committees are possible?

Well...: You want the number of *combinations* possible from 100 objects, taken 7 at a time. So: 1 0 0 SPC 7 MTH PROB COMB Result: 16007560800 possible committees.*

Another: How many different ways can you shuffle a regular deck of 52 playing cards? How many different 5-card poker hands can you draw?

Hmm... *Permutations* of 52 cards—taken all 52 at a time (for shuffling), or just 5 at a time (for poker):
5 2 SPC 5 2 PERM Result: 8.06581751709E67
5 2 SPC 5 PERM Result: 311875200

---

*Please do not pass this classified information on to your senator.

As you continue this little tour of your workshop's built-in *function* tools, keep in mind that you can include any of these in the algebraic objects you build. You'll soon get practice doing that—but first, a few more tools to discover....

PARTS of Numbers

The 48 has a big bunch of functions that you'll probably use only occasionally—but when you need them, they're great. Most of these work with real numbers, some with complex numbers, too. They're in the MATH menu (press MTH), in the PARTS toolbox (press **PARTS**). In one way or another, these functions all treat *parts* of numbers.

Back on page 167, you learned about **TRNC**. It is one of four functions that help you ***round*** a number....

- **FLOOR** — rounds a decimal *down* to the nearest lesser integer.
- **CEIL** — rounds a decimal *up* to the nearest greater integer.
- **RND** — rounds a decimal to a given number of decimal places or significant digits. It works on the elements of units, complex numbers, vectors and arrays, too.
- **TRNC** — truncates a decimal to a given number of decimal places or significant digits. It works on the elements of units, complex numbers, vectors and arrays, too.

RND and **TRNC**, require a *second* argument—to tell them *where* to do their rounding or truncating.

Try Some: FIX the display to four decimal places, then:

a. Round 5.9983675 to 6 digits.

b. Evaluate 6 sin 48°, rounded to 3 significant digits.

c. Truncate 4.98330929 to the current display setting.

Solutions: [←][MODES][4] **FIX** sets the display. Then...

a. [5][•][9][9][8][3][6][7][5][ENTER][MTH] **PARTS** [←][PREV][6] **RND**. Result: Your display says 5.9984, but press [←][EDIT] to confirm that the actual number is now: 5.998368 (then press [ENTER] to cancel the EDIT).

b. In DEGree mode, press [4][8][SIN][6][×][3][+/−] **RND**. Result: 4.4600. Using a *negative* number as an argument tells the **RND** function to round to that many *significant digits* instead of decimal places.

c. [4][•][9][8][3][3][0][9][2][9][ENTER][1][2] **TRNC**.... Result: 4.9833 (confirm with [←][EDIT]). The 12 tells the 48 to use the current display setting.

Question: What's the difference between FIXing 3 decimal places and RouNDing to 3 decimal places?

Answer: FIXing the display affects only the *display*; it's a mode setting that has no effect on actual object values. But *rounding* a number actually changes that object. This is why the rounding functions are indeed *functions*.

Dissecting Numbers

You've already used two functions (**IP** and **FP**) that selectively eliminate *part* of an argument. But there are eight different functions that do some sort of extraction (these examples assume STD mode):

IP — extracts the Integer Portion of a real number or unit:
[5][•][6][8][9] **IP** yields 5

FP — extracts the Fractional Portion of a real number or unit:
[5][•][6][8][9] **FP** yields .689

MANT — extracts the MANTissa of a number—as if it were formatted in scientific notation:
[4][•][8][9][3][EEX][+/-][8] **MANT** yields 4.893

XPON — extracts the eXPONent of a number—as if it were formatted in scientific notation:
[4][•][8][9][3][EEX][+/-][8] **XPON** yields -8

ABS — extracts the ABSolute value, magnitude or norm of a real number, unit, complex number, array or vector:
[3][•][4][+/-] **ABS** yields 3.4

SIGN — extracts the SIGN or direction* of a real number, complex number, or unit: [3][•][4][+/-] **SIGN** yields -1

RE — extracts the REal portion of a complex number or unit:
[←][( )][3][SPC][5][+/-] **RE** yields 3

IM — extracts the IMaginary component of a complex number:
[←][( )][3][SPC][5][+/-] **IM** yields -5

***SIGN** returns a unit vector in the "direction" of the complex number.

Comparing Two Numbers

There are six simple comparison functions—each needing arguments (reals or units) on the first two Stack levels. Then the arguments are consumed and the result goes on Level 1:

MIN — keeps the lesser of the two arguments:
[4] [•] [5] [SPC] [9] [•] [3] **MIN** yields 4.5

MAX — keeps the greater of the two arguments:
[4] [•] [5] [SPC] [9] [•] [3] **MAX** yields 9.3

MOD — divides the first real number by the second real number and reports the *remainder*:
[8] [7] [SPC] [7] **MOD** yields 3

% — multiplies the two arguments and divides by 100:
[2] [0] [SPC] [5] [4] **%** yields 10.8

%CH — calculates the % CHange in value from the first argument to the second:
[4] [0] [SPC] [5] [5] **%CH** yields 37.5

%T — (% of Total) calculates the percentage of the first argument represented by the second argument:
[8] [5] [0] [SPC] [1] [7] [0] **%T** yields 20

Symbolic Functions and Variables

All right—that gives you a fairly good feel for what tools you have at your disposal when building functions of your own. Now it's time to start doing that.

As you know, the real power of the 48 is unleashed when you use it with *symbolic arguments.* You can use symbolic arguments—i.e. your variables—within *algebraic* objects.

There are three types of symbolic objects:

Variable: the basic building block of algebraic expressions and equations—variables are the names into which you store values.

Expression: an algebraic containing at least one function with its arguments (and any of these arguments may be variables).

Equation: an expression equated (by a =) to another expression, or to a real number, complex number or unit.

It's time to examine each of these objects in greater detail...

Creating and Reviewing Variables

You already know how to build and name *variables*, but you'll need to do a few more now—to use later. Some names will contain objects; others will remain *formal* variables—names without objects.

Go: Create the following variables:

$X =$ (undefined) $\quad Y =$ (undefined)

$A = 4 \quad B = -3 \quad C = \sqrt{2}$

$D = 1 - 2i \quad E = 4 + 6i \quad L = B - A$

$V1 = 7\mathbf{i} + 4\mathbf{j} \quad V2 = -2\mathbf{i} - 5\mathbf{j} \quad V3 = 3\mathbf{i} - 2\mathbf{k}$

Press [→][CLR], then ['][α][X][←][PURGE]['][α][Y][←][PURGE] to dissociate values from the *formal* variables X and Y. Then:

[4]['][α][A][STO] [3][+/-]['][α][B][STO][2][√x]['][α][C][STO]
[←][()][1][SPC][2][+/-][▶]['][α][D][STO][←][()][4][SPC][6][▶]['][α][E][STO]
['][α][B][-][α][A][▶][SPC]['][α][L][STO][←][[ ]][7][SPC][4][▶]['][α][V][1][STO]
[←][[ ]][2][+/-][SPC][5][+/-][▶]['][α][V][2][STO]
[←][[ ]][3][SPC][0][SPC][2][+/-][▶]['][α][V][3][STO]

Now go to your VARiable menu—press [VAR]—and be sure they're all there (you'll have to use [NXT] to see all of them).

Question: How do you review the value stored in a variable?

Answer: You can press its menu key in the VAR menu. For example, pressing **V2** will put the current value of V2, which is `[ -2 -5 ]`, onto the Stack.

Or, you can press [←][REVIEW] to get a list of the items and values on the current menu page. Then, of course, you can use [NXT] and [←][REVIEW] again for the next page (and you can use [←][REVIEW] on any menu—not just VAR).

Creating Expressions

You can create algebraic expressions in three different ways—with the *Stack*, the *Command Line*, or the *Equation Writer.* Look at each method in turn....

Creating Expressions with the Stack or Command Line

You've already become acquainted with these two methods. Here's a quick comparison....

Do It: Build the expression sin(2*A*+*B*) , using the Stack.

Like So: VAR NXT 2 ENTER ' A ENTER × ' B ENTER + SIN

Easy—right? Indeed, you built a much more involved algebraic (the solution to a quadratic equation) back on pages 128-129.

Or: Build the same expression, sin(2*A*+*B*), using the Command Line.

OK: Press ' SIN 2 × A + B ENTER

Also very simple, no? But that's because it's a simple expression. When you encounter big, ugly expressions (lots of parentheses, radicals, exponents, teeth, hair, etc.), it's good to know your third option....

Creating Expressions with the Equation Writer

The Equation Writer is a built-in graphics program that allows you to see algebraic objects in the form you're used to seeing in a textbook.

And it's easy to use....

Do It: Build the expression sin(2*A*+*B*) , using the Equation Writer.

Go: Enter the Equation Writer ("EW") *environment* by pressing [←][EQUATION], whereupon you'll see the box cursor (▯) waiting for you to begin.

Start by pressing [SIN]....*Notice* right away that you don't need the ['] key in the EW to indicate that you're entering an algebraic (the 48 knows that—why else would you be there?)!

Press [2] [A]. Notice that you don't need to press [×] in the expression; The EW lets you get by with implied multiplication—knowing that when you say 2*A* you really mean 2×*A*.

Now finish the expression: [+] [B] ...and place it onto the Stack: [ENTER].... See? The finished expression goes onto the Stack exactly as it would if you had created it with the Stack or Command Line!

But, again, that's a simple case—which doesn't really show you the power of the Equation Writer....

Problem: Using Equation Writer, key in this expression:

$$n_0 + \frac{1}{\ln n}\int_A^B \left(4 - e^x\right)^{3n} dx$$

Solution: This is quite straightforward to do, but study each step carefully. Keep in mind that if you key in something wrongly, just press the backspace key ([←]) to undo it:

[←][EQUATION] gets you into the EW. [α][←][N][0] enters the first variable, n_0 (the EW doesn't use subscripts). [+][▲] (the [▲] begins the *numerator* of a fraction).

[1][▼] (the [▼] begins a *denominator* of a fraction).

[→][LN][α][←][N][▶] (the [▶] ends the current *subexpression* —here it's the parenthetical argument of the LN function). Press [▶] again to end the fraction subexpression (notice how the cursor tells you where you are). Now [→][∫] (the EW lets you *imply* the multiplication).

[A] [▶] [B] [▶] enters the limits of integration, then [←][()] begins a parenthetical subexpression: [4][−][←][eˣ] [α][←][X]. Note that exponentiating the natural base, *e*, is represented by the EW as EXP().

[▶][▶] ends the exponential argument, then the parenthetical subexpression. Then [yˣ][3][α][←][N][▶] creates the exponent, and [▶] ends the integrand subexpression and prepares for the variable of integration: [α][←][X]....Done!

Notice that the completed expression is too large to fit into the display—part of it has scrolled off to the left.

Question: What would you have to do to create this expression using the Command Line?

Answer: Press [ENTER] to put your expression onto the Stack and exit the EW. The 48 converts the EW's user-friendly display to the Stack's machine-friendly display:

```
'n0+1/LN(n)*∫(A,B,(
4-EXP(x))^(3*n),x)'
```

This is what you'd have to key in via the Command Line. Not as easy as with the EW, is it?

Another: Use the EW to enter $\dfrac{\sqrt{1-\cos^2 x}}{2}$

Solution: [←][EQUATION] enters Equation Writer; [▲][√x] begins the numerator and radical; [1][−] begins the radicand. Now, to enter the square of the cosine function, *either*: [COS][α][←][X][▶][y^x][2][▶] *or* [←][x²][COS][α][←][X][▶][▶]:

```
√(1-COS(x)^2 □)        √(1-SQ(COS(x))□)
```

[▶][▼] ends the radical and numerator subexpressions, and [2][ENTER] finishes the expression and sends it to the Stack. Its Stack form depends on your choice above, but the expression will evaluate the same either way.

Problem: Use the EW to create $4.72\frac{\text{amp}^2 \bullet \text{sec}^2}{\text{N} \bullet \text{m}}$

Solution: [←][EQUATION][4][•][7][2] enters the numerical part.

Then [→][_][▲] begins the unit's numerator; [α][A][yˣ][2][▶] enters the amperes; [α][←][S][yˣ][2][▶] enters the seconds; and [▼] ends the numerator and begins the denominator.

Then [α][N][×][α][←][M][ENTER] completes the expression.

Lastly: Create the following expression in the Equation Writer:

$4x^2 + y^2$ where $x = 3b - 2$ and $y = a + 1$

Do It: This uses "where" notation—a concise way to define both the main function *and functions defining its arguments.*

So press [←][EQUATION][4][α][←][X][yˣ][2][▶][+][α][←][Y][yˣ][2][▶] to build the main function. Then [←][ALGEBRA][NXT][|] enters the "where" syntax—that vertical bar—and [α][←][X][▶] begins defining the first variable (x). Notice that [▶] automatically ends the variable name and inserts an =.

[3][α][←][B][−][2][SPC] completes the function defining x (and notice that [SPC] automatically inserts a comma to separate the two variable definitions).

To finish: [α][←][Y][▶][α][←][A][+][1][ENTER].

Editing Expressions

As you know well, it's easy to make mistakes when entering complex expressions. Well, what if you discover a mistake "many keystrokes later"—when it's too late to conveniently use [⬅]?....

Editing with the Command Line

You've already seen this method for error correction; here's a quick...

Example: Use the Command Line to change the main function in the previous example to $5x^2 + 2y^2$.

Solution: Since the expression needing editing is still in Level 1 of the Stack (if not, rebuild it now), press [↰][EDIT] to start.

Now, replace 4 with 5 as the first coefficient of the function: Press **INS ■** so that you are replacing instead of inserting, and then [▶][5]

Return to insert mode (press **INS**) and press [▶][▶][▶][▶][▶] until the blinking cursor is on the y.... Now press [2][×] to insert the second coefficient, and put the edited expression on the Stack: [ENTER].

This should seem pretty familiar. But how would you do this editing with the EW?...

Editing with the Equation Writer

Actually, you can't edit directly using the Equation Writer. But it does include a number of features that makes editing expressions easier.

Try This: Create $\sum_{n=1}^{10}\left(\sqrt{1+\tan\frac{3\pi}{4}}\right)^{n}$ in the EW

Then, after you've completed the expression (but before you [ENTER] it onto the Stack), use the Command Line to change the upper limit to 25.

Solution: To create the expression: [←][EQUATION][→][Σ][α][←][N][▶][1] [▶][1][0][▶][√x][1][+][TAN][▲][3][←][π][▼][4][▶][▶][▶][yˣ][α][←][N]. To edit the expression: [←][EDIT] **INS ■** **←SKIP** **←SKIP** [▶][▶] [▶][▶][▶][▶][▶][2][5][ENTER]. You should see:

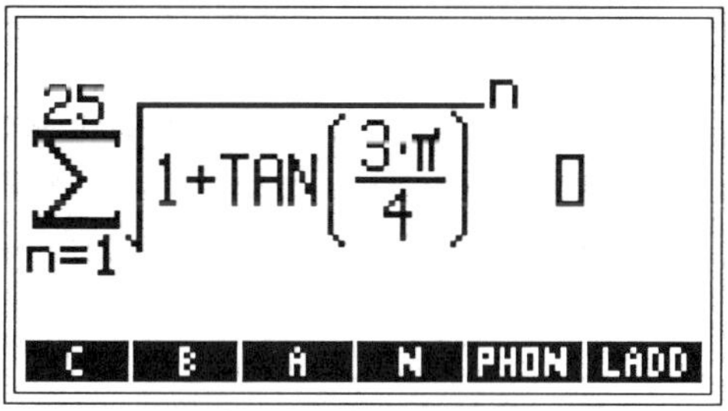

In this example, you brought the entire expression to the Command Line even though you needed to change only a small part of it. But the EW allows you *select* a part of an expression (a *subexpression*) to be edited on the Command Line and then returned to the overall expression. This selection process goes on in the *Selection Environment*.

Watch: Assuming that you're still in Equation Writer looking at the display of the previous summation expression, press ◄. Welcome to the Selection Environment.

Use the arrow keys to move the highlight around. You'll find that you can move "up" and "down" only when the highlighted subexpression has an "up-down" direction—as in the Σ term and the fraction here.

To use the Selection Environment well, you must understand what the 48 sees as a subexpression—what it will actually select:

A subexpression is one function plus its arguments. If one or more of those arguments contains other functions, then the selection will include those functions, also.

Question: In the Selection Environment, press the arrow keys until the division bar of the fraction is highlighted. Now, what subexpression is defined by this dividing bar?

Check: Press **EXPR** to highlight the entire subexpression (the fraction) determined by the dividing bar. Press **EXPR** again and just the division bar is highlighted. **EXPR** is a display option only; whether you *see* the entire fraction highlighted or just the division bar, it *is* the selection. So the *function* selected was the division (÷), along with its two *arguments*—the numerator and denominator.

Question: What subexpression is defined by the radical?

Find Out: Move the highlight to the radical by pressing ◀ four times. Then press **EXPR**. The radical subexpression is the square-root function plus its argument, $1+\tan\frac{3\pi}{4}$, even though its argument has two additional nested subexpressions.

Question: Press ▶. What subexpression is defined by the 1?

Find Out: Press **EXPR**.... Nothing happens—because the number is an argument, not a function, and therefore defines no subexpression.

When an ***argument*** is highlighted, only that argument is selected; but when a ***function*** is highlighted, the entire subexpression that it defines is selected—and you can actually see the entire subexpression via **EXPR**.

Editing Subexpressions

Now that you know what subexpressions are—and how to select them—look what you can do with them. You can:

- Remove a subexpression from the main expression in the EW, edit it in the Command Line, then put it back into the EW.
- Copy a subexpression to Stack Level 1.
- Take the subexpression sitting at Stack Level 1 and either *insert* it or use it to *replace* another within your EW expression.

So, make sure that you're still in the Selection Environment from the previous exercises, and then...

Try This: Select the fraction subexpression and, using the Command Line, change the denominator to 8.

Like So: Use the arrow keys to highlight the division line. Then press **EDIT**. Now just the *subexpression* is being edited. Press (←)(8) to change the denominator, and then (ENTER) to return the result back to the main expression.

Easy, right?

Another: Copy the argument of the radical onto the Stack.

Hmm... The argument of the radical is defined by the + function. So press ◀◀ to highlight the + and then SUB. Then press ENTER to see the copied subexpression. This will exit you from the Selection Environment to the Stack, copying the *entire* current expression to Level 1. And the *sub*expression you copied, '1+TAN(3*π/8)', should now be at Level 2.

That's an important distinction: Use ENTER—within either the EW or the Selection Environment—to return the complete expression to the Stack. But you use SUB within the Selection Environment to copy a selected *sub*expression to the Stack.

Question: How do you accomplish the reverse process—move expressions and subexpressions from the Stack to the EW and/or Selection Environment?

Answer: To move the expression at Stack Level 1 into the EW environment, press ▼ (do it now). Whenever you have an algebraic object (or unit object) on Level 1, pressing ▼ displays it in friendly EW style. But ▼ delivers only complete expressions. You can't use it to add to an expression already in the EW.

Challenge: Modify the expression to: $\sum_{n=1}^{25}\left(\sqrt{1+\tan\frac{3\pi}{8}}\right)^{n}-\left(1+\tan\frac{3\pi}{8}\right)$

Solution: Press [◄] to enter the Selection Environment, then [◄][◄] [◄][◄] to highlight the + function. Press [SUB] to copy the radicand subexpression to the Stack. Then [EXIT] the Selection Environment. Now [−][←][()] to begin the new term, and [→][RCL] to *recall* the subexpression on Level 1 and *insert* it into the expression at the cursor's location:

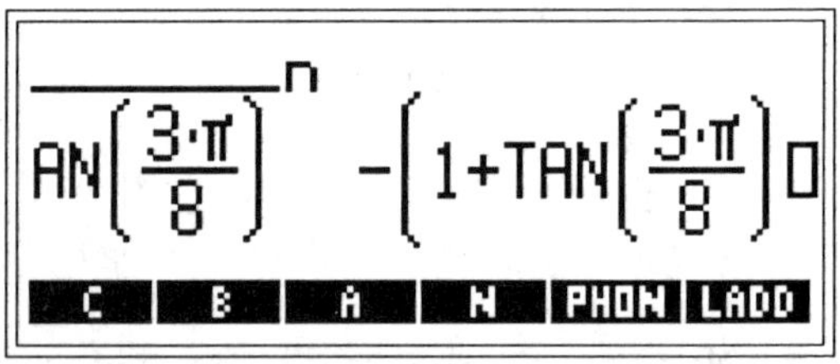

Since the expression is too big to fit in the display, press [←][GRAPH] and use the arrows to scroll around and view the parts that are hidden. When you're finished, press [←][GRAPH] again to continue your work.

Keep in mind the critical difference between [▼] and [→][RCL] when moving expressions from the Stack to the EW:

- [→][RCL] does it only from the EW environment. It recalls the expression from Stack Level 1 and *inserts* it at the EW box cursor.
- By contrast, [▼] does it only from the Stack, *overwriting* the entire contents of the EW with the expression in Stack Level 1. Thus [▼] is a shortcut for [←][EQUATION][→][RCL].

But [→][RCL] doesn't meet all your needs for expression modification. Yes, it *adds* to the existing expression, but how would you *replace* a subexpression with that in Stack Level 1?

Hmm: What if the proper trig function in this summation were sine, not tangent? Replace the TAN's with SIN's.

OK: Copy the tangent subexpression to the Stack: [◄][◄] SUB. Then exit Equation Writer, by pressing [ENTER]. This puts the main expression on Level 1 and the tangent subexpression on Level 2.

So [►] (SWAP) them and [←][EDIT] the subexpression: INS■ [►][α][α][S][I][ENTER]. Make an extra copy of this: [ENTER].

Now, reload the full expression into Equation Writer: [▲][▲][▲] PICK [ENTER] copies the full expression (currently sitting on Level 3) down to Level 1; then [▼] loads it into Equation Writer.

Re-enter the Selection Environment and highlight the first TAN subexpression: [◄][◄][◄][◄][◄][◄][◄][◄][◄]. Replace the TAN subexpression with the SIN subexpression you left at Stack Level 1: REPL. Now hop over to the other TAN subexpression and replace it, too: [►][►][►][►][►][►][►][►] REPL.

Can you use **REPL** to replace an *argument* as well as a *function*?

Try This: Change the fraction in the previous expression to 5π/8.

Solution: Assuming that you're still in the Selection Environment from the previous example, press [ENTER] [5] [ENTER] [ENTER] [▲] [▲] [▲] **ROLL** [ENTER] [▼] [◀] [▲] [◀] **REPL** [◀] [◀] [◀] [◀] [◀] [◀] [◀] [◀] [▲] [◀] **REPL**. This will change both occurrences of 3π/8 to 5π/ 8. Press [ENTER].

Do This: In the Equation Writer, create this expression:

$$\int_{2}^{9} \frac{1}{1+X}\, dX$$

Then, using **REPL**, change the upper limit to 5*A*.

Solution: Create the original expression: [◁] [EQUATION] [▷] [∫] [2] [▶] [9] [▶] [▲] [1] [▼] [1] [+] [α] [X] [▶] [▶] [α] [X] [ENTER].

Next, create its replacement: ['] [5] [×] [α] [A] [ENTER]

Now recall the original to the Equation Writer: [▶] [▼] Enter the Selection Environment and highlight 9, the upper bound: [◀] [◀] [▲] [▲] (this is not exactly intuitive: you can't move from the integral to its bounds, but you can from the integrand).

Press **REPL** [ENTER] to complete your task.

A Visual Review

Just in case all these keystroke combinations and environment changes have you reeling, here's an all-in-one shot of your options for creating and/or editing algebraic expressions:

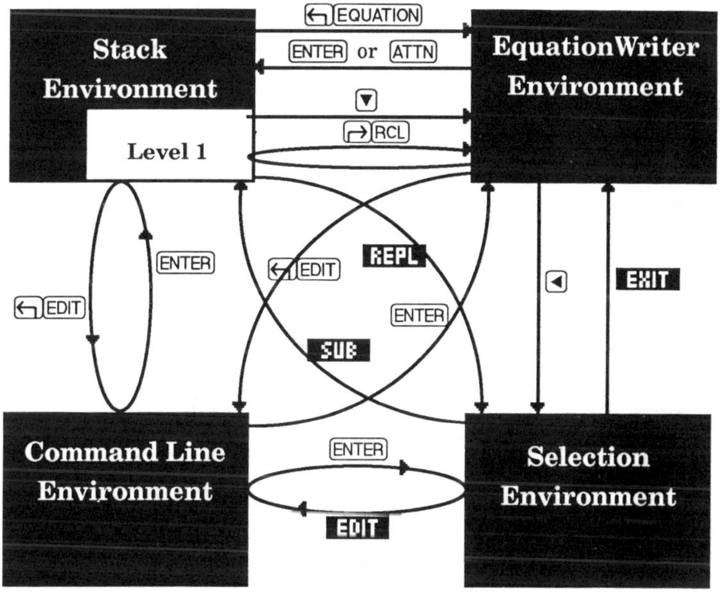

Saving Expressions

So far, you've been moving expressions created in the Equation Writer to the Stack by pressing [ENTER]. Once there, of course, you know how to give them a name and store them for a later date....

Do It: Assuming your expression is in either the Selection Environment or the EW, press [ENTER] to send it to the Stack.

Now, store it in the name 'MYINT': ['] [α] [α] [M] [Y] [I] [N] [T] [ENTER] [STO]. Press [VAR] to confirm that you indeed have the new variable.

No big deal, right? You've done this kind of naming of all sorts of objects by now—including algebraic expressions like this.

But the point here is this: When you press [ENTER] in the Equation Writer, you take an easy-to-*read* form of an expression and put it onto the Stack in its easy-to-*use* (-but-sort-of-ugly) Command Line form. And when you name ([STO]) the expression, you are indeed saving this Command Line version.

Hmm... but wouldn't it be nice to be able to save the big, friendly, easy-to-read EW version, too?

("yes, fans—that's right....")

Try This: Recall the expression you just saved into the Equation Writer by pressing **MYIN** [▼]. Now press [STO]. Then press [ATTN] to see what you've done.

Result: On Stack Level 2, you have: `Graphic 131 × 56`. This is a ***graphic object*** (or ***grob***). It's a picture—like a fax—of the EW expression. The picture has 131 columns and 56 rows of pixels (dots). And you can name this object: [▶][''][α][α][P][M][Y][I][N][T][α][STO]

Pretty neat, eh?

Well ...that depends on what you want to *do* with the expression. If you need to do any calculations with it, evaluate it, manipulate it, edit it, or some such thing, then the grob version is useless to you. It's just a "photograph" of an expression; and after all, you can't drive a nail with a *picture* of a hammer, can you?*

But if you want to see the "pretty" version of a completed expression, then use the grob version. Just remember the key distinction:

- The Command Line version acts like an algebraic expression. Press [ENTER] from the Equation Writer.
- The grob version acts like a picture—any picture. Press [STO] from the Equation Writer.

*The details about viewing, manipulating and editing grobs are not covered in this book, since they're almost exclusively used by programmers and other advanced users. If the material in the Owner's Manual isn't sufficient for you, Grapevine's book, *HP 48SX Graphics* (by Ray Depew), covers this and many other useful topics extensively.

Using Expressions

All right, already—so you know how to build and edit an algebraic expression—so what? It's time to look at the things you can *do* with these expressions.

You can do these three types of things:

- You can *evaluate* an expression—"crunch" it into a number as far as possible.
- You can *rearrange* an expression—transform it into an *equivalent* expression. The 48 offers you commands that follow algebraic rules for expanding terms, combining like terms, using the distributive, associative and commutative properties, etc.
- You can *symbolically solve an equation*—isolate a given variable out of an otherwise unsimplified expression; or reduce one side of the equation to a numerical value.

Look at each category, in turn....

Evaluating Expressions

You already know *how* to evaluate an algebraic object: With the algebraic at Stack Level 1 (or in the Command Line), just press [EVAL]. But you also need to better understand *what happens* when you do it....

Example: Create and then evaluate the expression $4A + 5B$

Solution: Just use the Command Line for this simple expression: ['][4][×][α][A][+][5][×][α][B][ENTER] creates it; then [EVAL]....
Result: `1.0000` This uses the VARiables you stored.

Another: Create and then evaluate the expression $4L + 5M$

Solution: ['][4][×][α][L][+][5][×][α][M][ENTER][EVAL]
Result: `'4*(B-A)+5*M'`
One of the variables (`M`) *contains no value.* And the other (`L`) contains another algebraic object—the expression `'B-A'`. Therefore (as you learned on page 131), you must evaluate the expression *again* to reduce `A` and `B` to numerical values: [EVAL] Result: `'-28+5*M'`

Remember: [EVAL] examines an algebraic expression and replaces each name with the value that name contains. If there's no value, then [EVAL] leaves the empty name in the expression; if the value is a number, the number is substituted; if the value is simply another name, then that name is also evaluated; if the value is an algebraic object, then that object is substituted *but not evaluated.*

There's also another type of evaluation available to you—one that gives you more control as to what is evaluated. The SHOW command (available via [←][ALGEBRA] **SHOW**) allows you to *choose* which objects to evaluate—useful for finding "hidden" variables....

Example: Given that $v = v_0 + at$ where v is velocity, v_0 is the initial velocity, a is the constant acceleration and t is time, and given that $x = x_0 + \frac{1}{2}t(v_0 + v)$, where x_o is the initial position and x is the position at time t, how is a related to x?

Solution: First, define V: ['][α][V][0][+][α][A][×][α][T][ENTER]['][α][V][STO]

Next, create the equation: [←][EQUATION][α][X][←][=][α][X][0][+][1][÷][2][▶][α][T][×][←][()][α][V][0][+][α][V][ENTER].

Indicate which hidden variable you want to SHOW after the substitution: ['][α][A][ENTER]....

And perform the substitution: [←][ALGEBRA] **SHOW**
Result: 'X=X0+1/2*T*(V0+(V0+A*T))'

Do you see what SHOW did here? The A, which had been hidden inside the V variable, is now explicitly a part of the equation for X.

Rearranging Expressions

The 48 contains a number of ways to *symbolically* rearrange an algebraic expression. Whenever you make rearrangements, the new expression is always equivalent to the old one—just as proper algebra demands. Of course, not all of the rearrangement tools are equally useful to you, but the 48's repertoire is quite extensive:

- You can collect like terms and combine whatever can be combined in order to simplify an expression.
- You can expand an expression to make all powers and products explicit.
- You can select a subexpression and move it around, associate it or distribute it differently, or a number of other things depending on the nature of the subexpression.
- You can define your own algebraic rule (or identity) to augment the built-in rules and apply that rule to an expression.

Try One: Create $2 + x + 4x^2 - 3x + 9 - x + 2x^2$ in Equation Writer: Then collect like terms.

Solution: [←][EQUATION][2][+][α][X][+][4][α][X][y^x][2][▶][−][3][α][α][X][+][9][−][X][+][2][X][α][y^x][2][ENTER]. Then [←][ALGEBRA] **COLCT** ...
Result: `'11+6*X^2-3*X'`

Now: Using the Interactive Stack (remember? press (▲)), go find the equation 'X=X0+1/2*T*(V0+(V0+A*T))' and copy it to Level 1 (press **PICK** while the pointer is pointing at the equation). Then exit the Interactive Stack (press (ATTN)). Your mission: Tidy up the equation with some rearrangements.

OK: First, notice that the two V0's can combine. Press **COLCT**.
Result: 'X=0.5000*(A*T+2*V0)*T+X0'

That's still not very pretty (even in the Equation Writer—press (▼) to see). So (back at the Stack), press **EXPA**, to EXPAnd the expression, by *distributing terms* wherever possible. Often you'll need to EXPAnd an expression like this before **COLCT** can do much tidying.
Result: 'X=(0.5000*(A*T)+0.5000*(2*V0))*T+X0'

The 0.5000 is distributed, but not the T. So **EXPA** again....
Result: 'X=0.5000*(A*T)*T+0.5000*(2*V0)*T+X0'

Now try combining like terms—press **COLCT**....
Result: 'X=0.5000*A*T^2+T*V0+X0'
Much better—and you can make it even prettier: (←)(→Q)(▼).
As a matter of fact, it might even look familiar.

Rearrangement using **EXPA** and **COLCT** works well for many expressions, but they aren't well-suited to make smaller, single-step, rearrangements. For those sorts of "microsurgeries," you'll need the set of algebraic tools collected in the **RULES** toolbox, available in the EW's Selection Environment.

Example: As nice as the previous equation ended up, you'd prefer to be consistent in the order of the coefficients. Since it's a quadratic in T, the coefficients of the powers of T should come first. Somehow, you need to switch the order of T and V0 in the second term. But how?

Solution: No amount of pressing **EXPA** and **COLCT** is going to make this happen; you need to use the **RULES**.

Assuming that you are looking at the Equation Writer version of the quadratic already, press ◀ to enter the Selection Environment. Then press ◀◀◀ to highlight the multiplication dot between T and V0. Just as before, you are selecting a subexpression for editing.

Press **RULES** NXT **↔**. This "commutes" (switches) the order of the arguments, so that V0 comes before T. Then ENTER returns you to the Stack.

That's just one example of the sorts of massaging you can do to your expressions—either in the EW or on the Stack. Here is a list of all the available RULES, which fall into three categories (these are the Stack versions of the results):

- Rules that apply to any selection (argument or subexpression):

DNEG	—	A	becomes	-A
DINV	—	A	becomes	(INV(A))
*1	—	A	becomes	A*1
^1	—	A	becomes	A^1
/1	—	A	becomes	A/1
+1-1	—	A	becomes	A+1-1
COLCT	—	collects like terms (in the selection only).		

- Rules that apply to subexpressions.

Commutation

←→	—	A+B	becomes	B+A

Distribution

←D	—	(A+B)*C	becomes	A*C+B*C
D→	—	A*(B+C)	becomes	A*B+A*C
←M	—	A*B+A*C	becomes	A*(B+C)
M→	—	A*C+B*C	becomes	(A+B)*C
→()	—	-(A+B)	becomes	-A-B
-()	—	A+B	becomes	-(-A-B)
1/()	—	A*B	becomes	INV(INV(A)/B)

Association

←A	—	A+(2*B+C)	becomes	A+2*B+C
A→	—	A+2*B+C	becomes	A+(2*B+C)

Moving Terms (arguments of +, −, *, /, or =)

←T	—	A+2*B+C	becomes	A+C+2*B
T→	—	A+C+2*B	becomes	C+A+2*B

Building and Moving Parentheses

(())	—	A+2*B+C+D	becomes	A+(2*B+C)+D
(←	—	A+2*B+(C+D)	becomes	A+(2*B+C+D)
→)	—	A+(2*B+C)+D	becomes	A+(2*B+C+D)

- Rules that apply only to *specialized* subexpressions:

Trigonometric Functions

→DEF — SIN(X) becomes (in radian mode)
(EXP(X*i)-EXP(-(X*i)))/(2*i)

TRG* — COS(X-Y) becomes
COS(X)*COS(Y)+SIN(X)*SIN(Y)

Exponential and Logarithmic Functions

L* — LOG(A^B) becomes LOG(A)*B

L() — LN(A)*B becomes LN(A^B)

E^ — ALOG(A*B) becomes ALOG(A)^B

E() — EXP(A)^B becomes EXP(A*B)

Fractions with Different Denominators

AF — A/D+B/C becomes (A*C+D*B)/(D*C)

Question: How can you possibly remember all these RULES?

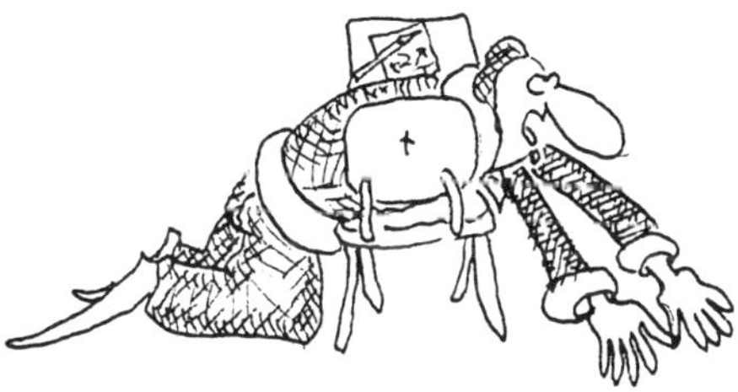

Answer: You'll soon learn the ones you use most often. As for the rest, don't bother to memorize them at all. Also, your 48 helps you select among them: On its RULES menu, it will offer only those rearrangement commands that apply to the situation you've selected. And even then, it won't let you do something mathematically "illegal" to your expression. So relax and explore the RULES....

Example: Given that $\frac{GMm}{(R+r)^2} = m\omega^2 r$; $R << r$; and $\omega = \frac{2\pi}{T}$, show that: $GM = 4\pi^2 r^3 T^{-2}$

Solution: Begin by keying in the first equation: [←][EQUATION] [▲][α][α][G][×][M][×][←][M][α][▼][←][()][α][R][+][α][←][R][▶][yˣ][2] [▶][▶][←][=][α][←][M][×][α][→][W][yˣ][2][▶][α][←][R][ENTER]

Now, since R is insignificant relative to r, eliminate it by storing 0 into it: [0]['][α][R][STO] and [EVAL]. Next, multiply by 'r^2' to clear the left-hand denominator: ['][α][←][R] [yˣ] [2] [ENTER] [×]. Then collect like terms: ([←][ALGEBRA] **COLCT**), divide by 'm' and collect: ['][α][←][M] [ENTER][÷] **COLCT** Result: 'G*M=r^3*ω^2'

Now define the variable ω and evaluate the equation: ['][2][×][←][π][÷][α][T][ENTER]['][α][→][W][STO] [EVAL].
Result: 'G*M=r^3*(2*π/T)^2'

Distribute the final exponent over the terms in parentheses: [▼][◀][◀] **RULES** **←D** [▲] **RULES** **←D**. Now return to the Stack and collect: [ENTER] **COLCT**...
Result: 'G*M=4*r^3*T^-2*π^2'

Finally (optionally) rearrange the terms on the right-hand side to exactly match the target: [▼][◀][◀][◀][◀] **RULES** **←T** **←T** [ENTER]....Result: 'G*M=4*π^2*r^3*T^-2'

Your use of algebraic rearrangements depends entirely on your needs. Often, it's quicker to do them by hand (or eye). But for a derivation or proof, they're awfully handy to check for careless errors.

With all the algebra already built into it, the 48 even goes one step further: It allows you to *define your own algebraic transformations.*

Try One: Define the following identity: $\cos^2\theta + \sin^2\theta = 1$

Like So: To define the identity, you create a *list* object that contains up to three algebraic expressions, in this order:

1. The expression you wish to replace.
2. The new expression to be substituted.
3. An *optional* expression (such as '&x>0') that puts a condition on when the replacement should occur.

So, begin the list with the first expression: [←][{ }]['][COS][α] [←][ENTER][α][X][▶][y^x][2][+][SIN][α][←][ENTER][α][X][▶][y^x][2][▶].

Notice that you're using a ***wildcard name***—a name beginning with the & character (&X in this case)—instead of θ, as your variable. This will allow your 48 to recognize the identity *no matter what variable name* is being used.

Next, enter the second expression—the replacement: [1]. And since there are no special conditions needed with this identity, you don't need any third expression, so just press [ENTER] to put the list onto the Stack.

Finally, give your list a name: ['][α][α][P][Y][T][H][α][STO].... and press [VAR] to confirm it.

Ready to test it? All right....

Problem: Use the PYTH identity to help you prove this one:

$$\frac{1}{\sin^2 A} + \frac{1}{\cos^2 A} = \frac{1}{\sin^2 A \cos^2 A}$$

Solution: Use the EW to create the left-hand expression: [⬅][EQUATION][1][÷][SIN][α][A][▶][y^x][2][▶][▶][+][1][÷][COS][α][A][▶][y^x][2].

Now, start the transformation: Press [◀][◀] RULES AF to add the fractions over a common denominator. Return it to the Stack and collect: [ENTER][⬅][ALGEBRA] COLCT

Now, test your customized transformation: Put PYTH into Level 1: [VAR] PYTH. Your current expression should now be in Level 2. Execute the MATch command—to perform the search-and-replace: [⬅][ALGEBRA][NXT] ↑MAT

Result: (Level 1) 1 (means that a match was found)
(Level 2) '1*COS(A)^-2*SIN(A)^-2'
(the transformed expression)

This is the target expression.... Q.E.D.

So that's the idea: You build a list containing a target, a replacement and (if necessary) a conditional expression—all using wildcard names for any variables. Then you use this list as one of the arguments (along with the expression to be transformed) with the MATch command.

Solving Equations of Expressions

Face it: The algebraic trickery of the previous section wouldn't be nearly so interesting if the 48 couldn't solve an *algebraic equation.*

On paper, the primary reason you perform algebraic rearrangements is to isolate a key variable on one side of the equal sign, with everything else on the other—i.e. to get something such as $x = \ldots$ or $y = \ldots$

But, if you had to imitate each minuscule step of algebra on the 48 just in order to solve for a particular variable, it would take you longer to use your calculator than to do it on paper.

Well, there's a shortcut: The ISOL command will automatically perform all the transformations necessary to isolate the variable.

Example: Enter 'A=B*C' and solve for C symbolically.

Easy: ['] [α] [A] [⇦] [=] [α] [B] [×] [α] [C] [ENTER] puts the equation on the Stack. Then, to solve for C, ['] [α] [C] and [⇦] [ALGEBRA] **ISOL**. <u>Result</u>: 'C=A/B'

ISOL is handy—for some cases. But it won't isolate any variable that appears *more than once* in an expression. If you ask it to, the 48 will beep at you and display the message: Unable to Isolate.

That's the bad news. The good news is that the ISOLate command can work on an *expression* (i.e. an algebraic without an equal sign), too.

Watch: Isolate t in the following expression: $2b-\frac{a}{t}$

Solution: Wait a minute! You can't isolate ("solve for") *anything* if you don't have an equation. You *must* have a mathematical sentence with a = in it.

True. So the 48 *simply assumes that the expression you've entered is equal to zero* and then proceeds to ISOLate the requested variable.

Enter the expression: ['] [α] [α] [←] [α] [2] [×] [B] [−] [A] [÷] [T] [ENTER].
Now enter the variable to isolate: ['] [α] [←] [T]
And **ISOL**.... Result: 't=a/(2*b)'

Try Another: Solve for t in the following expression: 2^t

Solution: ['] [2] [y^x] [α] [←] [T] [ENTER] ['] [α] [←] [T] **ISOL**....
...Ooops! What happened?
As usual, the 48 set the expression equal to zero: $2^t = 0$; But isolating t in this circumstance requires an impossible operation. You do have to be aware of these things when using **ISOL**.

In addition to ISOL, you can also use the QUAD command to "solve" for a given variable in some algebraic expressions:

- You can solve for a polynomial variable of the second order (i.e. the "x" in a quadratic);
- You can solve for an unknown polynomial variable of the first order (linear) which appears *more than once* in the expression or equation.
- You can approximate a solution for a polynomial variable of third order or higher.

Try One: Solve $\frac{1}{1+X} - (X-1) = 4$ for X, to 2 decimal places.

Solution: Create the equation: [←][EQUATION] [1][÷][1][+][α][X] [▶] [−] [←][()][α][X][−][1][▶][←][=][4][ENTER]. QUAD solves an equation incorrectly if the solution variable ('X' here) is in the denominator. So, multiply through by '1+X' before solving for X: ['][1][+][α][X][ENTER][×] [2][←][MODES] **FIX** [←] [ALGEBRA]['][α][X] **QUAD**.... Result: 'X=(4+s1*2.83)/-2

Notice the s1. A quadratic has *two* solutions, but a function in the 48 can return only one at a time. So the 48 creates the s1 to allow for the "±" part of a quadratic solution (or any solution pairs that vary only in sign).

Thus you can choose either result. First, let s1 = 1: [ENTER] [1]['][α][←][S][1][STO][EVAL].... Result: 'X=-3.41'

Now let s1 = −1: [▶][1][+/−]['][α][←][S][1][STO][EVAL]....
Result: 'X=-0.59'

This last example illustrates the difference between a ***principal solution*** and a ***general solution***. The 48's built-in functions always return the *principal* solution (given real or complex arguments):

- The square root of 16 is evaluated as 4, though ⁻4 is also correct;
- The arcsine of 0.5 is evaluated to be 30°, though there are an infinite number of angles whose sines are 0.5.

By contrast, whenever you use the **ISOL** or **QUAD** commands to isolate or solve for a variable, your machine assumes that you want the *general* solution—unless you specifically tell it otherwise....

Compare: Use **ISOL** to find the general solution for x: $\sin x° = 0.5$ Then tell your 48 to give you the principal solution.

Solution: ['][SIN][α][⬅][X][▶][⬅][=][·][5][ENTER] generates the equation. Duplicate: [ENTER]. Then make sure you're in DEG mode and press ['][α][⬅][X] **ISOL** to give the general solution....
Result: `'x=30*(-1)^n1+180*n1'`

To request just the principal solution for **ISOL**, you need to *set* system flag –1: [1][+/-][SPC][α][α][S][F][ENTER]. Then [▶] and solve the expression again: ['][α][⬅][X] **ISOL**....
Result: `'x=30'`

User-Defined Functions

To solve problems with algebraic expressions, you can simply create an algebraic object of the proper form and assign values (if any) to the names in it. When you evaluate this object, it combines the values as specified and you get a result. Fine and dandy.

But if the algebraic object contains lots of named objects, then assigning values to the names (using the [STO] procedure) can be a lengthy and error-prone process. That's where a UDF can come in handy.

A ***User-Defined Function*** (UDF) is a special kind of quasi-algebraic that allows you to stream-line the use of complicated expressions and create and name your own functions....

Create One: Define the following function: $f(x) = x^2 - 2x + 1$

Like This: When you define a UDF, you use exactly this kind of $f(x)$ function notation. The left side of the equal sign must include only the name of the function, with the names of the arguments in parentheses. The right side of the equal sign is the defining expression.

So...press [⬅][EQUATION] [α][⬅][α][α][F][⬅][()][α][X][▶][⬅][=] [α][X][y^x][2][▶][−][2][α][X][+][1][ENTER] to write the function. Then press [⬅][DEF] to define it and place its name in your VARiable menu.

Now Then: Set your display to STD (⬅ MODES **STD**), and use your new function, f, evaluating it at:

a. $x = 1$ **b.** $x = -2$

c. $x = 2 + 3i$ **d.** $x = \sqrt{2}$

Solutions:

a. VAR 1 **F** Result: 0

b. 2 +/- **F** Result: 9

c. ⬅ ( ) 2 SPC 3 **F** Result: (-8, 6)

d. 2 √x **F** Result: .17157287525

Notice that the UDF took its argument from the Stack here—just as a built-in function would have. And if it had required more than one argument—say, a function $P(A, B)$—it would have expected the arguments to go onto the Stack in the same order in which they appear in the parentheses in the function definition: A ENTER B ENTER. Thus, UDF's act just like built-in functions; they're additions to your 48 workshop.

Try Another: Define the following UDF: $q(x, y) = 2x + xy$
Then evaluate q for:

a. $x = -2y$ **c.** $x = t, \quad y = t - 1$

b. $y = -2x$ **d.** $x = z - 3y, \quad y = x - 3z$

Solutions: Define the function: [←][EQUATION] [α][←][α] [α][Q][←][()] [α][X][SPC][α][Y][▶][←][=][2][α][X][+][α][X][×][α][Y][ENTER][←][DEF].

Now evaluate:

a. ['][+/-][2][×][α][←][Y][ENTER] ['][α][←][Y][ENTER][VAR] [Q] [←][ALGEBRA][COLCT]

Result: `'-(2*y^2)-4*y'`

b. ['][α][←][X][ENTER][ENTER][2][×][+/-][VAR][Q] [←][ALGEBRA][COLCT] Result: `'-(2*x^2)+2*x'`

c. ['][α][←][T][ENTER][ENTER][1][−][VAR][Q] [←][ALGEBRA][EXPA][COLCT] Result: `'t^2+t'`

d. ['][α][←][Z][−][3][×][α][←][Y][ENTER]['][α][←][X][−][3][×] [α][←][Z][ENTER][VAR][Q] [←][ALGEBRA][EXPA][EXPA][COLCT]

Result: `'-(3*z^2)-3*x*y+x*z`
`+9*y*z-6*y+2*z'`

(Press [▼] to see it in the Equation Writer.)

Symbolic Arguments in a UDF

So far, you've used your UDF's (F and Q) with arguments, placing those arguments onto the Stack and invoking the names of the functions by themselves.

Question: How do you use UDF's in their algebraic functional form—with *symbolic* arguments? For example, is this valid? `'2*Q(A,B)+3*F(C)'`

Answer: Absolutely. It's just as valid as when you use two built-in functions: `'2*PERM(A,B)+3*TAN(C)'`

And when evaluated, both of these would use the values currently stored in the VARiables A, B and C.

Notice: The VARiable names you use as arguments (within the parentheses) when *invoking* a UDF have nothing to do with the names you use when DEFINing that UDF. When defining Q on the previous page, for example, you used the names x and y. But that was simply for the purposes of the definition (after all, how can you define a function without some sort of symbols for the variables?). But when it comes time to *use* the UDF, the names of the arguments you give it are unlimited—and their values (if any) will be taken from VARiables with those names.

Getting anxious to test your understanding of functions and expressions? All right—put it to practice with this quiz (answers follow)....

Math Anxiety

1. Evaluate: $\tan^{-1}\left(\dfrac{\sqrt{2}}{2+\sqrt{2}}\right)$ in radians, as a fraction of π.

2. Find all four solutions to $\sqrt[4]{8-8i\sqrt{3}}$.

3. In 1989, the worldwide consumption of petroleum was about 21.28 billion barrels. Total remaining oil resources available is estimated to be 1590 billion barrels. The formula,

$$A = \frac{A_0}{k}\left(e^{kT} - 1\right)$$

expresses an exponential growth rate where A is the amount of oil consumed over the next T years, A_0 is the annual amount of oil consumed currently, and k is the relative growth rate of annual consumption. Compute the "life expectancy" for oil, assuming that the rate of oil consumption grows annually by:

a. 1% **b.** 2% **c.** 3% (the predicted rate for this decade)

4. Around 1515, Italian mathematician Scipione del Ferro solved the cubic equation, $x^3 + px + q = 0$, deriving this general formula:

$$x = \sqrt[3]{\frac{-q}{2} + \sqrt{\frac{q^2}{4} + \frac{p^3}{27}}} + \sqrt[3]{\frac{-q}{2} - \sqrt{\frac{q^2}{4} + \frac{p^3}{27}}}$$

Using the Equation Writer, key in this monster expression and store it as `'QUBE'`. Use whatever shortcuts you want.

5. Expand the following expression to a polynomial of the fifth degree, using **EXPA** and **COLCT** :

$$\left(1+\frac{1}{X}\right)^5$$

6. Determine the term containing a^3 in the expansion of $(a-2b^3)^{11}$. With your experience from the previous problem, make use of the binomial theorem this time.

7. Create user-defined functions for the following triangle truths:

   a. Law of Cosines: $a=\sqrt{b^2+c^2-2bc\cos A}$

   b. Law of Sines: $B=\sin^{-1}\left(\frac{b\sin A}{a}\right)$

   c. Heron's Formula: $A=\sqrt{s(s-a)(s-b)(s-c)}$, where A is the triangle's area, and $s=\frac{1}{2}(a+b+c)$

8. Use the functions you created above to determine the remaining sides, angles, and areas of triangle ΔABC in each of these cases:

   a. $\angle A = 40°$ $b = 6.1$ cm $c = 3.2$ cm

   b. $a = 6$ $b = 7$ $c = 10$

Cool and Calculating

1. In STD display mode and RAD angle mode, build the expression: [2][√x][ENTER][2][+][÷][←][ATAN].... Result: `.392699081699`
Now convert this to a fraction of π: [←][ALGEBRA][NXT] **→Qπ**
Result: `'1/8*π'`

2. FIX the display to 2 decimal places. Remember that you can get multiple solutions only when you use **ISOL** or **QUAD** and are in *general solution mode*—i.e. flag –1 is clear. So press [1][+/–][SPC][α][C][α][F][ENTER]. And, because you want numerical results for symbolic constants only, set flag –2 and clear flag –3: [2][+/–][SPC][α][S][α][F][SPC][3][+/–][α][C][α][F][ENTER].

Next, because you must use **ISOL**, you must set up the expression as an equation, $x^4=8-8i\sqrt{3}$: [←][EQUATION][α][X][y^x][4][▶][←][=][8][–][8][α][←][I][√x][3][ENTER]. Now ['][α][X][←][ALGEBRA] **ISOL**....
Result: `'X=EXP((0.00,6.28)*n1/4)*(1.93,-0.52)'`

This is the general solution. To find each particular solution, you must give the variable `n1` the values 0, 1, 2, and 3 successively. So make 3 copies of the general solution ([ENTER][ENTER][ENTER]), then:

[0]['][α][←][N][1][STO][EVAL]	Result: `'X=(1.93,-0.52)'`
[◆][1][VAR][←] **N1** [EVAL]	Result: `'X=(0.52,1.93)'`
[◆][2][←] **N1** [EVAL]	Result: `'X=(-1.93,0.52)'`
[◆][3][←] **N1** [EVAL]	Result: `'X=(-0.52,-1.93)'`

3. First, purge your VAR menu of potentially interfering names: [←][{ }][α][α][A][SPC][T][SPC][←][K][ENTER][←][PURGE].
Next, create the growth formula: [←][EQUATION][α][A][←][=][α][A][0][÷] [α][←][K][▶][←][()][←][eˣ][α][←][K][×][α][T][▶][−][1][ENTER].
Now solve the equation for *T*: ['][α][T][←][ALGEBRA] **ISOL**
You want just the principal solution this time, so store 0 into n1 and [EVAL] (or, you can set flag –1 and use **ISOL** instead):
[0][VAR][←] **N1** [EVAL][→][LAST MENU] **COLCT**
Result: 'T=LN(1+A*k/A0)/k'
Now make copies of this expression ([ENTER][ENTER]), and explore the impact of various growth rates: [2][1][•][2][8][EEX][9]['][α][A][0][STO] [1][5][9][0][EEX][9]['][α][A][STO] defines the common variables. Then

a. [•][0][1]['][α][←][K][STO] [EVAL] Result: 'T=55.80'

b. [◆][•][0][2][VAR][←] **K** [EVAL] Result: 'T=45.70'

c. [◆][•][0][3][←] **K** [EVAL] Result: 'T=39.20'

So, depending on the consumption growth rate, the world's oil will be used up somewhere between the years 2030 and 2045.

4. Begin the expression: [←][EQUATION] [→][ˣ√y][3][▶] [+/−][α][←][Q][÷][2] [▶][+][√x][α][←][Q][yˣ][2][▶][÷][4][▶][+][α][←][P][yˣ][3][▶][÷][2][7][▶].
Now save yourself some work: Copy the cube root subexpression to the Stack ([◀][◀][◀][◀][◀][◀][◀][◀] **SUB**), move back to the Equation Writer (**EXIT**), enter the [+], and copy the subexpression from the Stack back into the expression ([→][RCL]). Now send the expression to the editor, [←][EDIT], and replace the fourth + sign with a − sign: [▲][▶] **DEL** [−][ENTER][ENTER]. Store the expression as QUBE: ['][α][α][Q][U][B][E][α][STO].

5. Create the expression: ['] [←] [( )] [1] [+] [1] [÷] [α] [X] [▶] [y^x] [5] [ENTER]. Now expand it as far as it will go—[←] [ALGEBRA], then press **EXPA** *17 times*—to get the following not-so-intuitive expression:

```
'1*(1*(1*(1*1)))+1*
(1*(1*(2*1*(1/X))))
+1*(1*(1*(1/X*(1/X)
)))+(1*(1*(1/X*(1*1
)))+1*(1*(1/X*(2*1*
(1/X))))+1*(1*(1/X*
(1/X*(1/X)))))+(1*(
1/X*(1*(1*1)))+1*(1
/X*(1*(2*1*(1/X))))
+1*(1/X*(1*(1/X*(1/
X))))+(1*(1/X*(1/X*
(1*1)))+1*(1/X*(1/X
(1/X*(2*1*(1/X))))+
1*(1/X*(1/X*(1/X*(1
/X))))))+(1/X*(1*(1
*(1*1)))+1/X*(1*(1*
(2*1*(1/X))))+1/X*(
1*(1*(1/X*(1/X))))+
(1/X*(1*(1/X*(1*1))
)+1/X*(1*(1/X*(2*1*
(1/X))))+1/X*(1*(1/
X*(1/(*(1/X)))))+(1
/X*(1/X*(1*(1*1)))+
1/X*(1/X*(1*(2*1*(1
/X))))+1/X*(1/X*(1*
(1/X*(1/X))))+(1/X*
(1/X*(1/X*(1*1)))+1
/X*(1/X*(1/X*(2*1*(
1/X))))+1/X*(1/X*(1
/X*(1/X*(1/X))))))
'
```

Now, *just* **COLCT** *it:* `'1+X^-5+5*X^-4+10*X^-3+10*X^-2+5/X'`

(Use the Equation Writer, [▼], to see it more clearly.)

6. The rth term in the expansion of $(a+b)^n$ is $\binom{n}{r-1} a^{n-r+1} b^{r-1}$

So create a function `TERM(n, r, a, b)` to calculate this formula:
Press [←] [EQUATION] [α] [α] [T] [E] [R] [M] [←] [( )] [←] [N] [SPC] [←] [R] [SPC] [←] [A] [SPC] [←] [B] [α] [▶] [←] [=] [MTH] **PROB** **COMB** [α] [←] [N] [SPC] [α] [←] [R] [−] [1] [▶] [α] [←] [A] [y^x] [α] [←] [N] [−] [α] [←] [R] [+] [1] [▶] [α] [←] [B] [y^x] [α] [←] [R] [−] [1] [ENTER].

Now DEFine this as a UDF: [←] [DEF]...and enter the arguments, $n, r, a,$ and b: [1] [1] [ENTER] [9] [ENTER] ['] [α] [←] [A] [ENTER] ['] [2] [+/−] [×] [α] [←] [B] [y^x] [3] [ENTER]...and execute the function: [VAR] **TERM**....
<u>Result</u>: `'165*a^3*(2*b^3)^8'` With some rearrangements (eight **EXPA**'s and a **COLCT**), this becomes `'42240*a^3*b^24'`

7. a. [←][EQUATION][α][α][C][S][L][W][←][()][←][B][SPC][←][C][SPC][A][α][▶] [←][=][√x][α][←][B][y^x][2][▶][+][α][←][C][y^x][2][▶][−][2][α][←][B][×][α] [←][C][COS][α][A][ENTER][←][DEF].

b. [←][EQUATION][α][α][S][N][L][W][←][()][←][B][SPC][←][A][SPC][A][α][▶][←] [=][←][ASIN][α][←][B][SIN][α][A][▶][÷][α][←][A][ENTER][←][DEF].

c. For *s*: [←][EQUATION][α][α][S][←][()][←][A][SPC][←][B][SPC][←][C][α][▶] [←][=][▲][α][α][←][A][+][←][B][+][←][C][α][▼][2][ENTER][←][DEF]. Then [←][EQUATION][α][α][H][E][R][O][N][←][()][←][A][SPC][←][B][SPC][←][C][α] [▶][←][=][←][()][√x][α][α][S][←][()][←][A][SPC][←][B][SPC][←][C][α][▶][◀] [◀][◀][◀] **SUB** **SUB** **SUB** **EXIT** [◆][←][()][→][RCL][−][α][←][A][▶] [←][()][→][RCL][−][α][←][B][▶][←][()][→][RCL][−][α][←][C][ENTER][←][DEF]

8. a. Set FIX 1 and DEG modes. PURGE A, B and C. Find side *a*: [6][•][1][←][UNITS] **LENG** **CM** [3][•][2] **CM** [4][0] [VAR] **CSLW** Result: 4.2_cm Find angle *C*: [3][•][2][→][LAST MENU] **CM** [▶][4][0] [VAR] **SNLW** Result: 29.4 Angle *B*: [1][8][0][ENTER][4][0][−][▶][−] Result: 110.6 Now use Heron's area formula: [4][•][2][→][LAST MENU] **CM** [6][•][1] **CM** [3][•][2] **CM** [VAR] **HERO** Result: 6.3_cm^2

b. Heron's Formula: [6][SPC][7][SPC][1][0] **HERO** Result: 20.7 Then find angle (a), using the Law of Cosines: [7][SPC][1][0][SPC] [α][A] **CSLW** Result: '√(149-140*COS(A))' Now equate this with its known length (6): [6][ENTER][▶][←][=] Then set flag −1 (principal solution) and isolate A: [1][+/−] [α][S][α][F][ENTER][α][A][←][ALGEBRA] **ISOL** Result: 'A=36.2' Knowing *A*, use the Law of Sines to get *B*: [7][SPC][6][SPC][3][6][•][2][VAR] **SNLW** Result: 43.6 Then *C* is: [1][8][0][ENTER][3][6][•][2][−][▶][−] Result: 100.2

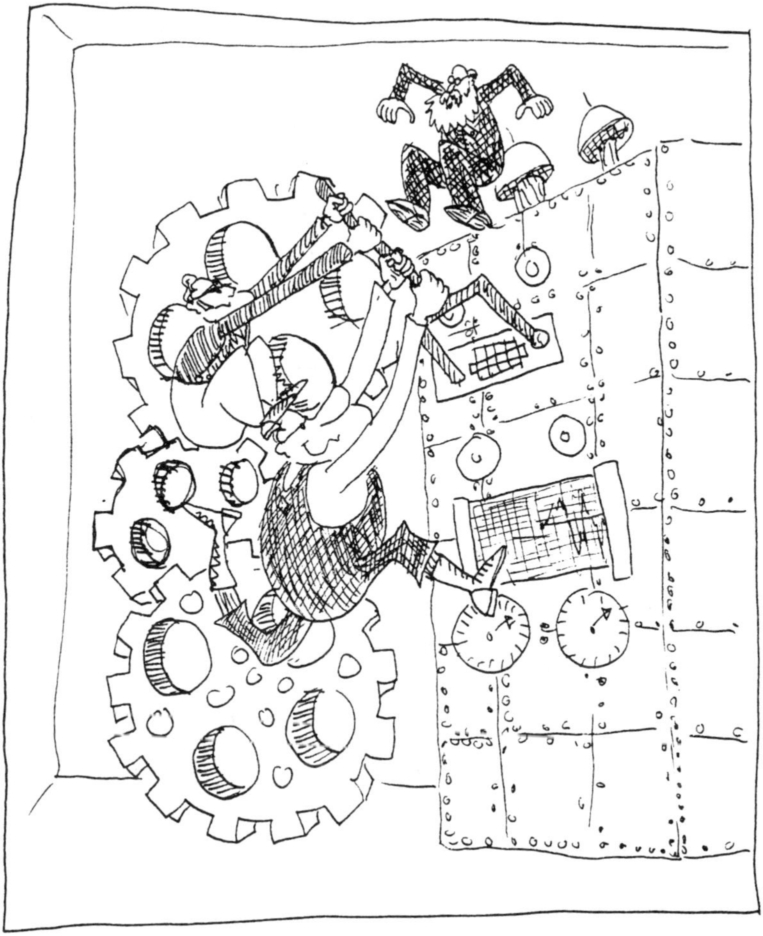

5 Solving, Plotting and Analyzing

Equations, Data and Graphics

For bigger jobs, you need bigger tools. Indeed, your 48 workshop has such "power tools," and it's time to learn how to use them.

You're going to see how to coordinate three powerful tools (SOLVE, PLOT, and STAT) and three special supporting "environments" (Equation Writer, Matrix Writer, and Graphics) to make short work of challenging real-world problems that, but a few years ago, couldn't be handled even by desktop computers.*

To begin, look at this schematic, which summarizes the multiple relationships between these tools and environments:

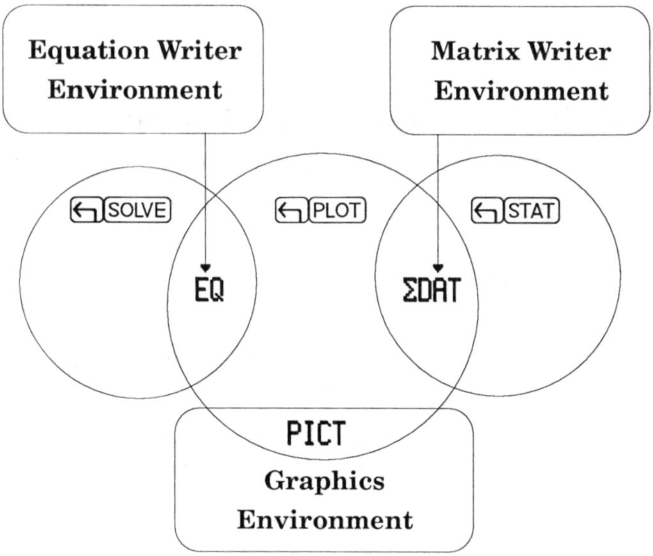

* Even today, computer software packages that give you the functionality of the 48 will set you back hundreds of dollars.

On that schematic, notice the three *reserved VARiable names* that you use to communicate between the three tools.

- EQ You store the *current equation* in the VARiable EQ. The SOLVE tool will solve only this equation, and the PLOT tool will plot only this equation. However, the word "equation" has a very flexible range of meanings here. As you'll see in this chapter, the SOLVE and PLOT tools will allow EQ to contain:

  - any real number, unit object, *algebraic expression* or *equation*;
  - any *program* that evaluates to a single real number or unit object;
  - a *list* of algebraic expressions and/or valid programs.

- ΣDAT You store the *current data array* in the VARiable ΣDAT. The tools in the STAT toolbox operate only on this array, and the PLOT tool plots statistical data only from this array. These tools require that ΣDAT contain a real-valued array with at least one element.

- PICT The *current graphics display* is stored in the variable called PICT. The PLOT tool calculates coordinates for functions it graphs, but the actual graph—the PICTure—is stored in PICT. PICT can contain only a graphic object. Whenever you view the Graphics display, you are viewing the graphic object currently stored in PICT.

Notice that each of these reserved variables is a different kind of object:

- EQ contains a *procedure* object (algebraic expressions, equations, and programs).
- ΣDAT contains an *array* object.
- PICT contains a *graphics* object.

Notice also that EQ and ΣDAT are appropriate *inputs* for the PLOT tool, while PICT is only a final *output*. That is, EQ and ΣDAT are the procedures and data from which the 48 calculates and outputs results. And one form of output is created chiefly for your eyes—the graphics display—stored in PICT. That form, similar to a paper print-out, is generally meaningless to the machine as data thereafter.

Of course, other forms of outputs can then become appropriate inputs. Besides building a graphics display in PICT, SOLVE, PLOT and STAT also generate numerical results on the Stack, which readily become the arguments for other functions.

That being the case, this chapter concentrates on the variables EQ and ΣDAT and their use with SOLVE, PLOT and STAT. Though you'll certainly use PICT and the Graphics environment to help you view your plots, you won't study it in much detail in this course.

To learn more specifically how to manipulate, modify, and dissect graphic objects (grobs), read Chapter 19 of your Owner's Manual or—better yet—read ***HP 48 Graphics*** (by Ray Depew), a book entirely dedicated to the topic (see the back of this book for more information).

Defining EQ, the Current Equation

Before you can use the SOLVE and PLOT tools, you must define the VARiable EQ. There are two ways to store an equation into it:

- Create an equation from scratch and store it into EQ;
- Choose an existing equation from the Equation Catalog and store it in EQ.

From Scratch: Create the following expression, named POLY, as the current equation: $x^4+3x^3-7x^2+4x-10$

Like So: Use the Equation Writer: [←][EQUATION][α][X][y^x][4][▶] [+][3][α][X][y^x][3][▶][−][7][α][X][y^x][2][▶][+][4][α][X][−][1][0] [ENTER].

To make it the current equation: [←][SOLVE] NEW ....
You'll see: Name the equation,
press ENTER

And the 48 goes into alpha mode (notice the annunciator), so type the name: [P][O][L][Y][ENTER]

Now you should see POLY listed as the current equation in the message area at the top of your display. And you can press [VAR] to confirm that POLY is now a named variable, too.

Question: What exactly is stored in EQ now?

Find Out: Remember that EQ is just a VARiable with a reserved name; you can do anything to it that you normally do to a VARiable. So press: [VAR] [←] [PREV] [→] **EQ**....

Result: 'POLY' The *name* of the equation—not the equation itself—is what you stored into EQ.

Hmm... Do you have to name *every* equation you want to store into EQ?

Not At All: For example, to create $5\sin(2x - \frac{\pi}{4})$ and store it, unnamed, into EQ, you would do this:

Create: [←] [EQUATION] [5] [SIN] [2] [α] [X] [−] [←] [π] [÷] [4] [ENTER]
Store: [←] [SOLVE] **STEQ**. Simple.

The **STEQ** (STore EQuation) command is just a shortcut for ['] [α] [E] [α] [Q] [STO].

When would you store a name—instead of the equation itself—into EQ?

Keep in mind that if you store an unnamed equation, it will be lost forever when you next store something else into EQ. So if you want to preserve your equation for future use, name it first and store the name into EQ. On the other hand, use **STEQ** for quick, temporary equation-solving—when you don't want to use memory to name an equation that you'll never use again anyway.

The Equation Catalog

Of course, you might not need to create an equation for EQ; maybe it exists already in your VARiable menu. And the easiest way to load an existing equation into EQ is to use the ***Equation Catalog***.

A ***catalog*** is just a subset of your VARiable menu, displayed so you can select an equation with a pointer like that of the Interactive Stack.

Watch: Press CAT.... You'll soon see a list of all of the algebraic expressions and equations in your VARiable menu. And a pointer (▶) should be pointing to POLY, like this:

▶POLY: 'X^4+3*X^3-7*X...

Use ▼ to move through the catalog. Look at the various names and objects listed. They fall into three categories:

- Algebraic objects
- Directories—which can lead to more equations
- Other types of objects (lists, complex numbers, programs, vectors, arrays)—anything with a name ending with .EQ.

That is, the 48 includes all algebraic objects and directories in the Equation Catalog, *plus* any object whose name ends with .EQ (you'll read more about this suffix soon).

Next: Move the pointer to POLY, and look at the menu. You can do several things once you're pointing to the equation:

PLOTR You can store the selection into EQ and jump immediately to the PLOTR menu to plot it.

SOLVR You can store the selection into EQ and jump immediately to the SOLVR menu, to solve for a variable or calculate the value of an expression.

EQ+ You can add the selection to a list, thus linking it with other objects.

EDIT You can edit the selection on the Command Line (and ENTER returns you to the Catalog when you finish).

→STK You can put a copy of the selection on Level 1 of the Stack. Try it—press →STK.

VIEW You can temporarily view the entire expression by holding down the VIEW menu key. Try it.

Do This: Press SOLVR. This is the "business end" of the SOLVE tool. Notice how the current equation is listed in the message area at the top of the display.

Question: How do you get back to the Equation Catalog now?

Answer: You could either press ← SOLVE CAT or use a *shortcut*, → ALGEBRA, to go to the Equation Catalog.

The SOLVR Menu

Press **SOLVR** to return to the SOLVR menu from the Equation Catalog. This menu is obviously different from other menus; it has "hollow" menu labels.

The different appearance is the 48's way to remind you that you're looking at a special *customized* menu. The SOLVR menu is customized for the particular object currently stored in EQ. Each time you change what's stored in EQ, the 48 changes the SOLVR menu.

Right now, POLY is stored in EQ. So the SOLVR menu contains just two selections, [X] and **EXPR=**. The [X] selection represents X, which is POLY's only variable (if there were other variables, they would appear in this menu, too).

Use It: Find the value of the POLY expression for $x = 0, 1, 2$, and 3.

Like So: Set FIX 3 display format: 3 ⬅ MODES **FIX** ➡ LAST MENU

Press 0 [X] **EXPR=**. Result: EXPR: -10.000

Press 1 [X] **EXPR=**. Result: EXPR: -9.000

Press 2 [X] **EXPR=**. Result: EXPR: 10.000

Press 3 [X] **EXPR=**. Result: EXPR: 101.000

EXPR= calculates the value of the expression, given the current values stored in all the variables. Notice that to store a value into a SOLVR variable name, you simply key in the value and press the appropriate hollow variable key. This is different than the VAR menu.

Question: Of course, you can use one named algebraic in another. How does the SOLVR menu handle this?

Find Out: Create another expression TPOLY: 'A*(POLY-B)'

Press: ['][α][A][×][⬅][( )][VAR] **POLY** [−][α][B][ENTER][⬅][SOLVE] **NEW** [T][P][O][L][Y][ENTER].

Now look at the SOLVR menu for TPOLY. Since it's the current equation—as you can tell from the message area—simply press **SOLVR**....

Answer: The SOLVR menu now includes the variables *directly* invoked in TPOLY ([A] and [B]), *and* those variables invoked *indirectly* in TPOLY, via POLY ([X]).

Thus, in the SOLVR menu, you'll always have access to any variables you need to solve an equation or expression, even if those variables are referred to only through other named algebraics.

Now it's time to practice solving equations....

Solving Equations with SOLVE

SOLVE allows you to solve an equation for one unknown variable as long as all other variables have known real or unit values (SOLVE does not find symbolic or complex solutions).....

To Wit: Use SOLVR to find a root of the POLY expression.

Easy: Make POLY the current equation ([→][ALGEBRA][▼]) and go to the SOLVR menu (SOLVR).

Now press [←][X].... Result: X: 1.713

Pressing [←] before a hollow variable key tells SOLVE to solve for that variable (since X was POLY's only variable, you didn't need to store any other knowns first).

Something should be bothering you about now: How can an *expression*, like *POLY*, be "solved" when it's not equated to anything?

Good point. The answer is that SOLVE equates the expression to *zero* to solve for the variable you request (just like ISOL and QUAD).

Notice the message in the display—Zero—indicating that the 48 has indeed found a *zero* (a *root*) of the POLY expression. You can confirm this now, simply by evaluating the expression itself—press EXPR=....
Result: EXPR: 0.000

However, POLY is a polynomial of the fourth degree and thus has at least one more real root. To find this other root, you must *guide* SOLVE as it looks for solutions.

Do This: First watch SOLVE as it searches for the root you just found: Press [0] [X] to begin the search, then quickly press [←] [X] [ENTER] and watch the message area.

Those numbers are the intermediate guesses that SOLVE is using to home in on a solution. You control its search pattern by telling it where to begin its guessing:

Like So: Store -10 into X ([1] [0] [+/-] [X]), so that the 48 will start its searching at –10. Now solve for *x* ([←] [X]).
Result: X: -4.746.

Ah—a new root ...or is it? Look at the message area. What's a Sign Reversal—and what does it mean?

A ***sign reversal*** occurs when a change in the value of the unknown variable causes the value of the expression to *change signs* (i.e. cross the *x*-axis, like a root) *without exactly equalling zero*. This can mean either that:

- you've found a *discontinuity* in your expression (an asymptote or stair-step, or something); or,
- you really have found a root, but the round-off accuracy of the calculator (and the SOLVE algorithm) couldn't find the value of the variable that made the value of the expression exactly zero.

OK: To quickly determine if the Sign Reversal message means that you've encountered a discontinuity or a root, simply press EXPR=.... Result: EXPR: -4.000E-10

In other words, at the value of x where your 48 found a sign reversal, the value of POLY is −0.0000000004—so close to zero that, in all likelihood, -4.746 is actually a root of POLY and not a discontinuity.

So, you've found two real roots of POLY. Are there any more?

Check: Enter other guesses for x (try −50, −3, 0.5, 10, 100), solving each time for x. As soon as you see Solving for X, press (ENTER) to watch the search....

Result: All your guesses except $x = 0.5$ give you one of the two roots you already know. But your guess of $x = 0.5$ locates an Extremum at $x = 0.421$.

So apparently you have a local maximum or minimum there—and the other two roots are complex. Confirm this by pressing EXPR= to make sure the value of POLY at the extremum is neither "approaching zero" (as with a root) nor "approaching infinity" (as with a discontinuity).

Solving Equations Involving Units

The SOLVE tool can solve for a variable *and its required units*, as long as two conditions are true:

- The units for all variables are dimensionally consistent.
- You must give at least one guess for the unknown variable—with the desired unit attached. However, after you've included the unit once in a guess, you can alter the guess simply by entering the numerical part. This is a time-saving feature, but remember that a variable will keep its value until you PURGE it. So if you need to use a variable name first for a value with units, then later for a value without units, you'll need to PURGE the first value, so that it's units aren't implicitly kept for the second one.

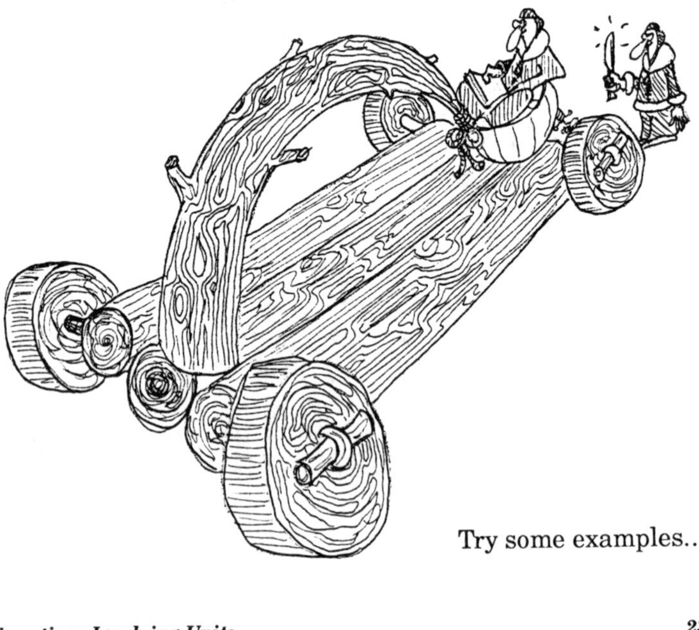

Try some examples....

Example: Create an expression, named IGAS, for the Ideal Gas Law: $PV - nRT = 0$, where P is the gas pressure; V is its volume; n is the number of moles of gas; R is the ideal gas constant; and T is the absolute temperature of the gas.

Given that 10.0 moles of an ideal gas fill an 8.2-liter jar at 273 K and 27.33 atm, use IGAS to find R in $\frac{\text{mmHg - gal}}{\text{mol - K}}$.

Solution: ['] [α] [V] [←] [PURGE] [←] [EQUATION] [α] [P] [×] [α] [V] [−] [α] [←] [N] [×] [α] [R] [×] [α] [T] [ENTER] [←] [SOLVE] NEW [I] [G] [A] [S] [ENTER] SOLVR.

Next, store the known values *and their units:*

[2] [7] [•] [3] [3] [→] [_] [α] [α] [←] [α] [A] [T] [M] [ENTER] [P];
[8] [•] [2] [→] [_] [α] [←] [L] [ENTER] [V];
[1] [0] [→] [_] [α] [α] [←] [M] [←] [O] [←] [L] [ENTER] [N];
[2] [7] [3] [→] [_] [α] [K] [ENTER] [T]

Now supply an opening guess for R—to establish its units:

[1] [→] [_] [α] [α] [←] [α] [M] [M] [←] [H] [G] [×] [G] [A] [L] [÷] [M] [O] [L] [÷] [←] [K] [ENTER] [R].

Now *solve* for R: [←] [R]....
Result: R: 16.481_mmHg*gal/(mol*K)

Press EXPR= to investigate the Sign Reversal....
Result: EXPR: -1.110E-7_mmHg*gal

That difference is negligible, so the answer is indeed a true solution; R is about 16.481 $\frac{\text{mmHg - gal}}{\text{mol - K}}$.

Now: What pressure (in mmHg) will result if you heat a closed 5-gallon jar, containing 20 moles of chlorine gas, to 600°F?

Hmm: Just key in your knowns: 6 0 0 ← UNITS NXT TEMP °F ← K (you must use an absolute temperature in the formula) → SOLVE T (a shortcut to the SOLVR menu); 5 → _ α α ← G ← A ← L ENTER V; 2 0 N (no need to include the unit here, because the correct one, _mol, is already stored in N from before).

Now key in a guess for the pressure, to establish the desired units: 1 → _ α α ← M ← M H ← G ENTER P
Then solve for the pressure: ← P....
Result: P: 38810.517_mmHg

One More: What pressure of chlorine gas will result if you release it—under the conditions of the previous example—into a sealed, evacuated room of dimensions 4m × 6m × 5m?

Simple: This time, the volume unit is the one to change:
4 ENTER 6 × 5 × ← UNITS VOL M^3 → SOLVE V.
Now solve for *P*: ← P.... Result: P: 6.121_mmHg

Solving Equations Using PLOT

Now that you have an idea about how SOLVE works, you'll appreciate how PLOT can make solving equations even easier. For one thing, you can find roots of equations from within PLOT itself....

Watch: Go to the Equation Catalog (remember that the shortcut is (→)(ALGEBRA)). Select POLY and press PLOTR. You'll see this:

```
Plot type: FUNCTION
POLY: 'X^4+3*X^3-7*X^…
Indep:'X'
x:      -6.500      6.500
y:      -3.100      3.200

ERASE DRAW AUTO XRNG YRNG INDEP
```

This display shows:

- the type of plot it's ready to draw (FUNCTION is the usual plot type for equation-solving);
- the name of the current equation and as much of the actual object as possible;
- the name of the independent variable—which will be plotted along the horizontal axis (x-axis);
- the display ranges for the horizontal (x) and vertical (y) axes of the plot (the ranges you see here are the default ranges with a scale of 10 pixels per unit).

Go Ahead: Plot POLY using the default ranges: press ERASE DRAW.

Result: After a few moments, you'll see this

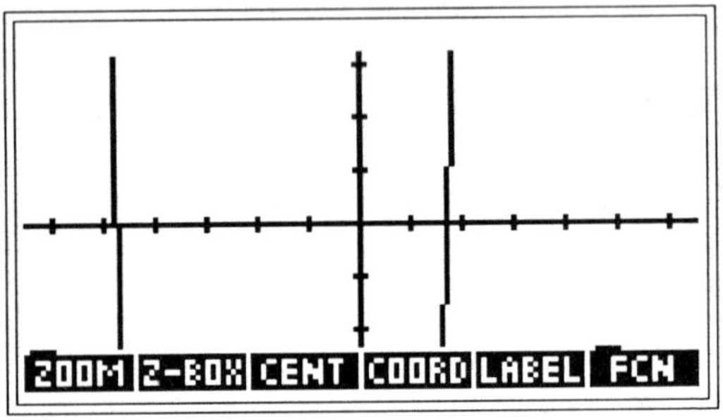

You can recognize the axes by the little hatchmarks, but it's a strange-looking plot—because you're not seeing the whole picture.

Zoom: To adjust your view, press ZOOM to see your zooming options. The vertical axis needs the adjustment, so press Y 1 0 ENTER to increase the vertical scale by a factor of 10.... After a few seconds, the revised plot appears. It shows more, but you still can't see all of the relevant area.

Zoom out again, say, by a factor of 5: ZOOM Y 5 ENTER.... Now you can see it all. You've increased the scale of the y-axis by a factor of 50; every vertical hatch mark represents 50 units.

And now that you can see the whole graph, take a moment to explore some of the tools available to you....

First: Label your axes: press **LABEL**. The numbers represent the values of the very edges of the display.

Next: Find your cursor. Press ▲ ▲ ▲ ▲ ▶ ▶ ▶ ▶ and find the small set of crosshairs just above and to the right of the origin of the axes. This is your cursor.

Then: Find the coordinates of your current cursor position: press **COORD**. You'll see a small ordered pair in the lower left-hand corner of the plot.

Now: Move the cursor around, using the arrow keys. Watch how the coordinates change as you move. Try pressing ↱ ▼ or ↱ ▶, etc.

Fifth: Cancel the coordinates display and return to the GRAPHICS menu by pressing any menu key.

Now you're ready to solve for the roots of POLY, using its graph.

Earlier, recall, you used a lot of trial-and-error guessing in SOLVE to discover that POLY has only two real roots. Now, one effortless glance at its graph tells you the same thing; it crosses the *x*-axis only twice.

So: Find the negative root of POLY using the graph.

OK: Use the arrow keys to move the cursor over to the vicinity of the left-most intersection of the graph and the *x*-axis (i.e. near the negative root). Then press **FCN** **ROOT**. This essentially calls upon the SOLVE root-finder, using the *x*-coordinate of your cursor position as its "guess" or starting point.

Thus, using a PLOT graph allows you to *visually* guide the SOLVER, thus eliminating your blind guessing.

Result: ROOT: -4.746 (lower-left corner of the display). The cursor is now sitting *at the root.* And this has also been copied to Level 1 of the Stack.

Then: Find the other root.

Easy: Press a menu key to get the menu back. Then move the cursor over to the vicinity of the positive root and press **ROOT** again. Result: ROOT: 1.713 (no surprise)

Now return now to the Stack ([ATTN] [ATTN]) to see what you've wrought.... Sure enough, the two roots have found their way to the Stack.

Recall that you plotted POLY back on page 239 by using **DRAW**, the main plotting command, which uses the currently established *x*- and *y*-ranges listed in the PLOT display. That's the most flexible approach.

But there's another way—a "quick-and-dirty" shortcut, called **AUTO**. It uses only the *x*-range specified in the PLOT display and then *automatically scales* the *y*-range so that the entire graph will fit into the display.

Try It: Press **AUTO**....

Result:

Given the current *x*-range, **AUTO** is a mixed blessing: The Good News is that the entire graph fits into the display with just one keystroke. The Bad News is that the resulting graph is scaled so that it's hard to tell how many roots there are without further investigation.

Just as before, you can improve things by zooming the y-axis until it looks approximately as it did before. But here's a chance to try another, more precise kind of zooming.

Blow It Up: Mark off a box on your graph and then zoom in on that box only—filling your display with it.

Here's How: Move the cursor anywhere to the left of the negative root and press **Z-BOX**. A cross will appear at the cursor. Next, press ⮡ ▶ to move the cursor (the cross stays put) to the right of the right-hand root. Then press ▼ until the cursor is nearly sitting on the menu.

You have a box marked out for zooming. The upper-left corner is determined by the cross; the lower-right corner by the cursor's current position. Press **Z-BOX** to fill the display with the contents of the marked-off box. Now you can better distinguish what's going on in this crucial region of the graph.

Again: Investigate the "flat" region: Move the cursor just to the left of that area and press **Z-BOX**. Then use ▶ until the cursor is just to the right of the flat region and press ⮢ **Z-BOX**....

Result: The plot's y-range is *auto-scaled* to fit within the the x-range you just selected. But still the plot is rather flat. Repeat the zooming process until your plot looks something like this:

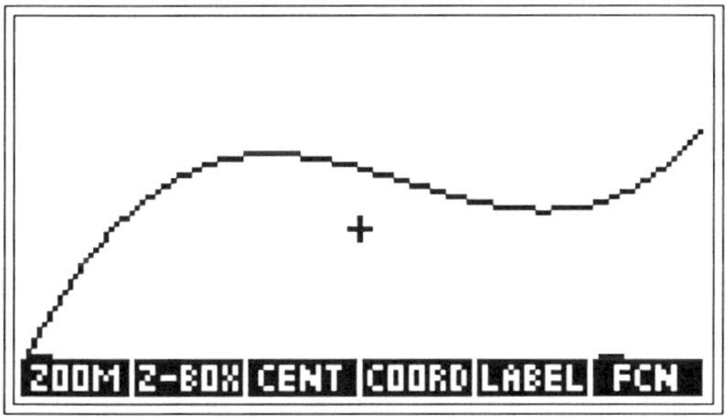

Challenge: Find the coordinates of those two local extrema.

Solution: Position the cursor on the maximum point and press **FCN** **EXTR**.... Result: `EXTRM: (0.421,-9.301)` (These are simply coordinates in the plot, not real and imaginary portions of a complex number.) Now position the cursor over the minimum point and press **EXTR**.... Result: `EXTRM: (0.704,-9.361)`

You can see how useful plotting a function can be: How many guesses would you have needed to isolate these extrema using only SOLVE?

Solving Two Expressions Simultaneously

Up to now, you've been using only *expressions* in SOLVE and PLOT. An equation is treated by these tools as *two* expressions—the left side and right side expressions—that are equal to each other.

Example: Create the following equation, name it EQUAT and make it the current equation (EQ): $4(\log x) = 5x^2 - 3$
Then use the SOLVE tool to solve for x.

Solution: Press [ATTN] [ATTN] to exit the Graphics environment.

Then [←] [EQUATION] [4] [→] [LOG] [α] [X] [▶] [←] [=] [5] [α] [X] [y^x] [2] [▶] [−] [3] [ENTER] creates the equation. [←] [SOLVE] NEW [E] [Q] [U] [A] [T] [ENTER] names the equation and stores it in EQ.

Now press SOLVR [←] [X] to solve for x.
Result: X: 0.684 Sign Reversal

Press EXPR= to find out if this is a root or not.
Result: LEFT: -0.659
RIGHT: -0.659

Because EQ contains an equation (i.e. *two* expressions), SOLVE attempts to find a value of the missing variable (x here) that equates both. Obviously, it was successful here—the Sign Reversal is indeed a root.

At this point, you could continue using the SOLVE tool to hunt for the other root. But, since you just learned how much more efficient it is to use PLOT for that kind of work, switch to the PLOTR display.

Do This: Press (→)(PLOT) to jump directly to the PLOTR display. Then, because the current ranges may not be appropriate for EQUAT, reset the default ranges by pressing (NXT) **RESET**.

Now press (NXT)(NXT) **AUTO**, and see a graph like this:

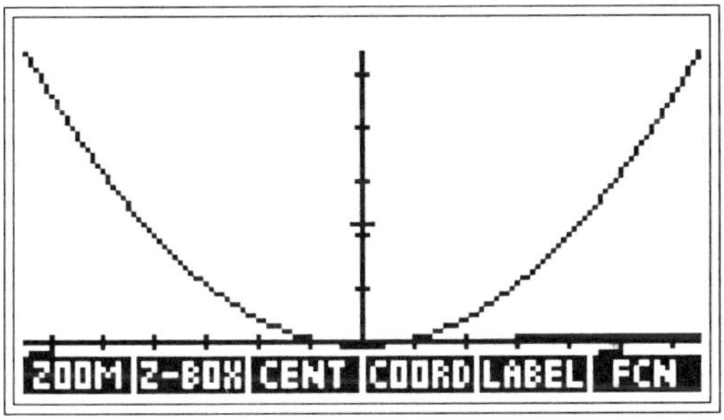

It's a little indistinct in the critical area where the two curves meet, so use **Z-BOX** to enlarge that area....

Now you should be able to see distinctly that the curves meet in two places, and that they cross the x-axis a total of three times.

So: Find the two points where the individual curves intersect.

Easy: Position the cursor over the right-most point of intersection and press **FCN** **ISECT**.... Result: I-SECT: (0.684,-0.659)

The first coordinate is the "solution" value of the variable. The second coordinate is the value of each expression at that point (compare with your SOLVE results).

Find the second solution similarly. Move the cursor over to the other intersection point and press **ISECT**....
Result: I-SECT: (0.199,-2.801)

Question: What will happen if you ask PLOT to find the *roots* instead of the *intersections* of the two expressions?

Answer: Try it—press any menu key to get the menu back, then **ROOT**.... Result: ROOT: 0.775

Notice that the cursor is sitting where the parabola intersects the positive x-axis. Whenever two expressions are plotted simultaneously, **ROOT** ignores the left-hand expression and finds the nearest root of the right-hand expression. Thus, if you move the cursor closer to the negative root of the parabola here, **ROOT** will find it. But it won't ever find the root of the logarithmic function.

All the functions in this menu except **ISECT** behave this way—working only on the *right*-hand expression.

Solving Programs and User-Defined Functions

At the beginning of the chapter, you learned that the current equation can be an algebraic object, a "proper" program, or a list combining algebraic objects and "proper" programs. You've seen how SOLVE and PLOT handle algebraic objects. Now it's time to see how they handle "proper" programs.

Question: What makes a program "proper" for SOLVE and PLOT?

Answer: To be acceptable, a program must do two things:

- It must take *nothing* off the Stack; it must use only named objects.
- It must return *exactly one result* to the Stack. That is, it must act as a mathematical function $f(x) = y$, where the $f(x)$ part is the program and y is the singular result (usually a real number or a unit object) that it returns.

In short, *SOLVE treats a program just like an expression.* That is, it lists all its variables in the SOLVR menu and attempts to find a value for the requested variable such that the program returns a result of 0.

Question: Why would you ever want to *solve* a program, anyway?

Answer: Some mathematical expressions don't lend themselves easily to a readable algebraic form. You might prefer to build them instead in the form of a program.*

Example: Create a program, PFUNC, that performs this function:

$$f(x)=\begin{cases} x^2+10 \text{ for } x<-3 \\ x^2-10 \text{ for } x\geq -3 \end{cases}$$

Solution:

```
«
 IF 'X<-3'
 THEN 'X^2+10'
 ELSE 'X^2-10'
 END
»
```

Key in the program:

[ATTN][ATTN][←][« »][α][I][α][F][′][α][X][α][←][2][+/-][3][▶]
[α][α][T][H][E][N][α][′][α][X][y^x][2][+][1][0][▶]
[α][α][E][L][S][E][α][′][α][X][y^x][2][−][1][0][α][α][E][N][D] [ENTER].

Now name the program as a *solvable program*: [←][PLOT] **NEW** [P][F][U][N][C].... Notice the .EQ suffix that the 48 appends to this name—so that PFUNC will be listed in the Equation Catalog. Now press [ENTER].

---

*You've already seen some rudimentary, "straight-ahead" programs in chapter 3, and you'll get a lot more practice in chapter 6. So don't worry too much if these particular programming commands are yet unfamiliar to you—just follow the general idea being illustrated. You'll also see in chapter 6 that you *could* build an algebraic expression for this example, too—if you prefer that form after all. It's nice to have options.

Now: Plot PFUNC and find any roots it may have.

OK: Press PLOTR (NXT) RESET (NXT)(NXT) AUTO.... Two roots?
Put the cursor over the left-hand "root," FCN ROOT....
Result: ROOT: -3.000
At the other "root," press ROOT.... Result: ROOT: 3.162

The only problem is that this plot deceives you. A "true" graph of the function would show a *discontinuity* at $x=-3$, instead of connected points. You can tell the 48 to show this discontinuity by changing a mode.

Do It: Exit the Graphics environment ((ATTN)(ATTN)). Then, at the MODES menu ((←)(MODES)(NXT)), press CNC■ to deselect the CoNneCT-the-dots mode (it should become CNCT).

Now return to the PLOTR ((→)(PLOT)), ERASE DRAW... better!

Then: Investigate the negative root by enlarging that region of the graph with Z-BOX.... It appears that -3.000 is not a root at all—the actual plot doesn't intersect the x-axis.

To check this, find the value of the function there: press FCN ROOT to move the cursor to the alleged root, then (NXT)(NXT) F(X) to evaluate the function at that point....
Result: F(X): 19.028

No, the function value is a long way from zero at $x = -3$. The sign change is not a rounding error at a root—it is indeed a discontinuity.

Properly constructed programs solve and plot so well that it seems as if user-defined functions (UDF's) ought to be useful, too. As you know, they're not valid when invoked with Stack arguments; taking values off of the Stack is a no-no for "solvability."

But you can always invoke a UDF in its algebraic form—as part of any ordinary solvable expression or equation.

Examples: `'COSLAW(b, c, A)'`

or `'a=COSLAW(b, c, A)'`

or `'5*x^2=COSLAW(b, c, A)'`

These are all just ordinary expressions and equations that happen to use a UDF—just as if it were a built-in function.

And these are all *solvable*, too—provided that they each have only one undefined name (at most). Keep in mind that those names refer to VARiables.

Multiple Equations with SOLVE and PLOT

Now you know how the SOLVE and PLOT tools manage one expression or one equation (two expressions) at a time. But to some degree, they can also handle more than one *equation* at a time.

- SOLVE can solve *a series of linked equations*, one at a time, to save you a lot of time and button-pushing.

  (Note: This is *not* the same as solving multiple equations *simultaneously*—such as a system of two equations in two unknowns; SOLVE cannot do that. For that you must use matrices—a topic covered later in this chapter.)

- PLOT can display plots of multiple equations simultaneously, provided that they all use the same independent variable. Similar to SOLVE, PLOT's analytical functions will work on the displayed equations *one equation at a time.*

  (Note: PLOT cannot find points of intersection *between* these different equations—a limitation analogous to the simultaneous solutions limitations on SOLVE).

So the main idea with multiple equations in SOLVE and PLOT is that you "load" them all at once for comparison and convenience; for the most part, you still analyze them one at a time.

To use multiple equations with SOLVE and PLOT, you name them and link them together in a *list*....

Example: Link PFUNC.EQ and EQUAT together in a list and store that list in EQ. Then, since both equations use 'X' as the independent variable, plot them on the same graph.

Solution: Of course, you could build a list from scratch and then store it into EQ. But there's an easier way—with the Equation Catalog.

Press [ATTN] [ATTN] [→] [ALGEBRA] to view the Equation Catalog. With the pointer at PFUNC.EQ, press EQ+.... A list will form in the message area: { PFUNC.EQ }

Next, select EQUAT and press EQ+ to add it to the list (the message area will confirm the addition). Press PLOTR to store the list into EQ. Then press [NXT] RESET [NXT] [NXT] AUTO to plot the two equations at once.

Notice that the first equation in the list—PFUNC.EQ—is drawn first. That first position is the privileged spot: Only the first equation is available for functional analysis (finding roots, slopes, points of intersection, etc.).

Question: Suppose you don't know which function needs further analysis until *after* you plot them. Can you choose which function is "active" (i.e. first in the list) without redoing the entire list-making procedure?

Answer: No problem—press **FCN** (NXT) **NXEQ**.

This rotates your list of equations so that EQUAT is now first and PFUNC.EQ is now second. Notice that the currently "active" equation is listed at the bottom of the graph so that you're in no doubt.

And you also confirm that you've rotated the list is to press (ATTN)(ATTN) and then evaluate EQ: (α)(E)(α)(Q)(ENTER). Result: { EQUAT PFUNC.EQ }

Sometimes you'll want to save a specially constructed list of equations for later or repeated use. But keep in mind that merely forming the list with **EQ+** does not *name it*. You must do that yourself—just as when you need to save any other object.

So: Name this list of equations TWO, so that you can use it later.

OK: Since the list is already sitting at Level 1 of the Stack, you don't need to recall it. Just press (⬅)(PLOT) **NEW** (T)(W)(O)(ENTER).

It certainly makes sense to *plot* a list of linked equations when they all share a common independent variable. But it makes more sense to *solve* a list of linked equations when they share one or more variables and are meaningfully related.

Example: There are two simple relationships which are often used in connection with the Ideal Gas Law:

$D = \frac{m}{V}$ where D is density; m is mass; V is volume.

$n = \frac{m}{Z}$ where n is the number of moles; m is mass; Z is molar mass.

Make an equation for each of these, naming them DENS and MOLE, respectively. Then combine them into a list along with IGAS and enter the SOLVR.

Solution: Create DENS: ['] [α] [D] [⇦] [=] [α] [⇦] [M] [÷] [α] [V] [ENTER] [⇦] [SOLVE] **NEW** [D] [E] [N] [S] [ENTER].

Create MOLE: ['] [α] [⇦] [N] [⇦] [=] [α] [⇦] [M] [÷] [α] [Z] [ENTER] **NEW** [M] [O] [L] [E] [ENTER].

Create the list: **CAT** shows the Equation Catalog; **EQ+** [▼] **EQ+** puts MOLE and DENS into the list. Then use the [▼] key to find IGAS and press **EQ+**. Finally, press **SOLVR**.

MOLE is the first equation in the list, so it becomes the "active" equation in the SOLVR (as indicated in the message area). But now press **NXEQ**....The active equation changes to DENS; and **NXEQ** again activates IGAS, etc.

Linking these equations in a list makes it very convenient to solve problems of the following kind:

Problem: An ideal gas has a molar mass of 95 grams. What is its density at 25°C and 800 mmHg, in g/m³?

Solution: Assume for a moment that you have 10.0 moles, and then use IGAS to calculate the volume:
[2][5][→][_][α][→][6][α][C] [ENTER][→][UNITS] UBASE [→][SOLVE]
[T], [1][0][•][0][N] [8][0][0][P] [1][→][_][α][←][M][y^x][3]
[ENTER][V] [←][V].... Result: 0.233_m^3

Now change the active equation to MOLE: [NXT] NXEQ. Then load the variable Z, indicating the mass units you desire (grams), and calculate the mass of the gas:
[9][5][→][_][α][α][←][α][G][÷][M][O][L] [ENTER][Z]
[1][→][_][α][←][G] [ENTER][M] [←][M]
Result: m: 950.000_g

Finally, switch to DENS and calculate the density (after specifying its units): NXEQ [1][→][_][α][←][G][÷][α][←][M][y^x]
[3][ENTER][D] [←][D] Result: D: 4085.774_g/m^3
What could be simpler?

Problem: What is the molar mass of an ideal gas if 0.52 g of the gas occupies 610 mL at 385 mmHg and 318 K?

Solution: Press NXEQ to switch the active equation back to IGAS. Then load the new values into the variables:

3 8 5 P
6 1 0 → _ α ← M α ← L ENTER V
3 1 8 T

Solve for *n*: ← N (result: n: 0.012_mol)

Now switch to MOLE, enter the mass, and solve for Z:

NXT NXEQ · 5 2 M ← Z
Result: Z: 43.928_g/mol

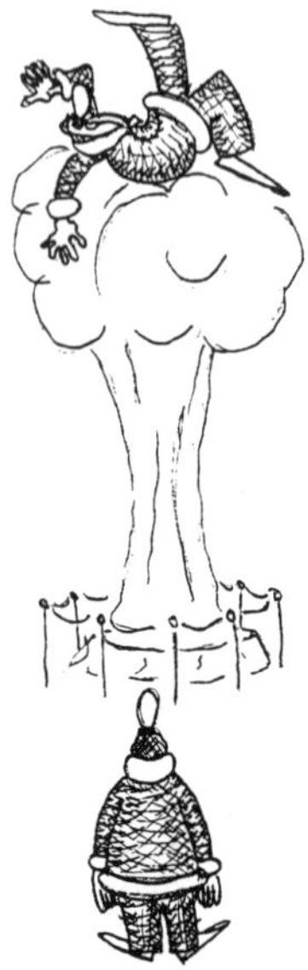

Solving Systems of Equations

Although its SOLVE and PLOT tools are limited to analyzing just one equation at a time, the 48 can indeed solve systems of equations—with matrices. So the next tool to learn about is the ***Matrix Writer***, a special matrix entry and editing environment.

Challenge: In STD display mode, solve this system of equations, using matrices created in the Matrix Writer:

$$4x - 3y + 2z = 40$$
$$5x + 9y - 7z = 47$$
$$9x + 8y - 3z = 97$$

Solution: First, convert the system to a matrix equation, **AX = B**:

$$\mathbf{A} = \begin{bmatrix} 4 & -3 & 2 \\ 5 & 9 & -7 \\ 9 & 8 & -3 \end{bmatrix}, \qquad \mathbf{X} = \begin{bmatrix} x \\ y \\ z \end{bmatrix}, \qquad \mathbf{B} = \begin{bmatrix} 40 \\ 47 \\ 97 \end{bmatrix}$$

Coefficients *Variables* *Constants*

Next, create matrices **A** and **B** with the Matrix Writer. Press ⮣MATRIX and see this:

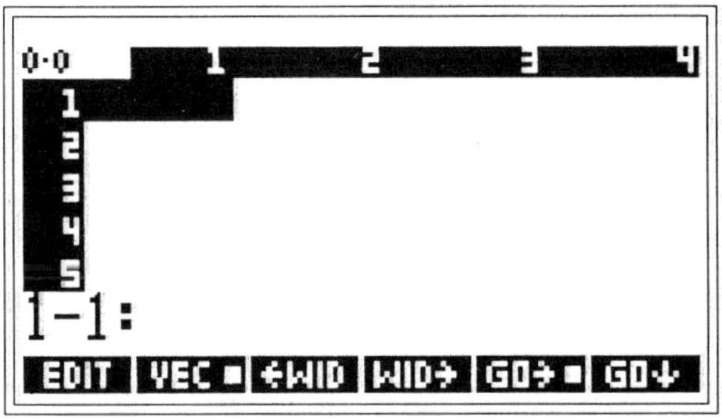

To enter matrix **A**: [4] [ENTER] [3] [+/-] [ENTER] [2] [ENTER] [▼]
[5] [ENTER] [9] [ENTER] [7] [+/-] [ENTER]
[9] [ENTER] [8] [ENTER] [3] [+/-] [ENTER]

Notice the little counter at the upper left that tells you the dimensions of the current matrix. It now reads `3·3`, indicating that **A** is a **3×3** matrix.
Now name and store matrix **A**: [ENTER] ['] [α] [A] [STO].

Enter and name matrix **B**: [→] [MATRIX] [4] [0] [ENTER] [▼]
[4] [7] [ENTER] [9] [7] [ENTER] [ENTER]
['] [α] [B] [STO]

Finally, divide matrix **B** by matrix **A** to get matrix **X**:

[VAR] [B] [A] [÷] Result:
```
[[ 10 ]
[ 2.00000000004 ]
[ 3.00000000006 ]]
```

Thus $x = 10$; $y = 2$; $z = 3$ is the solution (you can ignore the rounding error*).

Thus, solving a system of linear equations is as simple as solving the matrix equation, **AX** = **B** for **X**: **X** = **B/A**.

*The Owner's Manual (pp. 361-362) explains that you can improve the accuracy of the divide (/) function for matrices with the following short program (call it `MDIV`):

```
« → B A « B A / B A 3 PICK RSD A / + » »
```

To use MDIV instead of the regular divide in the last example, be sure that matrix B is on Level 2 and A is on Level 1 (just like the regular divide), then press [MDIV] from your [VAR] menu. The result will not show the rounding error; its calculation is a bit more precise. This fine-tuning may or may not be important to you.

Another: Solve the following system of linear equations:

$$4x-3y+2z-2r+9t=40$$
$$5x+9y-7z+3t=47$$
$$9x+8y-3z-7r+t=97$$
$$-4x+5y+z-2r+3t=68$$
$$x+y+z-3r-7t=23$$

Solution: Notice that the necessary matrices here are expansions of those in the previous examples. So, save some work—recall matrix **A** to the Matrix Writer: [α][A][ENTER][▼]... See? [▼] copies an array to the Matrix Writer—just as it copies an algebraic to the Equation Writer.

Now you can *expand* this **3×3** matrix by adding two rows and two columns, so that it will look like this:

$$\begin{bmatrix} 4 & -3 & 2 & -2 & 9 \\ 5 & 9 & -7 & 0 & 3 \\ 9 & 8 & -3 & -7 & 1 \\ -4 & 5 & 1 & -2 & 3 \\ 1 & 1 & 1 & -3 & -7 \end{bmatrix}$$

To add a column 4, move the cursor over to it: [▶][▶][▶]. Now [2][+/−] [ENTER]....(notice that the remainder of the new column fills with zeroes).

Now fill in the other values in that column: Element 2-4 should be a zero—no need to edit it. So move the cursor to element 3-4 ([▼][↱][▶]) and [7][+/−][ENTER].

Next, fill in the values in the two additional rows:

[4][+/-][ENTER][5][ENTER][1][ENTER][2][+/-][ENTER]
[1][ENTER][1][ENTER][1][ENTER][3][+/-][ENTER]

To add the fifth column, first move the cursor to element 1-5: [↱][▲][↱][▶][▶]. Then press **GO↓** to tell the cursor to move *down* (i.e. proceed column-wise) whenever you press [ENTER].

Now it's much easier to enter the values in the column: [9][ENTER][3][ENTER][1][ENTER][3][ENTER][7][+/-][ENTER] (and **GO→** to return to left-to-right—"row-major"—entry mode).

Inspect your work and then [ENTER] it onto the Stack.

Next, modify matrix **B**:
[α][B][ENTER][▼][▼][▼][▼][6][8][ENTER][2][3][ENTER][ENTER]

Finally, solve for matrix **X**: [▶][÷]

Result:
```
[[ 50.8814298158 ]
 [ 65.3897122915 ]
 [ 111.993025281 ]
 [ 77.7262423693 ]
 [ -3.98779424573 ]]
```

Thus, the solution set is (to two decimal places):

$x = 50.88$, $y = 65.39$, $z = 111.99$, $r = 77.73$, and $t = -3.99$

Analyzing Data: The STAT Tool

Equations are *solved*; data is *analyzed*. There's a decent analogy between the SOLVE tool and the STAT tool:

- The SOLVE tool works with the *current equation* (stored in the reserved name, EQ) that you've created either in the Equation Writer or on the Command Line.

- The STAT tool works with the *current data array* (stored in the reserved name, ΣDAT) that you've created either with the Matrix Writer or on the Command Line.

And the PLOT tool can help you visualize both kinds of information. It can draw five kinds of plots of EQ and three kinds of plots of ΣDAT.

So the task now is to learn to use ΣDAT to analyze some data.

Take a look at the World Survey table on the opposite page. It's full of interesting facts. Your exercises over the next few pages will be to *analyze* the data to find out what, if anything, is significant and/or related about these facts. That is, you will be analyzing what the data might *mean*.

After you've studied the numbers a bit, turn the page and have at it....

The World Survey					
Country	Pop. Density (per sq. mile)	% of GNP spent on Educ.	Literacy Rate	Per-Cap. Energy Use (kg coal equiv.)	Per Capita GNP
Australia	6	6.4%	99%	6700	$ 12,190
Bangladesh	2063	2.1%	29%	62	$ 150
Canada	7	7.7%	99%	9694	$ 15,910
Chile	44	4.5%	96%	921	$ 1,300
China	298	2.3%	76.5%	706	$ 280
Ethiopia	105	3.9%	35%	19	$ 110
India	658	3.6%	36%	272	$ 250
Italy	495	4.7%	93%	3211	$ 12,955
Japan	857	5.1%	99%	3625	$ 21,820
Mexico	114	2.1%	88%	1604	$ 7,253
Morocco	149	7.9%	28%	323	$ 510
Netherlands	1031	6.9%	95%	7200	$ 9,140
Nigeria	323	1.8%	30%	171	$ 520
Phillipines	560	1.7%	88%	246	$ 540
Portugal	293	4.4%	80%	1318	$ 3,393
South Korea	133	4.5%	95%	1625	$ 2,800
USSR	33	7.0%	99%	6389	$ 8,735
US	69	6.7%	96%	9489	$ 16,444
W. Germany	640	4.6%	99%	5672	$ 14,890
Yugoslavia	240	3.8%	90%	2440	$ 6,220
Zimbabwe	67	7.9%	77%	not avail.	$ 540

Creating the Data Matrix

First you need to enter the data into a matrix....

Do It: At the Stack, press [→][MATRIX] to enter the Matrix Writer with a new matrix. Then select GO↓, to enter the data by column. Also, press WID→ WID→ to decrease the number of columns displayed, allowing each column more room so that you can check your data (you can always rearrange the display later, once you've finished the entry process).

Now enter the first column's data—*Population Density*:
[6][ENTER][2][0][6][3][ENTER][7][ENTER][4][4][ENTER][2][9][8][ENTER]
[1][0][5][ENTER][6][5][8][ENTER][4][9][5][ENTER][8][5][7][ENTER]
[1][1][4][ENTER][1][4][9][ENTER][1][0][3][1][ENTER][3][2][3][ENTER]
[5][6][0][ENTER][2][9][3][ENTER][1][3][3][ENTER][3][3][ENTER]
[6][9][ENTER][6][4][0][ENTER][2][4][0][ENTER][6][7][ENTER]

Next, use the [▶] key to go back to the first row and move to the second column (*% of GNP spent on Education*). Enter this second column of data similarly, but when you finish, simply press [ENTER] to move to the top of the next column.*

Fill in the other columns likewise (skip the missing entry for Zimbabwe: [▶][→][▲]). Then press [ENTER] to place this data matrix onto the Stack, and name the new matrix WORLD and make it the current data matrix: [←][STAT] NEW [W][O][R][L][D][ENTER].

---

*You couldn't do this from the first column because the Matrix Writer would have taken the [ENTER] to mean "continue down the column." But now it knows the column length.

At the top of the display, you should now see these two lines:

```
WORLD(21)=[ 67 7.9 77…
WORLD(22)=
```

These tell you the name of the current matrix (WORLD), the number and contents of the last row (row 21), and the blank line indicating where the next data to be entered should go.

Try This: *Without using the Matrix Writer*, add the following data for Venezuela to the matrix:

Population density: 54 people per square mile
Percentage of GNP spent on education: 6.8%
Literacy rate: 88.4%
Per-capita energy consumption: 3,380 kg. coal equivalent
Per-capita GNP: $3,030

Solution: Press [5] [4] [SPC] [6] [•] [8] [SPC] [8] [8] [•] [4] [SPC] [3] [3] [8] [0] [SPC] [3] [0] [3] [0] [Σ+].

The [Σ+] command lets you add an entire row to the bottom of your current data matrix. Similarly [←] [Σ+] will *delete* the last row (but don't do this now).

And you can press [EDITΣ] to confirm that there are now 22 rows in your matrix (see the 22-5 at the upper left?).

Another: In the original data table (page 263), Zimbabwe was missing a value for its per-capita energy consumption. Further research has discovered that it's about 329 kg. coal equivalent. Edit the data matrix to insert this missing information.

Solution: While looking at the Matrix Writer view of WORLD, use the arrow keys to move the cursor to element 21-4 (row 21, column 4)—the location of the missing value. Notice that the Matrix Writer has put a zero there; it can't allow blank spaces in a matrix.

Now key in the proper value: 3 2 9 ENTER

Then: Press ENTER CAT to display the ***Data Catalog***, which is very analogous to the Equation Catalog. It's a list of all matrices in the current directory, plus any other accessible directory. You should see WORLD at the top of this list.

Once you select a matrix from the Catalog, you'll usually want to perform statistical tests on it or plot it. So your next task is to explore the WORLD data with the 48's built-in statistical tools.

The STAT Menu

The STAT Menu has five pages in all, divided logically:

- Page One: Entering and editing data matrices.
- Page Two: Single-variable statistical calculations.
- Page Three: Plotting statistical data (two-variable).
- Page Four: Two-variable comparative statistical calculations.
- Page Five: Summary statistics—the building blocks for other "customized" statistical tests.

Of course, normally when you press [←][STAT], you go to Page One—and you use [NXT] or [←][PREV] to switch to other pages—just as with any other multi-page menu in the 48.

But from the Data Catalog (where you should be now), you have some options:

- **1-VAR** selects the pointed-to matrix as the current data matrix and sends you directly to Page Two, so that you can do single-variable statistics.

- **PLOT** selects the pointed-to matrix and sends you directly to Page Three, so that you can plot the data.

- **2-VAR** selects the pointed-to matrix as the current data matrix and sends you directly to Page Four, to do two-variable regression and covariance analysis.

Single-Variable Statistics

With WORLD selected in your Data Catalog, press **1-VAR** to take you to the single-variable statistics (from some other menu, pressing (→)(STAT) will also take you directly to the single-variable statistics).

Challenge: Calculate the average and standard deviation of each variable in WORLD (say, to two decimal places: FIX 2).

Solution: Press **MEAN**. You'll get a vector (**1** × **5**) with the average for each column (variable) in WORLD. Press (▼) to display them in the Matrix Writer (use (▶) to show the complete version of each average in turn):

Result: [374.50 4.84 78.00
2972.55 6317.27]

Similarly, (ATTN) **SDEV** will compute the standard deviation for each column....

Result: [477.34 2.07 26.67
3153.61 6699.18]

Most of the other single-variable statistics work similarly to the mean and standard deviation.

BINS is an exception, however. **BINS** analyzes the distribution of a single, specified column of data—by dividing it into separate "bins."

Before pressing **BINS**, you must do four things:

- Identify the column you want to sort; **BINS** doesn't work with all of the columns at once.
- Enter the smallest possible value for the variable in question.
- Enter the size of each bin (they must be equally-sized).
- Enter the number of bins.

Try One: Set the display to STD. Then sort column 2 (percentage of GNP spent on education) into 7 bins that are 1.5 units (%) apart. The first bin begins at 0%.

Like This: Press NXT 2 **XCOL** to identify the second column as the current "*x*-column"—the independent variable.

Then: ← PREV 0 ENTER 1 • 5 ENTER 7 **BINS**.

Result: `[[ 0 ] [ 5 ] [ 4 ] [ 5 ]`
`[ 5 ] [ 3 ] [ 0 ]]`

and: `[ 0 0 ]`

Level 2 shows a *frequency distribution* for the variable—the number of data points in each bin, least-to-greatest. Level 1 shows the number of *outliers*—respectively, the number of data below and beyond the range of the bins.

Now plot this frequency distribution: Store it into ΣDAT (← PREV ← **STOΣ** 1 NXT NXT **XCOL**), then **BARPL**....
(Press ATTN when you're finished viewing the plot.)

Two-Variable Statistics

Of course, the most analytical statistical tests are not the *descriptive* statistics of one variable, but the kinds that compare *two* variables and infer relationships between them.

The analyses built into your 48 fall into three categories:

- Plotting
- Regression
- Test Statistics

These analytical tools can be used to compare just two variables at a time.* And you must designate the two variables you want to compare:

- `Xcol` designates the *x*-column—the column containing the *independent* variable data in the analysis you're conducting. If just one variable is involved (as with **BINS** in the previous section), then `Xcol` designates that column.
- `Ycol` signifies the *y*-column—the column with the *dependent* variable data.

*Actually, you can do multiple linear regression with matrices and the summation statistics in Page Five of the STAT menu, but it takes some programming to make it convenient.

Watch: Use NXT NXT NXT **CAT** to select WORLD as the current STAT array, then **PLOT** to return to Page Three of STAT. In the message area you'll see which columns are currently those of the independent and dependent variables.

Now make column 4 (per-capita energy consumption) the independent variable, and make column 5 (per-capita GNP) the dependent variable: 4 **XCOL** 5 **YCOL**.

The other item in the message line is Modl:LIN. This is the current regression model that STAT will use to search for the *best-fitting curve*—the mathematical function that approximates the data as closely as possible. The 48 can use any of these four basic regression models:

- LINear: $y = \boldsymbol{b} + \boldsymbol{m}x$
- LOGarithmic: $y = \boldsymbol{b} + \boldsymbol{m}(\ln x)$
- EXPonential: $y = \boldsymbol{b}e^{\boldsymbol{m}x}$ or $\ln y = \ln \boldsymbol{b} + \boldsymbol{m}x$
- PoWeR: $y = \boldsymbol{b}x^{\boldsymbol{m}}$ or $\ln y = \ln \boldsymbol{b} + \boldsymbol{m}(\ln x)$

In each case, the STAT tool will find an intercept, ***b***, and a slope, ***m***, that best fits the designated model to the data in the two selected columns.

Example: To find the LINear equation for the columns (to 2 decimal places—FIX 2), press **ΣLINE**....

Result: '1283.12+1.69*X'

So $\boldsymbol{b} = 1283.12$ and $\boldsymbol{m} = 1.69$

Now: Change the regression model you're using to EXP and recalculate the intercept and slope.

OK: Press (NXT) **MODL** **EXP** to select the model, then **LR**....
Result: `Intercept: 644.69`
`Slope: 4.37E-4`

That's another way to calculate the regression model: **ΣLINE** gives you the result as an algebraic expression; by contrast, **LR** gives you the result as two tagged objects that are immediately available for further calculations. The regression form you use depends on what you want to do with the result.

Now: Figure out which regression *model* will give you the "best" fit for your data—and find that correlation coefficient.

Sure: Press **MODL** **BEST**.... The 48 now chooses among its four models the one with the highest correlation coefficient.... It chooses PWR. Now press **CORR** (⬅)(x^2) to see how good that fit is.... Result: `.87`

So 87% of the variation in the data can be accounted for by correspondence to the calculated PWR model. Not bad.

Next: Generate a scatter plot of the data and plot the model regression curve on top of it.

Easy: Go to Page Three of the menu ((←)(PREV)) and press **SCATR**. Then zoom both axes up by a factor of 1.5: **ZOOM** **XY** (1)(•)(5) (ENTER).... and label the axes (press **LABEL**).

Then, to put the regression model on top of it, press **FCN**.

Aha: A few data points fall quite some distance from the regression curve. What does this tell you?

Simple: Remember that the vertical axis is the per-capita GNP; the horizontal axis, the per-capita energy use. So if a data point is *above* the regression curve, that country is producing more GNP for its energy use than "normal." Conversely, a data point below the curve represents a country whose GNP is below what its energy use would lead you to believe.

So, which countries do these points represent? Which are unusually efficient or inefficient in turning energy into GNP?

You can find out two ways. First, of course, you can position the cursor over a particular dot of interest, then press **COORD** to display those coordinates, and check your printed data to see which country has similar number. Or...

You can use the regression model to calculated the "expected" values of the variables....

Example: Japan's per-capita energy use is 3625 kg of coal equivalent. Based on the model, what per-capita GNP would you expect Japan to have?

Solution: Press ATTN NXT to go to the fourth page of the STAT menu. Then enter 3 6 2 5 (an x-value in the current model) and press PREDY to PREDict the Y-value.

Result: 6710.28

Japan's actual per-capita GNP ($21,820) is over three times higher than this expected value.

Try the same thing for the United States, W. Germany, USSR, Netherlands, Italy, and Venezuela:

Results:	*Expected GNP*	*Actual GNP*
Japan	6,710.28	21,820
US	16,587.83	16,444
W. Germany	10,223.54	14,890
USSR	11,434.64	8,735
Netherlands	12,794.83	9,140
Italy	5,986.96	12,955
Venezuela	6,282.86	3,030

Some countries appear to be much more energy-efficient in producing their GNP than do others.

Another: Explore your data for other relationships. Is there a correlation between per-capita GNP and literacy rate?

Find Out: Change the variables: [←][PREV][5] **XCOL** [3] **YCOL**.
Select the model: [NXT] **MODL** **BEST**.
Test the model: **CORR** [←][x²].... Result: 0.66

So while this is not as strong a correlation as that between energy use and GNP, it still accounts for two-thirds of the variability in the data.

Now plot the data and the model: [←][PREV] **SCATR** **FCN**

The graph suggests a fairly positive dependence: The only points far from the curve are *above* it—countries with high literacy rates for their GNP's. No country shows an unusually low literacy rate for its GNP.

One More: The data suggests some inverse correlation between population density and per-capita GNP: the less dense the country, the higher the GNP. Test this theory.

OK: Press [ATTN][1] **XCOL** [5] **YCOL** [NXT] **MODL** **BEST** to ascertain the model, then **CORR** to test the fit....

Well, the correlation is inverse (the coefficient is negative) all right, but (press [←][x²]) the model can account for only 8% of the variation—hardly convincing.

Two-Sample Statistical Tests

The other kind of two-variable analysis involves the kind of statistical hypothesis-testing used when a researcher compares similar data from *two differently treated* groups.

For example, suppose you're doing research in fish behavior. And in one experiment, you use two types of fish attractors, one made from vitrified clay pipes and the other from cement blocks and brush—during 16 different time periods spanning four years at a given lake.

From these numbers (fish caught per fishing day), can you determine whether one attractor is more effective than the other?

Period	Clay Pipe	Blocks and Brush
1	6.64	9.73
2	7.89	8.21
3	1.83	2.17
4	0.42	0.75
5	0.85	1.61
6	0.29	0.75
7	0.57	0.83
8	0.63	0.56
9	0.32	0.76
10	0.37	0.32
11	0.00	0.48
12	0.11	0.52
13	4.86	5.38
14	1.80	2.33
15	0.23	0.91
16	0.58	0.79

First: Create your data matrix using Matrix Writer. You should have a `16·2` matrix when you're done....

Call it `FISH`: [ENTER] [←] [STAT] **NEW** [F] [I] [S] [H] [ENTER].

Next: Calculate a *t*-statistic for the `FISH` data:

$$t = \frac{|\bar{x} - \bar{y}|}{\sqrt{\left(\frac{(n_x - 1)s_x^2 + (n_y - 1)s_y^2}{n_x + n_y - 2}\right)\left(\frac{1}{n_x} + \frac{1}{n_y}\right)}} \quad \text{where:}$$

$\bar{x}$ and $\bar{y}$ are the sample means

n_x and n_y are the sizes of each sample

s_x and s_y are the sample standard deviations

This suggests a UDF: `'TTS2(X,Y,NX,NY,SX,SY)=...'`:

[←] [EQUATION] [α] [α] [T] [T] [S] [2] [←] [()] [X] [SPC] [Y] [SPC] [N] [X] [SPC] [N] [Y] [SPC] [S] [X] [SPC] [S] [Y] [α] [▶] [←] [=] [▲] [MTH] **PARTS** **ABS** [α] [X] [−] [α] [Y] [▶] [▼] [√x] [▲] [←] [()] [α] [N] [α] [X] [−] [1] [▶] [α] [S] [α] [X] [yˣ] [2] [▶] [+] [←] [()] [α] [N] [α] [Y] [−] [1] [▶] [α] [S] [α] [Y] [yˣ] [2] [▶] [▼] [α] [α] [N] [X] [+] [N] [Y] [−] [2] [α] [▶] [←] [()] [1] [÷] [α] [N] [α] [X] [▶] [+] [1] [÷] [α] [N] [α] [Y] [ENTER] [←] [DEF].

Return to Page Two of the `STAT` menu ([→] [STAT]), calculate the means and put them onto the Stack: **MEAN** [←] [2D]. Then enter n_x and n_y: [1] [6] [ENTER] [ENTER]. Find s_x and s_y: **SDEV** [←] [2D].

Now, since you have the six arguments for TTS2 on the Stack in proper order, just invoke your function: [VAR] **TTS2**....
Result: `0.57`

Then: To *interpret* this result, you must now compare it to the whole t-probability distribution. The 48 has four functions (found on the second page of the MTH PROB menu) that compare a test statistic with a related probability distribution:

- Student t distribution (UTPT)
- Normal distribution (UTPN)
- Snedecor's F distribution (UTPF)
- Chi-square (χ^2) distribution (UTPC)

Therefore, you can use UTPT to finish the FISH analysis:

Level 2: the total degrees of freedom $= (n_x + n_y - 2)$
$= (16 + 16 - 2)$
$= 30$

Level 1: the calculated test statistic, 0.57.

So, press 3 0 ENTER ► MTH PROB NXT UTPT....
Result: 0.29

This is the probability that there is no significant difference between the two attractors. That's too high (usually 0.10 is the maximum allowable) to conclude that there is a significant difference.

Conclusion: Neither attractor is significantly more effective than the other.

Transforming Variables in the Data Matrix

Sometimes you may need to mathematically transform your raw data before performing a regression or statistical test.

Example: What if you want to calculate the *difference* between each pair of observations in your FISH data, then put these results into a third column in the matrix and use a single-variable version of the *t*-test on that column?

Solution: You could calculate and then enter each individual difference into a third column. Or, you could do this:

Transpose the FISH matrix, row-for-column: ⬅ STAT ➡ STOΣ α α T R N ENTER STOΣ. Then *extract* just the last two rows: ⬅ Σ+ ⬅ Σ+.

Next, do the transformation: ▲ ▲ NXT DUPN ENTER −.

Now *reassemble* the 3 row-arrays into columns in another matrix: ▲ ▲ ▲ ROLLD ENTER Σ+ Σ+ Σ+ ➡ STOΣ α α T R N ENTER NEW F I S H 2 ENTER.

Obviously, transforming columns in a matrix isn't a feature built into the 48. Whether it's easier to transform data element-by-element or via an array procedure like this last example depends on the size of your data matrix and the complexity of the transformation.*

*And this is an excellent example of a good use for a small program—stay tuned.

In any case, it's time to see what your efforts netted you...

So: Do a single-variable t-test on the new third column (the paired difference column) of FISH2. The single-variable t-statistic is:

$$t = \frac{\bar{y}\sqrt{n_y}}{s_y}$$

Go: Press [→][STAT], and be sure that FISH2 is still the current data matrix. Then: **MEAN** [▼][▶][▶][NXT] **→STK** [ATTN][←][1][6][√x][×] **SDEV** [▼][▶][▶][NXT] **→STK** [ATTN][←][÷].... Result: 3.05

Now compare this statistic with the probability distribution: [1][5][ENTER][▶][MTH] **PROB** [NXT] **UTPT**.... Result: 4.06E-3

Hmm...according to this test—with the differences—there's only a 0.41% chance that the blocks-and-brush fish attractor is *not* more effective than the clay pipe. That's a very different conclusion than that suggested by the previous test.*

*Mark Twain had a comment for such a situation—something about three kinds of falsehoods....

More Challenges

At this point, surely the vast possibilities of the 48's tools and workshop are evident to you. And there's no telling what *you* might want to do with them. So here's a group of challenge problems, grouped roughly by topic, to help you get more practice in using the SOLVE, PLOT and STAT tools (indeed, using most kinds of 48 tools, except for programming—that's the next chapter).

But these are more than just a set of review problems. Some illustrate techniques that you haven't yet seen. Some introduce entirely new categories of solvable problems. This is both your chapter quiz and an additional set of lessons. Learn by doing—and enjoy discovering....

1. Find the intersection(s) of the following two curves:

$$9x^2+4y^2-18x-8y-23=0 \quad \text{and} \quad x^2-y^2-4x+2y=6$$

2. Two particles start at the same instant, the first along the path

$$x_1(t)=\tfrac{16}{3}-\tfrac{8}{3}t, \qquad y_1(t)=4t-5 \qquad \text{with } t\ge 0$$

and the second along the elliptical path

$$x_2(t)=2\sin\tfrac{\pi}{2}t, \qquad y_2(t)=-3\cos\tfrac{\pi}{2}t \quad \text{with } t\ge 0.$$

At what points, if any, do the paths intersect?

At what points, if any, do the particles collide?

3. Solve the following linear system graphically:

$$\begin{aligned} 6x+2y &\le 36 \\ 2x+4y &\le 32 \\ 2x-y &\ge -6 \\ x &\ge 0 \\ y &\ge 0 \end{aligned}$$

4. Find the first and second derivatives of $f(x) = x^2 - \frac{1}{x^2}$. Then plot the function and both derivatives on the same graph.

5. Differentiate: $y = e^x(\cosh x + \sinh x)$

6. Find the curvature of $\mathbf{r}(t) = t\mathbf{i} + \frac{1}{2}t^2\mathbf{j}$ at the point $P(-1, \frac{1}{2})$

7. The standard cylindrical beverage can has a volume of 12 oz, or 26 cubic inches. What dimensions yield the minimum surface area? Find the minimum surface area.

8. A water trough with a vertical cross section in the shape of an equilateral triangle is being filled at the rate of 4 cubic feet per minute. Given that the trough is 12 feet long, how fast is the water level rising when the water reaches a depth of 1.5 feet?

9. Find the roots and the extreme values of

$$\left(\frac{x-2}{x+2}\right)^3$$

10. Evaluate the following definite integrals:

a. $\int_0^1 (1+x)^{2\pi}\,dx$ **b.** $\int_0^1 x10^{1+x^2}\,dx$

c. $\int_0^1 \frac{5x^{\sqrt{x+1}}}{\sqrt{x+1}}\,dx$

11. Calculate $\int \frac{xe^x}{(x+1)^2}\,dx$

12. Calculate $\int \frac{x+3}{x^2-3x+2}\,dx$

13. Find a 5th-degree polynomial equivalent to $3e^x$.

14. Find the area between these parabolas: $x = y^2$ and $x = 3 - 2y^2$

15. Find the arc length of $\mathbf{r}(t) = t\mathbf{i} + \log(\sec t)\mathbf{j} + 3\mathbf{k}$ from $t = 0$ to $t = \frac{\pi}{4}$

16. Find the surface area when the curve $y^2 - 2\log y = 4x$ from $y = 1$ to $y = 2$ is revolved about the x axis.

17. Graph the polar function, $r = 4\cos 8\theta$, and find the area it encloses.

18. Junior Beaver arrived home from Hydro Tech one spring to find his father furious and ranting as he watched his dam overflow:

"…#^*&*^$!!@ … ducks! That's the third year in a row them ducks've landed on th' pond so thick that the water level swamped my dam!"*

Now, Junior knew that something had happened the last few years to flood the dam, but he had his doubts about this theory.

"Pop, how much does the water level need to rise to overflow?"

"I build a half a meter of just-in-case at the top. I don't have enough material to do more n' that."

"Then I don't think the ducks could possibly be at fault. Let me run some calculations to see."

Junior then set out with his trusty 48 to test his father's theory:

- The surface of the pond—roughly rectangular—measured 70 meters by 13 meters.
- The pond was 3.5 meters deep (at its deepest) and roughly a half-cylinder in profile—like one half of a tall tin can.
- The average volume of a duck's bottom (d.b.) in water was 2.25 liters and its area on the surface averaged 450 cm^2.*

Were the ducks responsible for swamping the dam?

*For these sensitive and personal measurements, Junior Beaver wishes to thank several duck acquaintances who prefer to remain anonymous. They know who they are.

19. Evaluate the following expressions:

a. $\sum_{k=1}^{7} (-1)^{k+1} \left(\frac{1}{2}\right)^{2k+1}$

b. $\sum_{k=0}^{\infty} \frac{1-2^k}{3^k}$

20. Find the set of times—to the nearest hundredth of a second—during a 12-hour rotation of a clock in which the minute hand and hour hand coincide.

21. A car rental company has facilities at four airports: Los Angeles International (LAX), Burbank, Ontario, and Orange County. The following table shows the pattern of car returns.

	Fraction returned at			
Rented at	LAX	Burbank	Ontario	Orange C.
LAX	.85	.07	.03	.05
Burbank	.12	.70	.10	.08
Ontario	.10	.12	.69	.09
Orange County	.05	.03	.14	.78

If the company rents each of its 400 cars exactly once per day, how many should each airport have to maintain a steady supply?

22. Given the following data:

Investment Type	Sample Size	Mean Annual Return	Std. Dev. of Return (Risk)
Common Stocks	50	10.57	19.05
Corporate Bonds	35	4.38	5.52
US Government bonds	30	3.47	3.87
Municipal bonds	35	2.51	8.76

Do these data indicate significant differences in risk (i.e. in the standard deviation of annual returns) among these four types of investments? Use the data to predict the annual return of an investment type whose standard deviation is 11.67.

23. Assume that an economy is based on five industrial sectors:

Agriculture **B**uilding **E**lectricity **F**uels **W**ater

Each dollar of *output* from each sector requires a certain amount of *input* from each sector—including itself. The input values for all sectors are as follows:

	Output Sector				
Input Sector	A	B	E	F	W
A	.422	.100	.035	.235	.100
B	.089	.350	.082	.052	.180
E	.036	.075	.100	.224	.400
F	.098	.025	.380	.415	.115
W	.147	.115	.300	.107	.200

Projections of demand (needed output) were developed for two different scenarios:

	Demand Projection (in $billions)	
Sector	Scenario 1	Scenario 2
A	438	500
B	390	465
E	190	275
F	235	315
W	109	156

How much output value must each sector produce to satisfy the demand projections of each scenario?

More Solutions

1. The simplest approach is to find the intersection point(s) visually in PLOT and then check them in SOLVE:

   Create the two equations, CRV1 and CRV2. Then, at the Equation Catalog, combine them into a list and move to the plotter ([→] [ALGEBRA] EQ+ [▼] EQ+ PLOTR).

   These curves are both conics, so change the plot type to CONIC ([NXT] PTYPE CONIC) and be sure that flag −1 (Principal Solutions) is clear ([1] [+/−] [SPC] [α] [α] [C] [F] [ENTER]).* And [6] [SPC] [α] [α] [F] [I] [X] [ENTER].

   Each CONIC plot must have its dependent variable defined. The default is 'Y'—which you're using—so just RESET the display parameters, erase any previous plot ([NXT] [NXT] ERASE), and DRAW.

   Apparently, there's just one point intersection. Use Z-BOX to zoom in for better viewing (do this several times if necessary): Move the cursor just above and to the left of the area of intersection and press Z-BOX. Then move to the right and below it and Z-BOX.

   Press COORD to see the coordinates.... You should get something close to (-1.000000,1.000000). Press [ATTN] [→] [SOLVE] [1] [+/−] [X] [←] [Y] to move to the SOLVR and calculate y for $x = -1$....

   Result: Y: 1.000000 So (−1,1) is indeed the intersection point.

*Only half of the conic will be plotted if the Principal Solutions flag is set; this flag allows only one answer for each x, but a conic section requires two answers for each x.

2. First, create and name the expressions, X1, Y1, X2, and Y2. And PURGE 'T', set RAD mode, and turn off CoNneCT mode.

Next, using a *complex* form (this is how the 48 does parametrics), combine the equations into two parametric expressions, PAR1 and PAR2: 'X1+i*Y1' and 'X2+i*Y2'. Then combine PAR1 and PAR2 into a list (⮣ ALGEBRA **EQ+** ▼ **EQ+**), and **PLOTR**.

Now change the plot type to PARAMETRIC (NXT **PTYPE** **PARA**), **RESET** the display ranges,and declare the independent variable ('T') and its range ($0 \le t \le 5$): ⮢ { } α T SPC 0 SPC 5 ENTER ⮢ PREV **INDEP**.

Plot the two paths: **AUTO**.... You'll see an ellipse and a line. Use your cursor and **COORD** to obtain the coordinates for the intersection points.... <u>Result</u>: The paths intersect at (2,0) and (0,3).

Test those results: Recall X1 and create two equations based on the results: ATTN ATTN VAR NXT ' **X1** ⮢ = 2 ENTER ' **X1** ⮢ = 0.

Now solve each of these equations for 'T':
EVAL ' α T ⮢ ALGEBRA **ISOL** and SWAP EVAL ' α T **ISOL**.
So particle 1 reaches (2,0) at $t = 1.25$ and (0,3) at $t = 2$.

Now recall X2 into SOLVR and see where particle 2 is located at these critical times: VAR **X2** ⮢ SOLVE **STEQ** **SOLVR** 1 . 2 5 **T** **EXPR=** 2 **T** **EXPR=**....
Particle 2 is *not* at (2,0) at $t = 1.25$, but it *is* at (0,3) at $t = 2$.

<u>Conclusion</u>: The particles *collide* at location (0,3) at $t = 2$

3. To graph a system of inequalities, create one expression with all of them (AND, ≤ and ≥ are in the PRG TEST menu):

```
'6*X+2*Y≤36 AND
      2*X+4*Y≤32 AND 2*X-Y≥-6 AND X≥0 AND Y≥0'
```

Name it as the current equation: ← PLOT NEW I N E Q ENTER.

Now, this will be a TRUTH plot, so press: PTYPE TRUTH PLOTR. Enter plotting ranges: ← { } α X SPC 0 SPC 7 ENTER INDEP ← { } α Y SPC 0 SPC 1 0 ENTER NXT DEPN.
And display ranges: ← PREV 1 +/− SPC 1 0 XRNG 1 +/− SPC 1 5 YRNG. And plot it: ERASE DRAW....

4. First, create *f(x)* and make a copy of it on the Stack: ATTN ' α X y^x 2 − 1 ÷ α X y^x 2 ENTER ENTER. PURGE and enter the variable of differentiation: ' α X ENTER ENTER ← PURGE. Now differentiate and clean up the result: → ∂ ← ALGEBRA EXPA COLCT...
Result: '2*X^-3+2*X'

Duplicate this first derivative and repeat the differentiation: ENTER α X ENTER → ∂ COLCT...
Result: '2-6*X^-4'

Combine the three functions into a list, then designate that list as the current equation: ▲ ▲ ▲ →LIST ENTER → PLOT ← DRAW (← DRAW is equivalent to STEQ). Then change the plot type to FUNCTION: NXT PTYPE FUNC RESET NXT NXT. Now plot the three functions in the same display, adjusting the display as necessary: AUTO.

5. [ATTN], then PURGE X, and create the expression: [←][EQUATION][←][eˣ][α][X][▶][←][( )][MTH] HYP COSH [α][X][▶] [+] SINH [α][X][ENTER]. Then enter the variable of differentiation and differentiate: ['][α][X][ENTER][→][∂][←][ALGEBRA] COLCT....
<u>Result</u>: '2*(COSH(X)+SINH(X))*EXP(X)'

6. The curvature of a twice-differentiable curve $\mathbf{r}(t) = x(t)\mathbf{i} + y(t)\mathbf{j}$ is given by:

$$k(t) = \frac{|x'(t)y''(t) - y'(t)x''(t)|}{\left([x'(t)]^2 + [y'(t)]^2\right)^{\frac{3}{2}}}$$

So, create a user-defined function, KURV:

'KURV(X, Y)=ABS(∂t(X)*∂t(∂t(Y))-∂t(Y)*∂t(∂t(X)))/(∂t(X)^2+∂t(Y)^2)^(3/2)'

Keystrokes: [←][EQUATION][α][α][K][U][R][V][←][( )][X][SPC][Y][α][▶][←][=][▲] [MTH] PARTS ABS [→][∂][α][T][▶][α][X][▶][→][∂][α][T][▶][→][∂][α][T][▶][α][Y] [▶][▶][−][→][∂][α][T][▶][α][Y][▶][→][∂][α][T][▶][→][∂][α][T][▶][α][X][▶][▶][▶][▼] [←][( )][→][∂][α][T][▶][α][X][▶][yˣ][2][▶][+][→][∂][α][T][▶][α][Y][▶][yˣ][2][▶][▶] [yˣ][3][÷][2][ENTER][←][DEF]

Now prepare the Stack with the two function arguments:

Enter $x(t)$: ['][α][T][ENTER]
Enter $y(t)$: ['][α][T][yˣ][2][÷][2][ENTER]

Now PURGE T, evaluate KURV, and clean up the results: [VAR] KURV [EVAL][←][ALGEBRA] COLCT.
Since $t = -1$ at point $P(-1, \frac{1}{2})$, store -1 into 'T' and evaluate: [1][+/-]['][α][T][ENTER][STO][→][→NUM]. <u>Result</u>: .353553

7. The simplest procedure is to use a Lagrange multiplier to find the constrained minimum. You want to minimize the surface area of a cylinder ($S = 2\pi RH + 2\pi R^2$) subject to the volume constraint ($\pi R^2 H - 26 = 0$). So, create CANS: $2\pi RH + 2\pi R^2 - \lambda(\pi R^2 H - 26)$

PURGE the variables R, H and λ ([←][{ }][α][R][SPC][α][H][α][→][L][ENTER] [←][PURGE]), and find the partial derivatives with respect to each:

$\frac{\partial CANS}{\partial H}$: [VAR] **CANS** [α][H][→][∂]....

Result: '2*π*R-λ*(π*R^2)'

$\frac{\partial CANS}{\partial R}$: **CANS** [α][R][→][∂][←][ALGEBRA] **COLCT**...

Result: '-(2*R*λ*H*π)+4*R*π+2*H*π'

$\frac{\partial CANS}{\partial \lambda}$: [VAR] **CANS** [α][→][L][→][∂]....

Result: '-(π*R^2*H-26)'

Now you equate each derivative with zero and solve the resulting (nonlinear) system. First, isolate 'λ' from the ∂H derivative:
[▲][▲][▲] **ROLL** [ATTN][α][→][L][←][ALGEBRA] **ISOL** **COLCT**...
Result: 'λ=2/R' Save it: [←][DEF]

Next, isolate 'R' from the ∂R derivative, and save it:
[▶][EVAL] **COLCT** [α][R] **ISOL** **COLCT**...
Result (FIX 2): 'R=0.50*H' Save it: [←][DEF]

Now use the $\partial\lambda$ derivative to solve for 'H':
[EVAL][←][SOLVE] **STEQ** **SOLVR** [←][H]....Result: H: 3.21 (inches)
Then for R: [VAR] **R** [EVAL].... Result: 1.61 (inches)
Then **CANS** [→][→NUM] (to force the numerical evaluation of π)
Result: 48.58 (square inches)

8. When the water is x feet deep, the area of a vertical cross section of water is $\frac{\sqrt{3}}{3}x^2$. Since the trough is 12 feet long, the volume of the water is then $4\sqrt{3}x^2$. Thus, the volume at time t is:

$$V(t) = 4\sqrt{3}\left[x(t)\right]^2$$

PURGE `x` and `t`, then: ['] [α] [V] [←] [( )] [α] [←] [T] [▶] [←] [=] [4] [×] [√x] [3] [×] [α] [←] [X] [←] [( )] [α] [←] [T] [▶] [yˣ] [2] [ENTER].

Now differentiate : ['] [α] [←] [T] [ENTER] [→] [∂]....
Result: `'derV(t,1)=6.93*derx(t,1)*2*x(t))'`

Now just define the known functions, $V'(t) = 4$ and $x(t) = 1.5$, and the unknown `RATE` you're trying to find:
['] [α] [α] [←] [α] [D] [E] [R] [←] [V] [←] [( )] [T] [←] [,] [D] [T] [α] [▶] [←] [=] [4] [←] [DEF]
['] [α] [←] [X] [←] [( )] [α] [←] [T] [▶] [←] [=] [1] [•] [5] [←] [DEF]
['] [α] [α] [←] [α] [D] [E] [R] [X] [←] [( )] [T] [←] [,] [D] [T] [α] [▶] [←] [=]
[α] [α] [←] [α] [R] [A] [T] [E] [α] [←] [DEF]

Now [EVAL] the expression for the Volume's derivative:
Result: `'4=6.93*(RATE*2*1.5)'`

Then isolate `RATE`: ['] [α] [α] [R] [A] [T] [E] [ENTER] [←] [ALGEBRA] **ISOL**....
Result: `'RATE=0.19'`

Thus, the water level is rising at 0.19 feet per minute at the moment the water reaches a depth of 1.5 feet.

Note that you could have defined your *user-defined derivatives* `derV` and `derx` *before* differentiating `V(t)`, but you could not define `x(t)` until afterwards, because the 48 would have known how to differentiate the simple function `'x(t)=1.5'` and thus would have ignored the defined alternative, `derx`.

9. Turn off dot-CoNneCT mode (if it's on): [⬅][MODES][NXT] **CNCT**.

Then create the function: [⬅][EQUATION][⬅][()][▲][α][X][−][2][▼][α][X][+][2][▶][▶][y^x][3][ENTER].

Now set the display ranges and plot the function:
[➡][PLOT][⬅] **DRAW** [2][0][+/−][SPC][2][0] **XRNG**
[1][0][+/−][SPC][1][0] **YRNG** **ERASE** **DRAW**....

Now explore this plot: By inspection of the function definition, you know that the vertical asymptote is at $x = -2$. You can find a horizontal asymptote at $y = 1$ (for $x < -2$) via [➡][◀] **FCN** **EXTR**; and at $y = 1$ (for $x > -2$) via [➡][▶] **EXTR**.

To find the root, press **ROOT**.... Result: `Root: 2.00`
(**EXTR** will find this too, because it's an inflection point.)

10. Create the first expression in the EW: [ATTN][ATTN][⬅][EQUATION]
[➡][∫][0][▶][1][▶][⬅][()][1][+][α][X][▶][y^x][2][⬅][π][▶][▶][α][X][ENTER].

To evaluate the expression, you have two choices: [EVAL] evaluates the integral symbolically and *stepwise*. By contrast, [➡][→NUM] evaluates the definite integral completely and numerically (including the symbolic constant, π, which [EVAL] won't evaluate).

Try the latter: [➡][→NUM].... **a.** Result: `21.25`
Do the other two similarly (you can use [EVAL] and [➡][→NUM] from the Equation Writer).... **b.** Result: `19.68`*

c. Result: `1.76`

*This assumes a FIX 2 display mode. *The display setting limits the precision of the integration.* Calculating **b.** and **c.** in STD mode gives `19.54` and `1.77`, respectively.

11. Find this indefinite integral by using *integration by parts:*

Let $u = xe^x$ and $\partial v = \frac{1}{(x+1)^2}dx$

First, calculate v from ∂v by calculating $\int \frac{1}{(x+1)^2}dx$

But *all integration on the 48—even symbolic integration—requires limits.* So use the variable of integration as your upper limit and a "dummy" name as the lower limit, then drop the term with the dummy name in the result:

[→][CLR] and PURGE X, Y, U and V. Then [←][EQUATION][→][∫][α][Y] [▶][α][X][▶][1][÷][←][()][α][X][+][1][▶][y^x][2][▶][▶][▶][α][X][ENTER][EVAL][PRG] OBJ OBJ→ [◆][◆][◆][EVAL].... Result: '-INV(X+1)'

Store this result in V and store xe^x in U:

['][α][V][STO]['][α][X][X][←][e^x][α][X][ENTER][ENTER]['][α][U][STO].

Calculate ∂U: ['][α][X][ENTER][→][∂]. Result: 'EXP(X)+X*EXP(X)'

Simplify this with RULES: [▼][◀][◀][◀] RULES ←T [◀] RULES ←M [ENTER]. Store this in dU ['][α][←][D][α][U][ENTER][STO].

Now calculate the integral: $UV - \int VdU\,dx$

Find and simplify UV: [VAR] U V [×][←][ALGEBRA] COLCT

Find and simplify VdU: [VAR] V DU [×][←][ALGEBRA] COLCT

Then create the integral: [←][EQUATION][→][∫][α][Y][▶][α][X][▶][→][RCL] (recalls the simplified integrand from the Stack)[▶][α][X].

Now [EVAL][PRG] OBJ OBJ→ [◆][◆][◆][EVAL][−]....

Result: '-1/(1+X)*EXP(X)*X+EXP(X)' Thus,

$$\int \frac{xe^x}{(x+1)^2}dx = -\frac{xe^x}{x+1} + e^x + C$$

Use [▼] to view this in the EW, if you wish.

12. The 48 can't symbolically integrate the integrand as given, but in this case, you can modify it via partial fractions:

$$\frac{x+3}{x^2-3x+2}=\frac{5}{x-2}-\frac{4}{x-1}$$

So, create the integral with this modified integrand: [←][EQUATION] [→][∫][α][Y][▶][α][X][▶][5][÷][α][X][−][2][▶][−][4][÷][α][X][−][1][▶][▶][α][X][ENTER]

Now evaluate it: [EVAL][PRG] **OBJ** **OBJ→** [◆][◆][◆][EVAL]
<u>Result</u>: `'-(4*LN(X-1))+5*LN(X-2)'`

13. Use the TAYLR function, located in your [←][ALGEBRA] menu. First, create and enter the function: [3]['][α][X][ENTER][←][e^x][×].

Now enter the polynomial variable: ['][α][X][ENTER].
Then enter the degree of the polynomial: [5][ENTER].
Go: [←][ALGEBRA] **TAYLR**....
Then evaluate the coefficients: [EVAL]....
<u>Result</u>: `'3+3*X+1.50*X^2+0.50*X^3+0.13*X^4+0.03*X^5'`

Press [▼] to see the result in a clearer form, if you wish.

14. Create a third function that's the difference of the two parabolas: ['][3][−][2][×][α][Y][^][2][ENTER]['][α][Y][^][2][ENTER][−][←][ALGEBRA] **COLCT**

Now plot this function ('Y' is the independent variable here): [→][PLOT][←] **DRAW** [NXT] **RESET** [←][PREV][←][{ }][α][Y][SPC][2][+/−][SPC][2] [ENTER] **INDEP** **ERASE** **DRAW**...

The desired area is the area under the curve between its roots. So press [◄][◄] **FCN** **ROOT** to find the negative root and mark it (press [×]). Then go find the positive root ([→][►] **ROOT**) and press **AREA** to calculate the enclosed area between the two roots.*

Result: `AREA: 4.00`

15. The length of the curve is given by the formula:

$$L[\mathbf{r}(t)] = \int_a^b \|\mathbf{r}'(t)\| \, dt$$

The **i** and **k** terms of the derivative can be found by inspection. To calculate the **j** term: ['][COS][α][T][ENTER][1/x][→][LOG]['][α][T][ENTER] [→][∂][←][ALGEBRA] **COLCT**... Result: `'0.43/COS(T)*SIN(T)'`

That's 0.43 tan(t). So $\mathbf{r}'(t) = \mathbf{i} + (0.43 \tan t)\,\mathbf{j}$

To calculate the integrand: [←][x²][1][+][√x]

So $\|\mathbf{r}'(t)\| = \sqrt{1 + 0.19 \tan^2 t}$

Now create the integral (using the Stack is quickest) and evaluate: [0][ENTER][←][π][4][÷][▲][▲][▲] **ROLL** [ENTER]['][α][T][ENTER][→][∫] [→][→NUM].... Result: `0.81`

*Note that the AREA integration function in PLOT is sensitive to the scale of your display. For greater accuracy, use a smaller scale ("higher magnification").

16. The surface area of a revolution of a curve about the x-axis is:

$$S=\int_c^d 2\pi y(t)\sqrt{[x'(t)]^2+[y'(t)]^2}\,dt$$

when the curve is expressed parametrically. The given curve converts to: $x(t)=\frac{1}{4}(t^2-2\log t)$, $y(t)=t$ with $t\in[1,2]$

So PURGE T and calculate the integrand: ['] [α] [T] [ENTER] [←] [PURGE] ['] [←] [()] [α] [T] [y^x] [2] [−] [2] [×] [→] [LOG] [α] [T] [▶] [▶] [÷] [4] [ENTER] ['] [α] [T] [ENTER] [→] [∂] COLCT [ENTER] [×] COLCT [1] [+] [√x] ['] [α] [T] [ENTER] [×] [2] [×] [←] [π] [×].

Now create the integral and evaluate:
[1] [ENTER] [2] [ENTER] [▲] [▲] [▲] ROLL [ENTER] ['] [α] [T] [ENTER] [→] [∫] [→] [→NUM]
Result: 11.24

17. First, PURGE R and θ. Then set curve-filling mode (i.e. clear flag −31) and RADians mode. Now create the function as the current EQ in PLOT: ['] [4] [×] [COS] [8] [×] [α] [→] [F] [ENTER] [→] [PLOT] [←] DRAW.

Then change the plot type to POLAR ([NXT] PTYPE POLAR), change the independent variable to θ (['] [α] [→] [F] [NXT] [NXT] INDEP), and plot the graph: AUTO....

Now, the area enclosed by the curve is given by:

$$\int_0^{2\pi}\tfrac{1}{2}(4\cos 8\theta)^2\,d\theta$$

Create the integral and evaluate: [ATTN] [0] [ENTER] [2] [←] [π] [×] [VAR] [←] [PREV] EQ [←] [x^2] [2] [÷] ['] [α] [→] [F] [ENTER] [→] [∫] [→] [→NUM] (wait)... [←] [ALGEBRA] [NXT] →Qπ .... Result: '8*π'

18. First, Junior derived the formula* relating n ducks' bottoms ($nV_{d.b.}$), to the rise in the pond level:

$$nV_{d.b.} = 1000\int_{D}^{D+I} Lr^2 \cos^{-1}\left(1-\frac{h}{r}\right)-\frac{L}{2}(r-h)\sqrt{4h(2r-h)}\,dh$$

where $r = \dfrac{x^2+4D^2}{8D}$,

L = length of the pond

x = the initial width of the pond

h = the depth of the pond

D = the initial depth of the pond (before ducks)

I = the increase in pond level due to the n ducks' bottoms.

Next, he PURGEd the variable names: [←] [{ }] [α] [L] [SPC] [α] [N] [SPC] [α] [V] [SPC] [α] [R] [SPC] [α] [X] [SPC] [α] [H] [α] [D] [α] [I] [ENTER] [←] [PURGE].

Then he created the formula in Equation Writer, named it DAM, and made it the current equation:

[←] [EQUATION] [α] [N] [×] [α] [V] [←] [=] [1] [0] [0] [0] [→] [∫] [α] [D] [▶] [α] [D] [+] [α] [I]
[▶] [α] [L] [×] [α] [R] [^] [2] [▶] [←] [ACOS] [1] [−] [α] [H] [÷] [α] [R]
[▶] [▶] [−] [α] [L] [÷] [2] [▶] [←] [( )] [α] [R] [−] [α] [H]
[▶] [√x] [4] [α] [H] [×] [←] [( )] [2] [×] [α] [R] [−] [α] [H]
[▶] [▶] [▶] [α] [H] [ENTER]
[←] [SOLVE] **NEW** [D] [A] [M] [ENTER].

*It's a fascinating derivation, but unless you really want to prove it to yourself, you can take his word for it (he's been studying at Hydro Tech, remember). The point here is to notice that your unknown, I, is part of the *limit* of the integral—a new variation.

Then he created the subexpression and stored it into R:
['] [←] [( )] [α] [X] [y^x] [2] [+] [4] [×] [α] [D] [y^x] [2] [▶] [÷] [←] [( )] [8] [×] [α] [D] [ENTER]
['] [α] [R] [STO].

Junior entered SOLVR and loaded up his known variable values:
[SOLVR] [2] [•] [2] [5] [V] [3] [•] [5] [D] [7] [0] [L] [1] [3] [X].

But before he could solve for I—the increase in pond level caused by n ducks—Junior needed an estimate for n, the number of ducks. As a maximum, he divided the total surface area of the pond by the average surface displacement of a d.b.:
[7] [0] [0] [0] [ENTER] [1] [3] [0] [0] [×] [4] [5] [0] [÷] [N].

Result: 20,222.00 ducks—packed in like sardines.

Now, for the pièce de resistance: [←] [I].
Result: I: 0.02 (meters)

Just as he had surmised: Even if the pond were packed solid with ducks, the water level would rise only about 2 cm—not nearly enough to swamp his dad's extra 50 cm of dam.* (In fact—as he calculated later—even if all 20,222 ducks were to dive for food at the same moment, this still wouldn't be enough to do it.)

*It turned out, however, that the ducks weren't entirely blameless: After some further exploration, Junior and his dad discovered that the real problem was that his father was building his dam each year on a deeper and deeper layer of duck droppings accumulating on the bottom of the pond. The droppings were not as firm a base as the actual pond bottom, so at the spring thaw—with its sudden water rise—the dam would settle and slip. But it was pure coincidence that the ensuing overflows had happened around the same time as the annual arrival of the ducks.

19. **a.** Use the Equation Writer to key in the summation:
[←][EQUATION][→][Σ][α][K][▶][1][▶][7][▶][←][()][+/-][1]
[▶][y^x][α][K][+][1][▶][←][()][1][÷][2][▶][▶][y^x][2][α][K][+][1].
Evaluate: [EVAL].... Result: `0.10`

b. On the 48, you can often sum an infinite series by including an upper integration limit great enough to determine if convergence occurs (set flag –21 so that divergence overflow will stop the calculation: [2][1][+/-][SPC][α][S][α][F][ENTER]).
Create and evaluate the series: [←][EQUATION][→][Σ][α][K][▶]
[0][▶][5][0][0][▶][▲][1][-][2][y^x][α][K][▶][▼][3][y^x][α][K] [EVAL] ....
Result: `-1.50` (after 15 iterations)

20. The formula for the time—expressed in decimal hours is:

$$n+\frac{n}{12}\sum_{k=0}^{\infty}\frac{1}{12^k} \quad \text{where } 1 \le n \le 12 \text{ is an integer}$$

Create this expression as the current equation in SOLVE:
[←][EQUATION][α][N][+][α][N][÷][1][2][▶][→][Σ][α][K][←][=][0][▶][6][▶] (6 ought to be enough iterations for the required precision: .01 seconds is about 3×10^{-6} hours, and 12^{-6} is smaller than this)
[1][÷][1][2][y^x][α][K][ENTER][←][SOLVE] **STEQ**.
Fix 6 decimal places ([←][MODES][6] **FIX**). Then begin evaluating:
[→][SOLVE][1] **N** **EXPR=**.... Result: `EXPR: 1.090909`

Convert this to hours, minutes, seconds: [←][TIME][NXT][NXT] **→HMS**
Result: `1.052727` That's 1:05.27.27

Repeat for $n = 2\ldots11$ ($n = 12$ is a repeat).... Results:
`2.105455 3.162182 4.214909 5.271636 6.324364`
`7.381091 8.433818 9.490545 10.543273 12.000000`

21. This requires a Markov Chain approach. The matrix described in the problem is the transition matrix, CARS. So, in STD display mode, use the Matrix Writer to create CARS as a **4 × 4** matrix.

Then enter an arbitrary (**1 × 4**) *initial-state matrix*, that represents the car distribution on the first "morning" of your simulation: ⬅ [ ] ⬅ [ ] 2 5 0 SPC 3 4 SPC 7 5 SPC 4 1 ENTER (you can use any four numbers that sum to 400—but in an array, not a vector).

Now FIX the display to 0 decimal places, and then multiply the initial-state matrix by CARS to find the distribution of cars at the end of the first "day:" VAR CARS ×....
Result: [[226. 52. 68. 54.]]

Now repeat this sequence (CARS ×, CARS ×, etc.) until the resulting distribution stops changing—the steady-state matrix—for optimal distribution....Result: [[147. 76. 82. 95.]]

So the company keeps 147 cars at LAX, 76 at Burbank, 82 at Ontario, and 95 at Orange County, to best meet normal demand.*

*You might be thinking that this iterative method of solution ("start-with-any-combination-and-wait-until-the-result-becomes-steady") might work for the car company without any forethought or math at all; they could simply act out the iteration process in the course of their business. That's possible, but for the first couple of weeks, they'd probably have some dissatisfied customers at one or more airports—not so good for business. So, bring on the 48!

22. To compare risk, you must compare the variances of the samples. The variance of a sample is the square of its standard deviation. The F-statistic is a ratio (larger to smaller) of two variances:

$$F = \frac{s_1^2}{s_2^2} \text{ when } s_1^2 \geq s_2^2$$

Compare common stocks and municipal bonds (set FIX 3):

Input the degrees of freedom: [4][9][ENTER][3][4][ENTER], then the F-statistic: [1][9][•][0][5][←][x²][8][•][7][6][←][x²][÷] (4.729)
Compare this against the probability distribution:
[MTH] PROB [NXT] UTPF .... Result: 3.784E-6

That's a very significant difference in risk. Further comparisons will demonstrate that the differences in risk are highly significant across all investment types on the list.

To make a predictive model, create a data matrix, RISK, with two columns of variables—mean annual return and risk—and make it the current data matrix: [→][MATRIX]
[1][0][•][5][7][ENTER][4][•][3][8][ENTER][3][•][4][7][ENTER][2][•][5][1][ENTER]
[▶][1][9][•][0][5][ENTER][5][•][5][2][ENTER][3][•][8][7][ENTER][8][•][7][6]
[ENTER][ENTER][←][STAT] NEW [R][I][S][K][ENTER].

Now find the best regression model and its coefficient of determination: [NXT][NXT][1] XCOL [2] YCOL [NXT] MODL BEST LR CORR [←][x²].... Result: Modl:LIN Intercept: 0.569
Slope: 1.669
coefficient of determination: 0.795

The expected return for an investment with a standard deviation of 11.67 would be: [1][1][•][6][7] PREDX Result: 6.653

23. The first matrix in the problem is the **5 × 5** *technology* matrix (**T**). The second matrix is the *demand* matrix (**D**). You need to calculate the output matrix (**X**) that satisfies both internal and external demand:

Total Output		Internal Demand		External Demand
X	=	**TX**	+	**D**

Thus, $\mathbf{X} = (\mathbf{I} - \mathbf{T})^{-1}\mathbf{D}$.

So, to calculate **X**, first PURGE T and D (so that they'll appear together in your VAR menu), then create and name matrices T and D, using the Matrix Writer.

Next, create a **5 × 5** identity matrix, I: 5 MTH MATR IDN ....
And subtract T: VAR T − ....

Then invert the result matrix: 1/x ...
and multiply by D: D × ....

Result (FIX 0):

```
[[ 2672.  3329. ]
 [ 2006.  2518. ]
 [ 2061.  2684. ]
 [ 2676.  3466. ]
 [ 2046.  2638. ]]
```

6 Building Your Own Tools: Programming

Your "Automation" Options

Now that you've seen some of the "smarter" tools HP has built into the 48, it's time to learn how to build some for yourself.

A tool in your 48 is an *automated process*—a set of operations, recorded somehow, so that you don't need to re-do them every time you want a similar result. Keep in mind that there are *several* ways to do such "automation"—some of which you've used extensively already:

- By **naming an object**, you effectively record the keystrokes you used to build or calculate its value in the first place. You can reproduce or re-use that value whenever you invoke the name.

- An **algebraic** expression or equation tells the machine to execute a given set of *algebraic operations*—on a given set of *VARiables*—whenever you EVALuate that algebraic object.

- A **postfix program** tells the machine to execute a given set of *commands*—on a given set of *VARiables*, *Stack arguments*, and/or *system parameters*—whenever you EVALuate that program.

- A **list**'s elements can be any objects *and any commands*. And whenever you EVALuate a list, each of its elements is evaluated sequentially, so this is another way to record and execute *commands* on *VARiables*, *Stack arguments* and *system parameters*.

Compare the various methods of "automation" with this table:

Object	Allowed Actions	Source of Values	Range of Results	How You "Run" It
Named Object	EVALuate	any available VARiables	a single value: the value of the object stored in the name	invoke its name
Algebraic Object	any functions	any available VARiables	a single value: the result object	EVALuate it
Postfix Program	any commands	any Stack arguments, available VARiables, system parameters	any value(s), objects and system conditions	EVALuate it or invoke its name
List	any commands	any Stack arguments, available VARiables, system parameters	any value(s), objects and system conditions	EVALuate it

Consider, therefore, how you might best use each type of "automation:"

- To record an object's value, of course, just **name** it as a VARiable.

- To do math with VARiables and functions—generally, any "crunching" intended to give you *a single result*—use **algebraic objects**. They're generally easier than postfix programs to build, read, use, troubleshoot and understand.

  However, though an algebraic is handy, it's not especially "smart." It can do only *functions* (calculations describable in the 48's algebraic syntax). And of course, not all functions are defined for all object types: You can add two strings named a and b with 'a+b', but you can't subtract them with 'a-b'. You'll get an error (and an algebraic generally cannot test for or avoid an error). Also, remember that, unlike most object types, you can't EVALuate an algebraic simply by invoking its name. That just puts it onto the Stack; you must then EVALuate it explicitly.

- Whenever you need to get *multiple results*, manipulate objects or the Stack, adjust system settings (flags, directory structures, etc.)—i.e. *do any non-mathematical but nevertheless "recordable" kinds of operations*—these are jobs for **programs** or **lists**.

  Of the two, a program is the more tailor-made for ready execution, because it does EVALuate when you invoke its name (not so with a list). On the other hand, once you've built a program, you can't *modify* it (edit it) under any sort of automation—only "by hand." But you can readily edit a list via "recorded" commands.

The point here is to choose the most straightforward method for the job. When names and algebraics will suffice, use them. As you learn about programming, remember to save it for when you really need it.

Local Names

To recall the basic idea of building and naming a program, keep your place here, and look back for a moment at pages 132-135.... Of course, not all programs are so simple as those you first built. Sometimes you'll need loops and conditional tests, error traps, etc. And you'll learn about all of those things in this chapter. But first,...

Do This: Clear your 48's Stack and recall the User-Defined Function named q—the one you built on page 214.

Solution: Press VAR ⬅ PREV ⬅ PREV ⬅ PREV ➡ Q and see:*

« → x y '2*x+x*y' »

A UDF is really a postfix program; the DEFINE command built it from your algebraic definition. A UDF must be a program in order to take arguments from the Stack.

Question: What's that → x y before the algebraic?

Answer: That's to tell the UDF *how* to take your function's arguments off the Stack whenever you evaluate it. The x and y are ***local names***—names (having nothing to do with VARiable names) that the 48 associates *temporarily* with Stack objects.

---

*For the sake of space, this Course will not necessarily show programs formatted identically to your 48's displayed version, but they are entirely equivalent. Line breaks—here and in the machine's display—carry no significance; they are merely formatting for visual clarity.

Keep in mind that you can use a UDF just like any built-in function: Either you put its arguments onto the Stack and invoke just the name: [4] [ENTER] [5] [Q]; or, you invoke the name and arguments in an algebraic: 'q(4,5)' [EVAL]

When you invoke the function's name, [Q], the 48 EVALuates the program, q. The first set of instructions it encounters is → x y Essentially, this says to the 48: "Take the objects from the bottom two levels of the Stack (upper one first—it was on the Stack first), and *temporarily* identify them with the names* given after the →."

With the algebraic form, q(4,5), the *parentheses* tell the 48: "Take the arguments from within the ( ) and put them onto the Stack—in order." At that point, then, the situation is the same as when *you* placed the arguments onto the Stack: q executes, and the → x y instructions proceed as usual.

So that's what a User-Defined Function really is—a postfix program that does just two things:

(i) assigns one or more Stack arguments to local names;

(ii) uses those local names in calculating a single result.

*There's absolutely no requirement to use *lower-case* letters for local names—but it's probably a good habit to develop. It's a convenient reminder that they are indeed *local* names (as opposed to *global* VARiable names, for which you'll likely use *uppercase* characters more often, since the VAR menu displays only in uppercase).

Question: Do you *have* to use DEFINE to build a UDF?

Answer: Not at all. For example, you could have built the q function yourself: [←][«][→][→][α][←][X][SPC][α][←][Y][SPC]['] [2][×][α][←][X][+][α][←][X][×][α][←][Y][ENTER]['][α][←][Q][STO].

Now test it: [4][ENTER][5] [Q]
or ['][α][←][Q][←][()][4][←][,][5][ENTER][EVAL] *No difference.*

Question: Does the "crunching" portion of a UDF have to be a single algebraic object?

Answer: No. In fact, you don't need to use an algebraic at all. This postfix form would work just as well:

```
« → x y
« 2 x * x y * +
»
»
```

Key that in:
[←][«][→][→][α][←][X][SPC][α][←][Y][←][«][2][SPC][α][←][X][×] [α][←][X][SPC][α][←][Y][×][+][ENTER]['][←][Q][STO].

Then try it: [4][ENTER][5] [Q]
or ['] [Q] [←][()][4][←][,][5][ENTER][EVAL]

Question: Why the "program within a program"—the extra set of « » inside this last version?

Answer: To declare and assign local names, you use the →, followed by the ordered listing of those names. Then, somehow you must signal the *end* of that listing. The two allowed signals are an algebraic object or the beginning of a program. Thus, these programs are valid:*

```
« → x y 'SIN(45)+x/y' "Bye" »
« 45 → x y c « c SIN x y / + » "Bye" »
« "Hi" → m « "Good-" » "bye" »
```
(unused names are "legal")

But these are "illegal:"

```
« → x y "Hi" 'SIN(45)+x/y' »
« → a b "Hi" « a √ b - » »
```

Question: *Why* is an algebraic object or program segment the only allowed signal for ending a local names declaration?

Answer: *Because it also defines the only environment in which those local names exist.* The names are *local* (and thus not in conflict with your global VARiables) because of the strict boundary you draw around their "jurisdiction." And that boundary is the *defining procedure*—the algebraic object or postfix program—*immediately after the names declaration.*

---

*They're valid programs, but notice that they're *not* usable as UDF's: Each of them leaves more than one result on the Stack—a definite no-no for a function.

Make no mistake: Local names are indeed name objects. But each is born, lives and dies *with its defining procedure*. To illustrate...

Example: Write a program to calculate $(x+1)(x-1)$, taking x from Stack Level 1.

Solution(s):

(i) `« DUP 1 + SWAP 1 - * »`
Direct, but unclear that it uses an argument.

(ii) `« 'X' STO X 1 + X 1 - * »`
The argument is more obvious if you name it.

(iii) `« → X « X 1 + X 1 - * » »`
Looks a lot like **(ii)**.

(iv) `« → X '(X+1)*(X-1)' »`
The clearest of all, visually.

Cases **(ii)** and **(iii)** do look similar. Indeed, `'X' STO` and `→ X` *are* similar in effect: both store the argument into a name, `X`. But that name is something entirely different in each case.

In case **(ii)** `'X'` is a *global* name and will remain in the current VARiable directory after being used. At the very least, this clutters up that directory, but what if you've already used the name `'X'` to store some other important value? Case **(ii)** would overwrite (destroy) that value.

By contrast, in cases **(iii)** and **(iv)**, the *local* name, `X`, never exists in any VARiable directory; storing the argument in it during its defining procedure does not affect any global name, `'X'`. And the local `X` *disappears* at the completion of its defining procedure.

So you can see that local names are just as handy as global VARiables for "calling up" input values whenever you need them—so that you needn't try to keep track of them in the Stack meanwhile.

"Ah: So invoking local names works just like invoking global VARiable names?"

No: Recall that when you invoke a VARiable's name, this triggers an automatic EVALuation of the object contained in the name (except if it's an algebraic or a list). But when you invoke a *local* name, there's never an automatic EVALuation; the object contained in the local name is simply put onto the Stack.

You can demonstrate this difference. Try this program that, given two arguments (the old name and the new), renames an existing VARiable in your current directory:

```
« → old new « old RCL
new STO old PURGE » »
```

The fact that this program works at all (try it*) says a lot: When it first invokes the local name, `old`, this simply puts the object *contained* in `old` onto the Stack. That object is a *global* (VARiable) name—the name you're changing. And clearly this isn't evaluated; if it were, the *value* in that name (whatever it might be) would probably produce an error when the 48 tried to execute `RCL` with that value as its argument.

---

*You won't see many explicit keystrokes from now on. If you're still not sure how to key in and use a program like this, you may want to review Chapter 3, pages 132-135.

One more thing to keep in mind about local names: Since you can "nest" one program segment inside another, you can therefore "nest" the defining procedures of local names. So, to train your eye to see local name *environments*, look at these examples:

```
« → b c '√(c^2-b^2)' »
```

The simple case: Local names c and b exist only inside the defining procedure. This could be a UDF—named LEG or something similar.

```
{ → b c '√(c^2-b^2)' }
```

Don't forget that lists can do it, too. If you EVALuate this list, a local environment with c and b will be established for the algebraic immediately following—just as with the program version above.

```
« → s « s SQR s 4 * »
→ a p '22*(a/9+p/30)'
»
```

This is a *sequence* of local name environments: Assigning a single argument (the side of a square) to the local name, s, the first defining procedure then uses s to leave *two* results on the Stack (the area and perimeter of the square). Though the math is easy enough, you can't use an algebraic to generate more than one result, so the first defining procedure must be a program. Then, after it finishes (s and its environment are gone), the two results are assigned to another set of local names, a and p, for the final calculation in an algebraic procedure form.

```
« → x y z « x SQR y SQR + √
→ r 'π*r^2*z' '√(x^2+y^2+z^2)' »
SWAP »
```

This is a *nesting* of local environments: The first procedure takes three arguments and assigns them to x, y and z. Then it does a calculation on x and y and assigns that to another, *inner* procedure environment (the first algebraic), to complete a cylindrical volume calculation.

The end of that algebraic is the end of the inner environment; at that point, r disappears. But the outer environment still exists, so the program can continue to use x, y and z until it encounters a » to end *that* environment. And of course, even after that, the program itself can continue.

Notice that the local names from the outer procedure (x, y and z) exist within the inner procedure, too—*because they existed in the environment where the inner environment was being created.*

```
« → b c '√(c^2)-√(b^2+LEG(b,c)^2)' »
```

Here, within an environment with local names b and c, you invoke LEG (from the previous page). So LEG EVALuates, thus creating an environment for *its* local names, b and c.

Do those conflict with the b and c created above? No. Unlike nesting (where all commands creating the inner environment are executed *within* the outer environment), when you invoke the name of another program, any local environment(s) that program creates will be *outside* the invoking environment, Therefore, LEG cannot "see" the local names created above. It will interpret the b and c in LEG(b, c) as the *global* VARiables names 'b' and 'c' and assign *those* to its local names.

Program Design

Obviously, you can do a lot more with a 48 program than just straight-ahead arithmetic with a few arguments. It's time to explore the 48's inventory of programming tools—loops, conditional tests, etc. But first, some general comments....

No matter what kind of machine you're programming, you generally work through certain basic considerations when *designing* the program—before you even begin to write the code itself.

A *general* program design checklist might look something like this:

Define the outputs	Identify the results the machine is to calculate—the acceptable **ranges** of values and their **order** and **format** of presentation.
Define the inputs	Identify the information the user will supply to the machine—acceptable **ranges** of values and the **order** and **format** of input.
Set your strategy	Identify the critical approach and processes.
Subdivide tasks:	
Prepare	Prepare memory, system parameters;
Get inputs	Prompt for, check and store inputs;
Process inputs	Calculate, trap undesired errors;
Give outputs	Format, recall results;
Clean up	Reset memory, system parameters, etc.

This Course isn't a programming techniques manual; that could easily fill another book. But this checklist can help when you're programming the 48, especially the step where you **set your strategy.** If you clearly define that strategy first, you'll have no problem matching it properly with specific tools in the 48.

Also:

- There's no way around it: In postfix programs, you'll have to use some postfix notation. And it's not intuitively easy to read:

  `1 2 +`   instead of   `1+2`

  So *in every solution you see here*, force yourself to "walk" mentally through the program steps: Envision the Stack (do it on paper if it helps) and track the arguments as they come and go. If you want to be a programmer, you must learn the language.

- What's the difference between a built-in command and a program that you build and name?   ...Think about it....

  Not much, right? So if you don't find, say, a certain handy Stack command already built-into the 48—no problem—build it and name it yourself! In this way, you can literally *add to the tool box of commands* in your 48. And then, of course, you can use those tools to create still others, and so on.

  The 48 is well suited for such *modular* programming: no single program structure need be very long or intricate. Instead, it can invoke other small programs *as commands*, which, if you've designed them consistently, will behave as such (take arguments, return results, generate predictable errors). Your design strategy simplifies immensely if you consistently mimic built-in tools.

First, look at some "warmer-uppers" to see how that design checklist applies to your modular 48 workshop....

Problem: Write two programs, LMAX and LSUM, that do for lists what the commands RNRM and CNRM do for vectors.

Solution: Outputs. Each program should return a real number.

Inputs. Each program will take one argument (Stack Level 1)—a list of real or complex numbers (one type only). Any type error should be reported

Strategy. Convert the list to array; then RNRM or CNRM.

Subdivide tasks. No need to prepare anything. These programs should use the current memory configuration and flag settings, just like built-in commands. No prompt for the input—postfix commands assume the argument is on the Stack already. And no input checks; CNRM or RNRM will catch object-type errors. Each program consumes its argument and leaves its result on the Stack—just like a built-in command. No need to clean up—you didn't mess up anything.

The code.

```
LMAX:   « OBJ→ →ARRY RNRM »
LSUM:   « OBJ→ →ARRY CNRM »
```

All the formal design may seem like a lot of fuss over those rather simple programs, but—like anything else—if you do it consistently, it will become automatic.

More to the point, notice how many of the steps in the design checklist are taken care of by using or mimicking the built-in commands. Now LMAX and LSUM will behave as commands, too—especially if you've stored them in the HOME directory (so that they're accessible from any other directory). Try some more....

Problem: Write a program to compute a unit vector in the same direction as a given vector.

Solution: `UNIT: « DUP ABS / »`

This consumes the argument and leaves a result—for any non-zero real number, unit, complex number, vector or array (and depending on flag –3, an empty name or algebraic could be acceptable, too). For other argument types—or zero values—you'll get an error. *All of this is consistent with the behavior and definitions of the built-in ABS function.*

Problem: Write a program to double an array and subtract 1 from every element.

Solution: `DS1: « 2 * DUP 1 CON - »`

Again, this consumes the argument and leaves a result. And it works on several argument types.

When you need multiple arguments—or need to do more "horsing around" on the Stack—that's when to consider using local names to keep things clear and tidy....

Problem: Write a program that splits a given character string into two substrings. Make the split before the given character position.

Solution:

```
SPLIT:  « → s p
          « s 1 p 1 - SUB s p s
          SIZE SUB »
        »
```

Follow the progress of events on the Stack (work on your postfix reading skills). Notice how the program prepares two arguments for the built-in command, SUB.

As usual, the program consumes its own arguments. Indeed, local names accomplish this very nicely: they remove the arguments from the Stack right away, keeping them available by name, then disappearing with them when their procedure ends.*

Notice also that the two results (the two parts of the original string) are left on the Stack so that *the reverse process* (combining them) *is as easy as possible* ([+]). This, too, is a typical trait of the built-in commands (recall how OBJ→ works so well in this respect).

---

*But is SPLIT a User-Defined Function? No—it leaves more than one result.

You've been designing new commands that relied upon built-in commands they invoke to set their input limits and generate errors. But what if you want to create a command with *more flexible* tolerances ("smarter") than any built-in command it invokes?

Conditional Tests

The most basic kind of program flexibility is a machine's ability to *make decisions*. That is, it can change its course of action "on the fly"—basing its decisions upon information it encounters *during execution*. The 48 makes a decision by asking a question that can be answered by "yes" or "no." The command that asks the question is a *conditional test*, and it returns a 1 result for "yes" or a 0 result for "no."

Do This: Press (PRG) **TEST** and look through the resulting menu....

Each item asks a question* answerable by "yes" or "no" (1 or 0). And most of these questions *compare* one value with another, therefore demanding two arguments.**

For example, the > command asks: "Is the object in Stack Level 2 *greater than* that in Level 1?"

---

*Actually the SF, CF, TYPE and NOT commands are *not* tests (yes-or-no questions) at all, but you use them so often in conjunction with the other tests that they appear on this menu for convenience.

**There are a few *single*-argument tests, however—the flag tests (FS?, FC?, FS?C and FC?C)—where the only argument needed is the number of the flag to be tested.

Of course, when you're conducting such comparative conditional tests, the two argument objects must be *comparable.* You can't compare apples with oranges; nor an array with a character string. In general, the two objects being compared should be of the same type.

Examples: Stack arguments — Test

Stack arguments		Test
2:	11	<
1:	19	
Result: 1	"*Yes*—the object in Level 2 is *less than* the object in Level 1."	
2:	11	→ a b « a b < »
1:	19	
Result: 1	The same test as above, but using local names and a program procedure.	
2:	11	→ a b 'a<b'
1:	19	
Result: 1	Same again, using an algebraic procedure.	
2:	11	>
1:	19	
Result: 0	"*No*—Level 2 is *not* greater than Level 1."	
2:	"AARDVARK"	<
1:	"zymurgy"	
Result: 1	For strings, "less than" means *alphabetically first* (note: "Z" comes *before* "a").	

Stack arguments		**Test**
2:	(11,0)	==
1:	11	

Result: 1 == tests for *equality of value* (the single = symbol is for building algebraic equations).

2:	(11,0)	SAME
1:	11	

Result: 0 SAME tests for *exactly identical* objects.

2:	'B^2'	≥
1:	'4*A*C'	

Result: 'B^2≥4*A*C' A test comparing expressions acts as an *operator*, combining the two arguments into a new expression (recall that you built a quadratic expression similarly: 'B^2-4*A*C'). To get the yes-or-no (1 or 0) answer to the inequality test, you must EVALuate it with numerical values in each VARiable (A, B and C).

2:	44	AND
1:	0	

Result: 0 The logical operators can test combinations of real values. Each value is taken simply as non-zero (true) or zero (false).

2:	0	→ a b '(a OR b) AND b'
1:	64	

Result: 1 You can build tests of your own like this.

Branching

So now you know how to tell your 48 to test values—ask questions....

Question: How do you tell it *what to do* with the answers? How do you give the program one set of commands ("Plan A") for a "yes" answer and another set ("Plan B")—or maybe none at all—for "no"?

Answer(s): You use one of the four IF program structures, all available in the PRG BRCH (BRanCH) menu:*

```
Answer          IF Answer
PlanA           THEN PlanA
IFT             END
```

In each of the IF-THEN structures, the 48 evaluates PlanA only if the Answer to the test is *true* (1). If Answer is false (0), the structures do nothing.

```
Answer          IF Answer
PlanA           THEN PlanA
PlanB           ELSE PlanB
IFTE            END
```

In each of the IF-THEN-ELSE structures, the 48 will evaluate PlanA if the Answer is true (1). But if the Answer is false (0), the 48 evaluates PlanB instead.

---

*The various menus in the PRG toolbox offer a wealth of typing aids for programmable commands (for STacK, DiSPLay, etc.), many of which you can use in this chapter. Be sure to use them—and explore them, including their shifted menu items—as you build programs here.

Example: Write a program that squares the Level-1 argument only if its absolute value is between 1 and 5 (inclusive).

Solution:

```
« → x « 'ABS(x)≥1 AND ABS(x)≤5'
'x^2' IFT » »
```

IFT ("IF Then") is the postfix version of IF-THEN. It looks on the Stack for its arguments:

```
2: 'ABS(x)≥1 AND ABS(x)≤5'
1:                      'x^2'
```

The first argument is the test, which evaluates either to 1 or 0. The second argument is your "Plan A"—the object to be evaluated only if the test evaluates to *true* (1). Note that in either case—like other commands—IFT *consumes* its arguments.

Or, your "Plan A" (the second argument) could be a program (or any other object) instead of an algebraic:

```
« → x « 'ABS(x)≥1 AND ABS(x)≤5'
« x SQ » IFT » »
```

Here's the Stack as the IFT would find it in that case:

```
2: 'ABS(x)≥1 AND ABS(x)≤5'
1:                  « x SQ »
```

Programs and algebraics are both valid object types for *procedural* arguments such as these.*

---

*You could, of course, use a program rather than an algebraic for the conditional test, too: `« x ABS 1 ≥ x ABS 5 ≤ AND »` But the algebraic form is much more readable.

Question: How would the solution to the previous problem look if you were to use the more readable IF...THEN...END structure rather than the strictly postfix IFT?

Answer: Probably something like this:

```
« → x « IF 'ABS(x)≥1 AND ABS(x)≤5'
THEN x SQ END » »
```

IF...THEN...END doesn't expect Stack arguments; it's probably easier to read.

Question: Is readability the only advantage of IF...THEN...END?

Answer: Part of its readability makes it convenient to key in, too: Since it doesn't look for Stack arguments, it doesn't force you to put your "Plan A" into the form of a procedure object (program or algebraic). Instead, the 48 simply takes all instructions between the THEN and the END to be part of your "Plan A." Thus, at the very least, it can save you the keying in of the extra pair of ' ' or « ».

So IFT and IF...THEN...END are your two options for using the result of a test to decide whether or not to execute a certain set of instructions.

Often, though, you want to use a single test to choose between *two* different courses of action ("Plan A" and "Plan B")....

Problem: Write a program that negates (changes the sign of) the Level-1 argument if it's a real-valued array* but drops it from the Stack if it's anything else.

Solution:

```
« DUP TYPE → x t
« 't==3' '-x' 0
IFTE » »
```

IFTE is just like IFT—except that you need an extra argument for the "else" case:

```
3:              't==3'
2:               '-x'
1:                  0
```

The first argument onto the Stack is the conditional test ('t==3' asks "is t equal to 3?"). Next comes the "Plan A" object (for a *true* answer), then the "Plan B" object (for *false*). IFTE consumes all of its arguments.

Alternatively, IFTE can be used in algebraic form—as a *function:*

```
« DUP TYPE → x t 'IFTE(t==3,-x,0)' »
```

Just as with any other function, the arguments in IFTE's argument list correspond to the arguments you would normally prepare for it on the Stack. IFTE is unique among the four IF-THEN structures in having this allowable function form.

*To test the type of the given object, use the TYPE command: It will return a 3 for a real-valued array (look up and read about TYPE in your HP manuals to see all the various values it can return).

IF...THEN...END is a more readable version of the formal, argument-oriented IFT. No prizes for guessing what IF...THEN...ELSE...END is good for....

Yep: IF...THEN...ELSE...END is a more readable form of the more formal, argument-oriented IFTE.

Watch: Here's how you might solve the previous problem by using the IF...THEN...ELSE...END structure:

```
« DUP TYPE → x t « IF 't==3'
THEN '-x' ELSE 0 END »
»
```

Or (without local names):

```
« IF DUP TYPE 3 ==
THEN NEG
ELSE DROP 0
END »
```

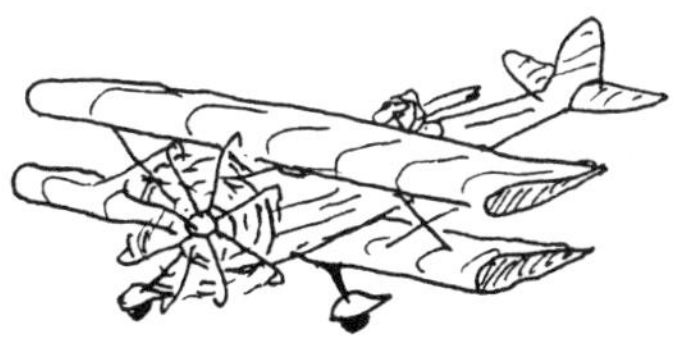

So those are your four choices for branching *one* or *two* ways, depending upon the outcome of one conditional test. But what if you want to branch one of *several* different ways—using several tests?

Problem: Write a program to return a character string describing the magnitude of a given real value.

Solution: Use a CASE statement:

```
« ABS XPON → m «
CASE
  'm≤0' THEN "Ones" END
  'm==1' THEN "Tens" END
  'm==2' THEN "Hundreds" END
  'm==3' THEN "Thousands" END
  'm==4' THEN "Tens of thousands" END
  'm==5' THEN "Hundreds of thousands" END
  'm==6' THEN "Millions" END
  "Several gadzillion" 1000 .1 BEEP
END » »
```

See how this works? Each case has its own test; the items following it (all those between each THEN and END) are evaluated only if that test result is *true*. The final items—without any test—are optional, in case you want some action(s) taken if *none* of the test results are true.

Very handy, no? Between IF statements and CASE statements, you can get your 48 to branch its execution just about any way you wish!

You've seen how to use conditional tests and branching to check object types and ranges and proceed accordingly. But what if you don't know all the possible problems? Somehow, you need to try your commands and deal with the errors as they arise....

Problem: Write a program to perform a simple division—consuming the arguments and generating a result—but substitute a character string if the attempted division causes an error for any reason.

Solution:

```
« IFERR /
THEN DROP2 "Not a number"
END »
```

IFERR (IF ERRor) is much like the IF-THEN command, but rather than obtaining a conditional test result from the commands between it and THEN, IFERR checks to see if those commands generate an error. If so, IFERR causes a skip to the THEN part (DROP2 "Not a Number" here). If there's no error, the original commands (/) are completed and those between THEN and END are skipped.

There's also IFERR...THEN...ELSE...END. So now you can trap errors—even if you can't predict in advance what they might be.

That's your basic repertoire of branching devices. Don't worry—you'll get lots more practice in the quiz coming up. But first, consider another important set of programming structures....

Looping

One of the most valuable features of any computing device is its ability to accurately and tirelessly *repeat* a series of commands....

Look: You can use one of these six loop structures on the 48:

```
Go                      Go
Stop                    Stop
START Commands          START Commands
NEXT                    Increment STEP
```

To repeat a set of Commands *a known number of times*, you can *count* from one value, Go, to another value, Stop—by ones (START...NEXT) or by any Increment (START...STEP).

```
Go                      Go
Stop                    Stop
FOR Index Commands      FOR Index Commands
NEXT                    Increment STEP
```

You can also *name the loop counter* (here it's Index), so that you can use its changing value in your repeated Commands.

```
WHILE 'NOT Done'        DO Commands
REPEAT Commands         UNTIL Done
END                     END
```

Or, for an *unknown number of repetitions*, just repeat until a given exit *condition* is satisfied: WHILE...REPEAT...END tests for the exit condition at the beginning of the command loop; DO...UNTIL...END tests for it at the end of the loop.

Try some examples of each kind of loop....

Problem: Write a program to sum the elements of a given list.

Solution: `« OBJ→ 2 SWAP START + NEXT »`

This uses the START...NEXT loop—where you simply want to repeat a set of commands a known number of times. Name this program SUML, and try it on this list:

`{ 27 8 9 43 }`

The first command, OBJ→, puts the list's elements and their *element count* (4) onto the Stack:

```
                          6:    27
5:    27                  5:     8
4:     8                  4:     9
3:     9                  3:    43
2:    43                  2:     2
1:     4                  1:     4
```

Next, the program puts a 2 onto the Stack and SWAPs positions with the 4. Your loop counters are now ready. The START will read (and consume) them, thus counting from 2 to 4* and performing the commands inside the loop (in this case it's just +), once for each count.

---

*Notice that the number of additions necessary to sum all the elements is one less than the number of elements. This is why your loop count goes from 2 to 4, not 1 to 4. You could, of course, count from 1 to 3 (or –45 to –43, or any other 3-count interval), but it's simplest to use the element count (4) produced by OBJ→ as the "end" of the count.

Question: How could you change the SUML program so that it would correctly ignore any error arising from trying to add with an "unaddable" type of object?

Answer: Put an IFERR...THEN...END structure inside the loop:

```
« OBJ→ 0 1 ROT START IFERR
+ THEN SWAP DROP END NEXT »
```

In this version, you put an extra value (0) onto the Stack—so that the program will start with a valid "running total" even if the very first list element it encounters is "unaddable." So here's the Stack as START finds it:*

```
7:    27
6:     8
5:     9
4:    43
3:     0
2:     1
1:     4
```

The commands inside the loop are now the IFERR structure, which will allow the + if that doesn't cause an error, but will substitute a SWAP DROP to dispose of any element causing an "unaddability" error.**

---

*Since you've inserted your own starting value (0), the number of additions necessary to sum all elements is now *equal* to the number of elements. So your count goes from 1 to 4 this time.

**Still, your "sum of all elements" may not turn out to be a real number: Recall what + does with character strings, complex numbers, etc.: Those object types will *not* cause errors here.

Problem: Write a program to count (in the display) from any two given real values, with any real increment.

Solution:

```
« → i j d
« i i j START DUP 1 DISP
1 WAIT d + d STEP » »
```

This solution uses the START...STEP loop—where you specify the *increment* of your count as well as its starting and ending values. Name the program COUNT and try it with various starting, ending and increment values.*

The program begins by taking your three arguments (your desired beginning, ending and increment values, respectively) from the Stack and putting them into local names. Then it puts the beginning value (i) back—as the first running total to be displayed—then the beginning *and* ending values (i and j), as consumable arguments for START.

Then, inside the loop, you DISPlay the running total on display line 1 and pause via the WAIT command for 1 second. Then you add the increment value, d, to the running total, then give d also as the consumable argument for STEP (so that it knows how to increment its own count), and that ends the loop.

*How does it handle negative values? Non-integer values? Non-real values?

So one solution for the COUNT program is to build and increment your own counter on the Stack. You must do that if you use a START...STEP loop, because the count it conducts is hidden and inaccessible to you. But is there another, easier way to display a count?

Sure: Use a FOR...STEP structure instead. In that kind of loop, its own count *is* accessible to you—via the *name* you give it.

Watch:

```
« → i j d
« i j FOR c c 1 DISP 1 WAIT
d STEP » »
```

After assigning arguments to local names, you enter a FOR loop, supplying begin and end count values (i and j). In a FOR loop, you declare a *local name* (existing only inside that loop), to represent the current value of the loop's count. So, first you *declare* the count name (c); then you *use* it (c again)—putting the count onto the Stack for display.

So there's no need for any explicit addition to increment the Stack count: When you end the loop (giving d as the argument for STEP—as before), on the next cycle, the *loop structure itself* will have incremented its own count, c. So, simply invoking that name, c, puts the current count value onto the Stack; the displayed count *is* the loop count.*

---

*Notice that if COUNT were to offer an increment of 1 only, you'd use a FOR...NEXT structure and dispense with d. Realize also that, within the loop, you can do any calculation you want with c; it's an entirely usable local name—with a local environment *nested* inside that of i, j and d.

So that's how to design programs to cycle through a known number of loops. But what if you *don't* know that number?

Problem: Write a program that drops objects off the Stack until it encounters a character string or empties the Stack.

Solution:

```
« IF DEPTH THEN
WHILE DUP TYPE 2 ≠
REPEAT DROP END END »
```

First, notice the IF...THEN...END structure surrounding the WHILE...REPEAT...END structure: Only if the Stack is not empty (i.e. if DEPTH gives a non-zero value) will the program even enter that structure.

WHILE...REPEAT...END tests its condition first: "The Level-1 object is not a character string (does not have a TYPE value of 2)." The commands between the WHILE and the REPEAT make this test, which must be true (1) before the loop itself (the commands between REPEAT and the first END) is evaluated for that cycle. When the test returns a false (0) result, the loop cycling will end.

Notice, therefore, that if the WHILE test returns 0 on very first time, the program will end without the commands in the loop having executed even once. This suits the problem: With a character string already at Level 1, indeed the program *shouldn't* do anything.

Again: A WHILE...REPEAT...END loop tests its condition before entering the loop itself. By contrast, consider this...

Problem: Write a program that produces two *odd* random integers between 0 and 100.

Solution:*

```
IRAND:   « RAND 100 * IP »

ODD?:    « 2 MOD »

« 0 0
DO DROP2 IRAND IRAND
UNTIL DUP2 ODD? SWAP ODD? AND
END »
```

Unlike WHILE...REPEAT...END, a DO...UNTIL...END loop is appropriate here, since it always executes its loop commands *at least once* (even if your first two values come up odd, you do need to generate them, no?). So the conditional test comes *after* the loop's commands.

Practice your postfix reading as you follow the commands. Notice how you put two start values (0 and 0) onto the Stack before entering the loop. This is to allow for the first commands inside the loop, which keep the Stack clean by dropping two previous, unacceptable values.

---

*Notice how you assist the program with two smaller programs: IRAND generates a random integer between 0 and 100; and ODD? tests an integer value for "odd-ness," returning a truth value (i.e. either 0 or not 0)—just like a built-in test. Of course, you could instead include their contents twice in the main program, but that's not as good a use of the 48's modular extendability.

Quiz

That's a brief tour of the programming structures available to you. Now put it all together with these practice problems.

1. Write two programs, one with local names and one without, to calculate $\frac{(A+B)(A-B)}{C}$, given arguments A, B, C (in that order).

2. Unlike the two-argument comparative tests, the four built-in flag tests (FS?, FC?, FS?C and FC?C) are not valid in functional (algebraic) form. That is, you can't build expressions such as 'FS?(-2) AND FC?(-3)'—though these might indeed be handy in your programs. So, *write your own:* write four UDF's to allow you effectively to use flag tests in algebraics. In general, how might you make various system flags more convenient?

3. Write a new conditional test, called LIST?, that tests whether a given object is a list. Then use LIST? to write another test, called FLST?, that tests whether a given object is a non-empty list.

4. Write programs that take a given string and:

- **(i)** reverse the order of the characters;
- **(ii)** change all lowercase characters to uppercase;
- **(iii)** change all uppercase characters to lowercase;
- **(iv)** change both cases simultaneously.

5. What's the primary use of a list as a procedure object?

6. Write a program that deletes from a given string...

   (i) all leading occurrences
   (ii) all trailing occurrences

   ...of a given character (another string—the second argument).

7. Write a program that waits for you to press the [α] key.

8. Write a program that takes a given list and a given conditional test procedure (in that order) and applies the test to each element of the list, returning a "filtered" version of the list—containing only the elements that satisfy the test.

9. Recall the alphabetical directory structure described in problem **36** on page 149. Write a program that returns the object stored in a given name in one of those 26 alphabetical directories.

10. How would you build your own version of OBJ→?

11. Remember page 279 (transforming data in ΣDAT)? Now write four programs that take a given real-valued array (but not a vector) and extract/insert a specified row/column.

Quiz Answers

1. As is usually the case with programming, there are many ways to solve a given problem. First, using local names:

```
« → a b c « a b                or   « → a b c
+ a b - * c / » »                      '(a+b)*(a-b)/c' »

« → a b c « a                  or   « → a b c
SQ b SQ - c / » »                   '(a^2-b^2)/c' »
```

Then, without local names:

```
« ROT ROT DUP2 +               or   « ROT SQ ROT SQ -
ROT ROT - * SWAP / »                SWAP / »
```

2. Simply "repackage" each built-in command:

```
fs?:     « → f « f FS? » »
fc?:     « → f « f FC? » »
fs?c:    « → f « f FS?C » »
fc?c:    « → f « f FC?C » »
```

You can build little routines to test sets of system flags. For example, flags –45 through –48 represent the number of decimal places in the current display format; flags –49 and –50 represent the format itself. So you could write routines, DGTS? and FMT?, to test these parameters (recall how you extracted the binary wordsize similarly from its system flags on page 104).

3. LIST?: « TYPE 5 == »

```
FLST?:  « IF DUP LIST?
          THEN SIZE 0 >
          ELSE DROP 0
          END
        »
```

4. (i)

```
« → s « "" 1 s SIZE
FOR i s i i SUB SWAP
+ NEXT » »
```

(ii)

```
« → s « "" 1 s SIZE
FOR i s i i SUB NUM
→ n 'IFTE(n≥97 AND
n≤122,n-32,n)'
CHR + NEXT » »
```

(iii)

```
« → s « "" 1 s SIZE
FOR i s i i SUB NUM
→ n 'IFTE(n≥65 AND
n≤90,n+32,n)' CHR + NEXT » »
```

(iv)

```
« → s « "" 1 s SIZE
FOR i s i i SUB NUM
→ n 'IFTE(n≥97 AND
n≤122,n-32,IFTE(n≥65 AND
n≤90,n+32,n))' CHR + NEXT » »
```

Follow the Stack closely. Also, notice the use of the FOR loop counter, i. And notice the nested IFTE structure in **(iv)**.

5. Lists are useful to evaluate chiefly as directory PATHs. For example, what if your program needs to DOSTUFF, which is in a directory, DIR1, that's *not* in the current PATH? No problem: simply *save* the current PATH (it's represented as a *list* of directory names, remember) and then later, *EVALuate* it—to get back to that PATH—when you've concluded your work in DIR1:

```
... PATH → whereiwas « HOME DIR1
  DOSTUFF whereiwas EVAL » ...
```

6. (i)

```
« → ch « WHILE DUP
NUM CHR ch == REPEAT
2 OVER SIZE SUB END »
»
```

(ii)

```
« → ch « WHILE DUP
SIZE DUP2 DUP SUB
ch == REPEAT 1 SWAP
1 - SUB END
DROP » »
```

A WHILE loop is appropriate for each of these, since you don't know right now whether you'll need to trim off *any* characters from the given string (so the test comes *before* the action).

Notice that only one of the two arguments (the character to be trimmed) is put into a local name; it's too difficult otherwise to place it onto the bottom of the Stack when you need it. As for the original string, it's simply "whittled down" (with SUB) by one character each cycle through the loop; the result of the previous cycle becomes the "given string" for the next cycle.

7. Here's one way:

```
« DO DO UNTIL KEY END
UNTIL 61 == END »
```

The KEY command returns a 0 ("false") if no key is pressed or a key location (row-column) code and a 1 if a key has been pressed. Therefore, you're looking for key code 61 (row 6, column 1). To do so, you use a nested pair of indefinite loops (DO...UNTIL's). The inner loop repeats until any key is pressed; the outer loop repeats until the *correct* keycode (61) is detected. You might want to read in your HP manuals more about the WAIT command, too.

8. LFLTR:

```
« → list test « { }
1 list SIZE FOR i list
i GET DUP IF test EVAL
THEN + ELSE DROP END
NEXT » »
```

This is just another FOR-loop problem; you know the number of cycles through the loop from the SIZE of the given list. Notice that you must EVALuate the test procedure explicitly (remember that invoking a local name won't do this for you).

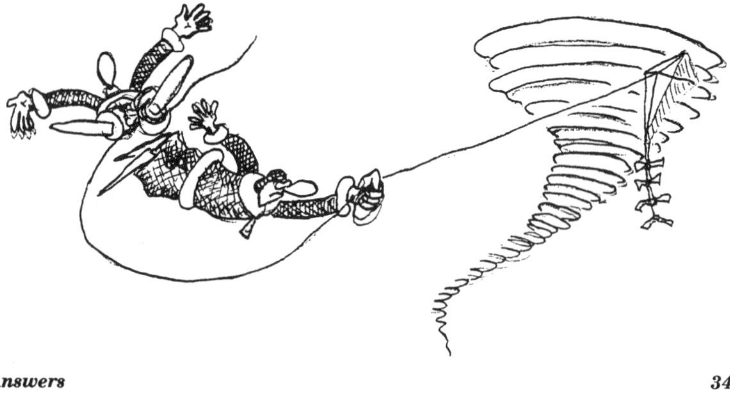

9.
```
« → n « { HOME }
n →STR 1 2 SUB
OBJ→ + n + RCL » »
```

The strategy here is to build a PATH list to the given name and then RCL that path—rather than EVALuate it—thus staying in the current directory (alternatively, you could use the "remember-and return" strategy shown in problem **5**). Notice how you extract the single-letter directory name by first converting the given name to a string.

10. You could do this:

```
obj→:  « DUP TYPE CASE
  0 == THEN real→ END
  1 == THEN cplx→ END
  2 == THEN str→ END
  3 == THEN rarr→ END
  4 == THEN carr→ END
  5 == THEN list→ END
            ...     (etc.)
  END »
```

Or this:

```
obj→:  « → ob « { real→
cplx→ str→ ...(etc.)... }
ob TYPE GET
EVAL END » »
```

Of course, you also need to define each of the specific routines, `real→`, `cmplx→`, etc. And then to change how a certain object type "decomposes," you'd simply edit that specific routine—not `obj→`.

11. GETRW:
```
« → i « DUP SIZE 1 1
SUB 1 SWAP + 0 CON
i 1 PUT SWAP * » »
```

GETCL:
```
« SWAP TRN SWAP GETRW
TRN »
```

Notice the assumed order of inputs: Array, row/column number. Notice that GETCL uses GETRW; TRN (TRaNspose) makes it easy. But GETRW doesn't check for bad inputs (what happens if you ask GETRW to extract, say, row 20 from a **3×12** array?). How might you trap or correct such problems? Also, what if you want to allow for vectors? You'd need to include a test to handle them, since they require different arguments than arrays.

INSRW:
```
« 1 - → r i
« OBJ→ OBJ→ DROP
→ n m « n i - m *
→LIST r OBJ→ DROP
m 1 + ROLL OBJ→ DROP
{ 'n+1' m } →ARRY
» » »
```

INSCL:
```
« ROT TRN ROT TRN
ROT INSRW TRN »
```

The inputs: Array, new row/column array, row/column number. INSRW decomposes the existing array onto the Stack, moves the rows after the "i th" row out of the way, inserts the new row and recomposes the array, one row larger. Notice how it decreases the specified row number by 1 to simplify the math. Again, notice that neither vectors nor bad inputs are detected.

INSCL just uses INSRW—via TRN.

7 Customizing Your Workshop

Labor-Saving Devices

A calculator as powerful as the 48 is certainly a labor-saving device. But that very power offers you so many choices that the keystrokes simply to *make* those choices soon become laborious, too—unless you take advantage of certain built-in features.

For example, it's great to be able to build and name a lot of new commands. But then you may have several pages in your VARiable menu to "leaf through" whenever you want to use one of those commands—which defeats the convenience of the menu for quick typing/execution. What to do? Use *custom menus* to group together the commands you typically *use* together, thus reducing your need for [NXT]'s and [←][PREV]'s.

This is just one example of the many labor-saving devices the 48 offers you. You set up certain assumptions about your particular needs and work habits, so that the machine will do more of what you want with fewer keystrokes.

So as you study (and in some cases, review) these features, consider how you might best use them. Weigh the labor you save with a tool or configuration against the labor you expend to build it and use it. That's the key question to ask yourself. This chapter on customizing is really about *optimizing* (not maximizing or minimizing); the best solution for one situation isn't necessarily that same for another.

Input Shortcuts

You've already seen most of the ways to ease and shorten your use of the 48's densely-packed keyboard, but here's a good one-glance recap.

Alpha Modes

[α] *Normal single-stroke alpha mode.* Normally, pressing [α][N] yields N; pressing [α][←][N] yields n; and pressing [α][→][N] yields µ. Thus, each key may have three alpha "meanings." But the alpha mode only lasts for the next keystroke.

[α][←][α] *Lower-case single-stroke alpha mode.* When you need to input many lower-case alpha characters, you can change what the [←] key does by pressing [α][←][α]. Thereafter, until you press [ENTER] or [ATTN], [α][N] yields n and [α][←][N] yields N. The [ENTER] or [ATTN] returns the alpha-shift keys to normal. The alpha mode lasts just one keystroke.

[α][α] *Normal alpha-lock mode.* This locks the keyboard into alpha mode until a third press of [α] (or [ENTER] or [ATTN]) releases it.

[α][α][←][α] *Lower-case alpha-lock mode.* This locks the keyboard into lower-case alpha mode for the duration of the Command Line.

Flag –60 affects the action of the four alpha modes. When it's clear, they operate as described above. But when it's set, the single-stroke alpha modes are disabled; single [α] enters alpha-lock mode until a second press of [α] (or [ENTER] or [ATTN]) releases it.

[▲] Allows you to review the contents of the Stack and manipulate it directly Among the many handy Stack tools are these:

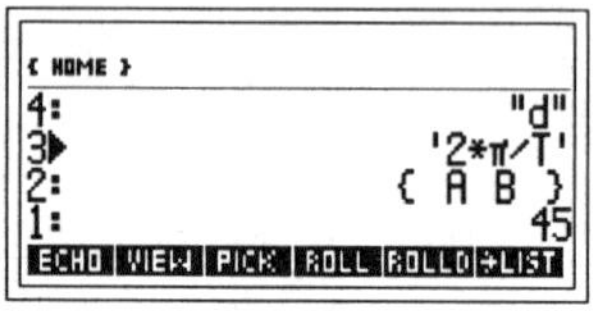

PICK

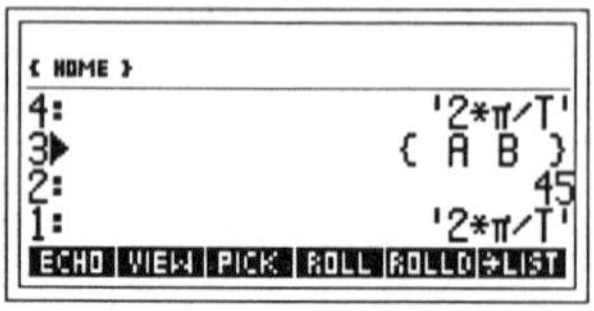

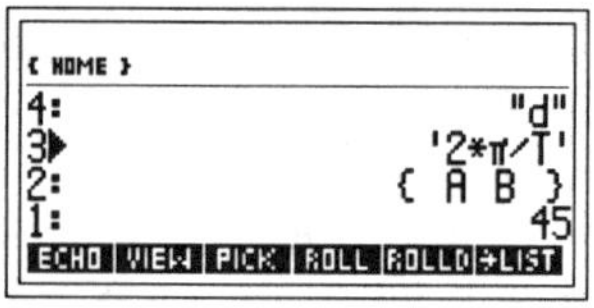

ROLL

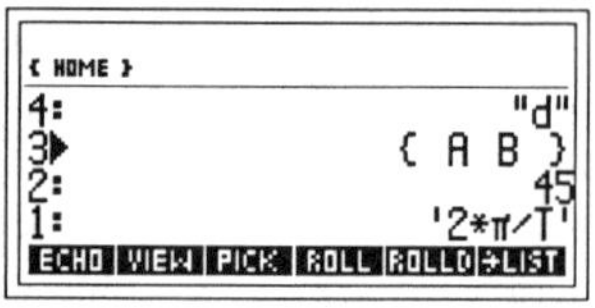

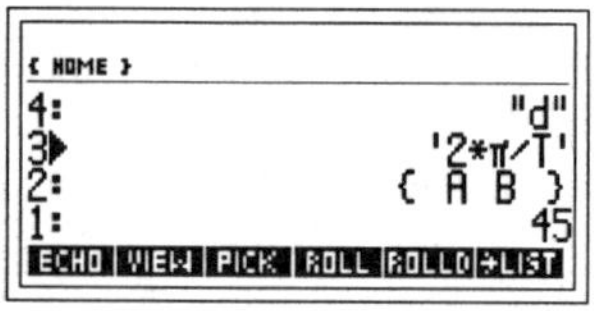

ROLLD

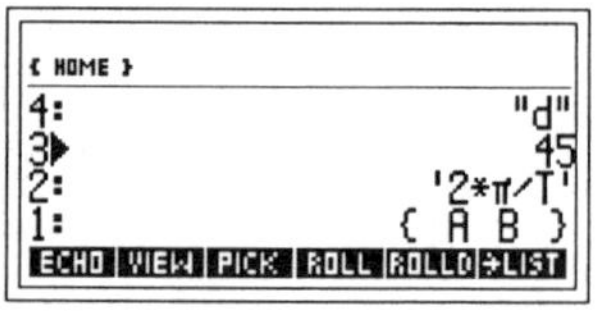

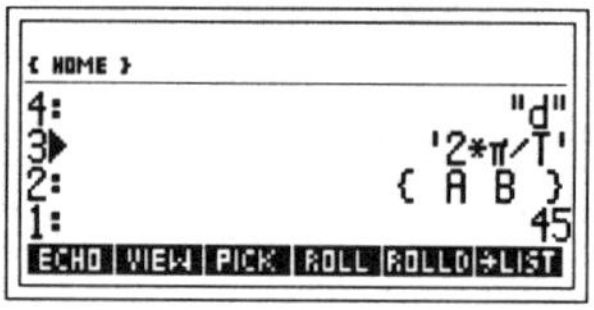

→LIST

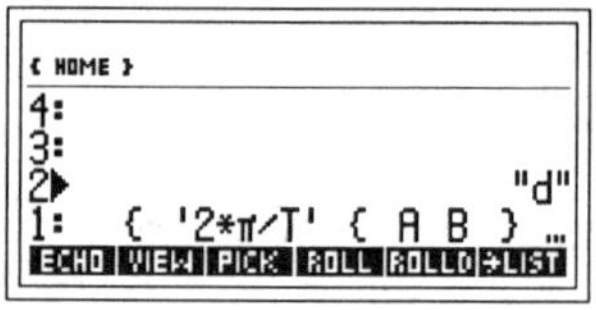

Remember, too, that **ECHO** copies a selected level of the Stack right into your Command Line, to save you from retyping it. With the 48, there are more than one way to do most things.

A built-in menu item normally evaluates immediately, making it impossible to use it as a typing aid. In fact, the only keystrokes that won't normally evaluate immediately are numbers and characters. Thus, [4][SPC][5] [+] results in a 9.

PRG You can activate this mode by starting a list ([⬅][{ }]) or program ([⬅][« »]) or via [➡][ENTRY]. When you see the **PRG** annunciator, any menu key for any *command*, *function*, or *VARiable* will—instead of evaluating—insert its name, surrounded by spaces, at the cursor on the Command Line. A keyboard command or function (such as [+]) behaves similarly: its name goes into the Command Line, surrounded by spaces. Thus, [➡][ENTRY][4][SPC] [5] [+] results in `4 5 + ◆` on the Command Line.

ALG You activate this mode by starting an algebraic object or name ([']). Now any key or menu item that is a *function* or *VARiable* (i.e. anything allowed in an algebraic object) will be inserted, *without spaces*, at the cursor on the Command Line. Thus, ['] [4][+][5] results in `'4+5'` on the Command Line.

ALG PRG You can turn on this mode by pressing [➡][ENTRY][➡][ENTRY] while in normal mode, or ['] while in **PRG** mode, or [➡][ENTRY] while in **ALG** mode. Here, any *command* key or menu item behaves as it would in **PRG** mode, while any *function or variable* key or menu item behaves as it would in **ALG** mode.

You cannot type an *operation*, such as [ATTN], into the Command Line (that's the difference between *commands* and *operations*). To determine if a keystroke is an operation, command, or function, see the Operation Index in your HP manual.

[→][MATRIX] The Matrix Writer, which you used in Chapter 5, makes entering and editing two-dimensional arrays extremely easy and intuitive. You are less likely to make careless mistakes if you use the MW instead of the Command Line to enter arrays.

[←][EQUATION] The Equation Writer, which you learned about in Chapter 4, allows you to enter any algebraic object—however complex—in a visual format similar to that on paper. The EW itself has a special entry mode:

[←][{ }] Within the EW, you can disable the implicit parentheses by pressing [←][{ }]. This allows you to enter polynomials without having to press [▶] after each exponent. You can then reactivate the normal, implicit parentheses feature by pressing [←][{ }] once again.

The VAR Menu and its Catalogs

Each directory has its own VAR menu, where all of the objects you create in that directory are listed. Whenever you need quick access either to the object's name or the object itself, it's usually easiest to use the VAR menu (via [VAR])—after putting the 48 into the proper entry mode (see page 352) to accomplish what you intend.

If you forget what's in a variable, press [⬅][REVIEW] to get a brief list of the six items shown on the current *page* of the current VAR menu. And remember also that the 48 presents special subsets of the current VAR menu—called *catalogs*:

[➡][ALGEBRA] [⬅][PLOT] CAT [⬅][SOLVE] CAT	Any of these three key sequences take you to the Equation Catalog, a special environment that lists all objects in the current VAR menu that are usable with the SOLVE and PLOT tools (see page 228). You use a pointer (like that in the Interactive Stack) to select the object you wish to make active.
[⬅][STAT] CAT	This leads to the Array Catalog, which lists all array objects in the current VAR menu—any of which might be candidates for the current statistical array. As with the Equation Catalog, you select the array you want with the list pointer.
[⬅][TIME] CAT	This leads to the Alarm Catalog, which lists all of the currently set alarms and allows you to selectively view and/or edit any particular alarm.

The LAST Commands

There are four operations grouped together (as the left- and right-shifted options) on the [2] and [3] keys that can:

- Save you time
- Save you grief from errors

[←][LAST CMD]

The 48 saves the last *four* most recently entered Command Lines in a special part of its memory—just in case you need to retrieve a long, hairy Command Line, make one small change, and re-enter it.

Example: Create these algebraics:

(a) `'-√((X+6)/(X^2-5))+X^2'`
(b) `'√(X^3-8)'`
(c) `'√((X+6)/(X^2+5))-X^2'`

Solution: ['][+/-][√x][←][()][←][()][α][X][+][6][▶][÷][←][()][α][X][yˣ][2][−][5][▶]
[▶][+][α][X][yˣ][2][ENTER] ['][√x][←][()][α][X][yˣ][3][−][8][ENTER]
[←][LAST CMD][←][LAST CMD][▶][DEL]
[→][ENTRY][→][ENTRY][→][▶][◀][◀][◀][◀][⬅][−][◀][◀][◀][◀][⬅][+][ENTER]

[←][LAST CMD] retrieves the *most recent* Command Line first and works backward in time from there.

[⬅][LAST STACK]

Try This: Assuming the three algebraics from the previous example are still on the Stack, press [+] to add two of them. Oops...you didn't really want to do that. Now what? How can you recover from such an error?

Solution: Use [⬅][LAST STACK] to retrieve the Stack as it was before the most recent command (that was [+] here).

[➡][LAST ARG]

Calculate: $(4 \times 5) + 4^5 - (4 + 5)$

Solution: [4][ENTER][5][×][➡][LAST ARG][y^x][➡][LAST ARG][+][−][+].
Result (FIX 3): 1,035.000 [➡][LAST ARG] returns all of the arguments consumed by the last command.

Another: Evaluate $\sqrt{\frac{1+x}{x^2+7}} - x$, for $x = 3$. Then press [➡][LAST ARG].

Solution: [⬅][EQUATION][√x][▲][1][+][α][X][▼][α][X][y^x][2][▶][+][7][▶][▶][−][α][X][ENTER][3]['][α][X][STO][EVAL][➡][LAST ARG].... Results:
-2.500 (Level3) 0.500 (Level2) 3.000 (Level1)
The arguments of [−]—the last command—return to the Stack (the radical evaluates to 0.500).

[→][LAST MENU]

Often, switching back to a previous menu involves only one or two keystrokes, in which case [→][LAST MENU] is no shortcut. But to switch easily to the back "pages" of a menu—or into the interior of a nested set of menus, [→][LAST MENU] is a lifesaver.

To Wit: 2.351 Å/sec + 4.56 µ/min = _??_ m/yr

Solution: [2][•][3][5][1][←][UNITS] **LENG** [←][PREV] **Å**
[←][UNITS] **TIME** [→] **S**
[4][•][5][6][→][LAST MENU] **µ** [→][LAST MENU][→] **MIN** [+]
[1][→][LAST MENU][NXT] **M** [→][LAST MENU][→] **YR**
[→][UNITS] **CONV**....

Result: 2.406_m/yr

Customizing Your Workspace

Keyboard shortcuts are handy, but they can't do it all for you. Customizing your workspace can also go a long way toward reducing your keystrokes and headaches.

But before you leap into it, remember one caveat:

Customization should make you more organized, not less.

As obvious as this advice seems, it's quite easy to get lost in the levels of customizing options that 48 provides—so that you end up making more work for yourself.

Briefly then, here are some specific ways you *can* customize your 48:

- Organize your workspace into *directories*.
- Create custom *menus*.
- Create custom *keyboard layouts*.
- Create custom *flag setups* (mode settings).
- Customize your SOLVR menu.
- Customize your PLOT and STAT tools for each directory.
- Create custom *tools*.

How much of this customizing you *should* do depends on your needs. The remainder of this chapter is devoted to introducing you to these customization approaches and how they best fit together into an optimization approach.

Directory Structure

You've dealt with directories briefly in this Course, but here's a more "full-blown" scenario to consider: Assume for a moment that you're an engineering student with a wide range of basic problems and subjects in your courses. Therefore, the most important organizational decision you make on your 48 is probably your directory structure.

One option is simply to use your **HOME** directory for everything. To see where this gets you, take a look at your **HOME** VAR menu right now. If you've done all the examples and problems in this book, that menu now has nearly *twenty* pages. You'll wear out your NXT key (and your patience) looking for any given VARiable if you insist on dumping everything in your **HOME** directory. Not only that, you'll be limited to keeping only *one* variable named 'V' or 'X' at a time—despite the vast numbers of equations that use these common variable names.

A better option is to subdivide your work into a structure of meaningful groups and subgroups. After careful thought, you—the engineering student—might come up with something like this:

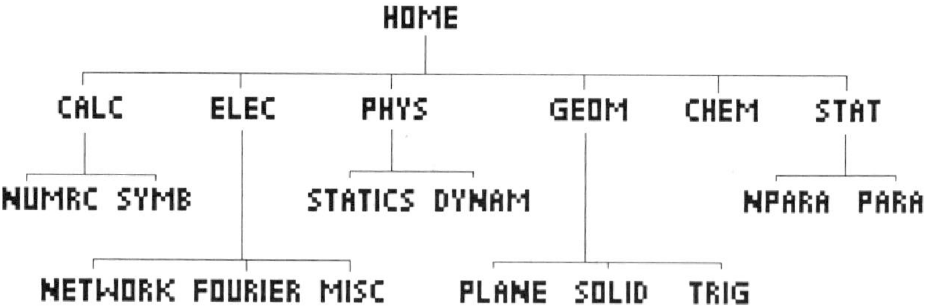

Do It: Create that directory structure and return to HOME directory.

Go: ['] [α] [α] [C] [A] [L] [C] [α] [←] [MEMORY] CRDIR
['] [α] [α] [E] [L] [E] [C] [α] CRDIR ['] [α] [α] [P] [H] [Y] [S] [α] CRDIR
['] [α] [α] [G] [E] [O] [M] [α] CRDIR ['] [α] [α] [C] [H] [E] [M] [α] CRDIR
['] [α] [α] [S] [T] [A] [T] [α] CRDIR [VAR]
STAT ['] [α] [α] [N] [P] [A] [R] [A] [α] [←] [MEMORY] CRDIR
['] [α] [α] [P] [A] [R] [A] [α] CRDIR
[→] [HOME] [VAR] GEOM ['] [α] [α] [P] [L] [A] [N] [E] [α] [←] [MEMORY] CRDIR
['] [α] [α] [S] [O] [L] [I] [D] [α] CRDIR ['] [α] [α] [T] [R] [I] [G] [α] CRDIR
[→] [HOME] [VAR] PHYS ['] [α] [α] [S] [T] [A] [T] [I] [C] [S] [α] [←] [MEMORY] CRDIR
['] [α] [α] [D] [Y] [N] [A] [M] [α] CRDIR
[→] [HOME] [VAR] ELEC ['] [α] [α] [N] [E] [T] [W] [O] [R] [K] [α] [←] [MEMORY] CRDIR
['] [α] [α] [F] [O] [U] [R] [I] [E] [R] [α] CRDIR ['] [α] [α] [M] [I] [S] [C] [α] CRDIR
[→] [HOME] [VAR] CALC ['] [α] [α] [N] [U] [M] [R] [C] [α] [←] [MEMORY] CRDIR
['] [α] [α] [S] [Y] [M] [B] [α] CRDIR [→] [HOME].

Now you can tidy up your HOME directory's VAR menu, by PURGing the unwanted variables and moving those that you do want to keep.

Tidy Up: Write a program, MOVV, to move a variable to another directory and PURGE it from the original directory.

Like So: MOVV:

```
« → a b « PATH a DUP
RCL SWAP b EVAL STO
EVAL a PURGE » »
```

MOVV expects the *name* of the object on Level 2 and the PATH list of the target subdirectory at Level 1 of the Stack.

For example, to move 'DAM' (remember Junior Beaver?) to the **NUMRC** subdirectory of **CALC**, you'd press ['] [DAM] (in your VAR menu) [ENTER]; then [←][{ }][→][HOME][α][α][C][A][L][C][SPC][N][U][M][R][C][ENTER], and [VAR] [MOVV]. Then, to see your results, press [NXT] [CALC] [NUMR] and see [DAM] on that directory's menu. *Notice* that MOVV does not check to see if a VARiable of the same name is already stored in the target subdirectory. If so, you'll lose the contents of that VARiable when MOVV executes.*

And: While you're at it, create a program, COPY, in your **HOME** directory, that copies a variable into another directory *without* purging it from its current directory.

```
COPY: « → a b « PATH a DUP
      RCL SWAP b EVAL STO
      EVAL » »
```

Use It: Use MOVV and COPY (and [←][PURGE]) to shorten the VAR menu of your **HOME** directory to 2-3 pages.

Most of those variables have been stored for this Easy Course and aren't going to be useful to you in the future, so you can purge them (save any you think you may use). When cleaning house, remember that [←][REVIEW] allows you to quickly view the variables on one menu page.

---

*Of course, you could modify MOVV so that it does check for a pre-existing VARiable by that name.

Custom Menus

Now that your directories are in place, it's time to make some *custom menus* that will serve you conveniently in your engineering student "career."

A menu is just a list of objects that the 48 associates with the menu keys and a menu display via the MENU command.

Watch: To go to the first page of the MODES menu, you could, of course, press [←][MODES]; *or* you could press [2][0][PRG] **CTRL** [NXT] **MENU**.

The MENU command understands that a real number argument refers to a *built-in menu*. Most built-in menus have corresponding numbers (see pages 697-698 of your Owner's Manual).*

Another: Use your Owner's Manual (pp. 697-698) and the MENU command to go to page 5 of the STAT menu.

Solution: [4][0][•][0][5] [→][LAST MENU] **MENU**. The page number of the menu is given by two digits after the decimal point (if none are given, the 48 assumes `.01`).

---

*There are a few other menus—Matrix Writer, Selection, Rules, Graphics—that are not accessible from a program and thus aren't given menu numbers.

Notice that the CST (CuSTom) menu has the number 1. That is, the list of objects currently stored in the variable named CST *in the current directory* is assigned the menu number 1 by the 48.

This is your *custom* menu—custom because you can readily change the list stored in that VARiable CST. And keep in mind that:

- You can have a different CST VARiable in every directory;
- You can create many lists in a directory—lists that can be menu lists whenever you decide to store them into CST.

Try One: Move to the { HOME CALC SYMB } directory and create a custom menu containing the functions COLCT, EXPAN, ISOL, →Qπ, and two short programs, PRINC and GEN that set and clear flag –1, respectively.

OK: VAR NXT CALC SYMB.

Then: ← « » 1 +/– SPC α S α F ENTER ' α α P R I N C ENTER STO ← « » 1 +/– SPC α C α F ENTER ' α α G E N ENTER STO. These will appear on the VAR menu in the SYMB directory.

Next, create the menu list and store it into CST: ← { } ← ALGEBRA COLCT EXPA ISOL NXT →Qπ → LAST MENU GEN PRINC ENTER ' α α C S T ENTER STO.

Now test it—press CST. Presto!

Now go back to the HOME directory ([→][HOME]) to see what custom menu you get.... It's probably blank (if you don't have anything stored into CST at the HOME level yet) or it's some other menu. But no matter what, *this is not the same menu you just created.* That one is available only when you're in the SYMB subdirectory.

Now, the thought may occur to you that this list could be useful as a custom menu in several of your engineering directories. So, should you copy the list to the CST VARiables in the other directories?

Probably not. There's only one CST in each directory and you don't want to monopolize all of them with copies of the same menu. A better approach is to store that particular menu list into some other name, and make it available to all of the directories, so that when you need it, you can store *its name* into the CST variable at that time.

Try It: Move to the SYMB subdirectory again and retrieve the list stored in CST. Name it CALG and store it as a variable in the HOME directory—so that it's accessible to all directories (remember how directory paths work?).

Simple: [VAR][NXT] CALC SYMB CST [→][HOME]['][α][α][C][A][L][G][ENTER] [STO]. Now, from any directory, you need only to store the name CALG into the local CST variable (either with [STO] or with the MENU command), and then press [CST] to activate your custom menu.*

---

*Note, incidentally, that when you use [CST], if the name CST is not defined in the current directory, the 48 will use CST from the parent directory.

Actually, you really ought to name all of your custom menu lists. This allows you to switch easily between different custom menus.

Some—like CALG—may be useful for many directories and therefore you store them in the **HOME** directory so that they're accessible by all. But if you have other menu lists whose use is more specific to a given directory, you would store those list names there. The point is—as with any VARiable—you control the universality of access to a custom menu list by where you store it.

Keep in mind, too, that even if the 48 can find your custom menu list name to store into CST, this doesn't guarantee that it will be able to find the *menu items* named in that list.

Try This: At **HOME**, press CST **PRINC**.... What happens? Instead of executing PRINC (i.e. setting flag –1), you get the empty name, 'PRINC'. The 48 can't find any object associated with that name.

Of course not—the VARiable, PRINC, is stored *down* the hierarchy in the **{ HOME CALC SYMB }** directory. That's not in the PATH of the **HOME** directory, so it's currently invisible to the 48. So use MOVV to move PRINC and GEN back to the **HOME** directory where they now belong.

No matter how you invoke it (by typing it or via a VAR menu or custom menu), a VARiable name can be evaluated only if it's in the current PATH.

Custom menus work much like the built-in menus—including [STO] and [RCL] for [←] and [→]—unless you have other uses for the shift keys....

Example: Modify CALG so that instead of using three menu keys for COLCT, EXPAN, and ISOL, you use just one. Make COLCT the normal (unshifted) choice, EXPAN the left-shifted ([←]) choice and ISOL the right-shifted ([→]) choice.

Solution: Create this list: `{ { "C,E,I" { COLCT EXPAN ISOL } } →Qπ GEN PRINC }`

Note the format for each item with shifted meanings:
`{ "`*item name*`" {` action [←]-action [→]-action `} }`

This list-within-a-list appears wherever you wish it to appear (first position in this case) in the custom menu. Store this list in `CALG` (at **HOME**), and use [CST] to test it.

This is how to pack more functionality onto six menu keys. Of course, your custom menus can have multiple pages, too—but after a couple of pages, you'd be playing hide-and-seek again with all the choices.

Do This: Turn CALG into a one-stop custom menu packed with useful goodies gathered from various built-in menus:

Item name	C.E.I	MISC	DRG	FLG	DIGIT	STAK
Normal	COLCT	1_m	DEG	FS?	FIX	ROLL
Left-shifted	EXPAN	1_ft	RAD	SF	STD	ROLLD
Right-shifted	ISOL	IFTE	GRAD	CF	RND	PICK

Solution: Store this list as CALG in the **HOME** directory:

```
{ { "C,E,I" { COLCT EXPAN ISOL } }
{ "MISC" { 1_m 1_ft IFTE } }
{ "DRG" { DEG RAD GRAD } }
{ "FLG" { FS? SF CF } }
{ "DIGIT" { FIX STD RND } }
{ "STAK" { ROLL ROLLD PICK } } }
```

CALG is now a very useful custom menu list, so useful, in fact, you might want it available any time—without overwriting the CST in the current directory. That is, you might want CALG as a *temporary* custom menu:

Look: « CALG TMENU », stored as CMEN in your **HOME** directory, lets you use CALG *without putting it into* CST. You invoke a *temporary* menu with the TMENU command. Like any other menu, it remains active until another menu replaces it. It's just a custom menu that doesn't use any CST VARiable.

Custom Keyboards

With custom menus, you redefine the menu keys—including their shifted versions. But what about the rest of the keys on the keyboard? HP has laid out the keyboard on the 48 to make it maximally useful for most people. But in case you're not "most people," or in case you have a special program or application, HP has also made it possible to completely "redo" the keyboard.

In fact, you've already seen examples of this: Whenever you enter a special environment—such as the Equation Writer or Graphics—the keyboard is reassigned. Only a few of the keys are functional and their operations change to fit the special needs of the environment.

It's done like this: Each and every physical key is identified by its row and column numbers. The [VAR] key is 24 because it's the fourth key in the second row. Similarly, [ENTER] is 51; [y^x] is 45; [3] is 84; [←] is 55, etc.

Then, each physical key location has up to six standard definitions—corresponding with its six shift positions (recall page 28). For example, key location 73 ([5]) has the following six definitions:

1	Unshifted ([5]):	the number 5
2	Left-shifted ([⬑][STAT]):	page one of the STAT menu.
3	Right-shifted ([⬏][STAT]):	page two of the STAT menu.
4	Alpha ([α][STAT]):	the character "5"
5	Alpha left-shifted ([α][⬑][STAT]):	the character "£"
6	Alpha right-shifted ([α][⬏][STAT]):	the character "¥"

Plus, *you* can assign to each key location up to six more definitions (*user-assigned* definitions), which become active whenever the 48 is in User mode. Thus a physical key location may have up to twelve definitions assigned to it—six built-in (active in normal mode) and six user-assigned (active in User Mode).

To make a key assignment, you assign an object to a key number. For example, in the standard (built-in) keyboard definitions, the character "£" is assigned to the key 73.5, where the 73 is the key location and the .5 indicates which shift position. The codes for the shift positions correspond to the list above—except that the unshifted position is designated by either .1 or .0 (or no digit at all).

Try It: Change [⬅][→Q] so that it executes →Qπ instead.

Easy: Enter the object: [⬅][« »][⬅][ALGEBRA][NXT] **→Qπ** [ENTER]
Enter the desired location and shift mode: [3][3][•][2][ENTER]
Assign the key: [➡][MODES] **ASN**.

Then, you access User mode much the same as you do alpha mode: Press [⬅][USR] once and your keyboard is the user keyboard for just the next keystroke. Press [⬅][USR][⬅][USR] and you're in User mode until you press [⬅][USR] a third time.

Try both now, and test your key assignment....

You can *change* your custom keyboard, too: Just as the current custom menu refers to a *list* named or stored in CST, so the current custom keyboard refers to a *list* of key assignments stored in memory.

Look: Press RCLK to retrieve the current user keyboard list.

Result (STD mode): { S « →Qπ » 33.2 }. The S means that the user keyboard is the same as the Standard keyboard *except* for the items following it in the list (i.e. with no key assignments at all, RCLK would yield simply { S }).

That means that you can use named lists to store and save special keyboard settings—ready to "install" them when you need them.

Example: Redefine these keys to produce audio tones at specified intervals in the musical scale, given a starting pitch:*

Key	Interval (half-steps)	Key	Interval (half-steps)
ENTER	0		
▼	–1	◁ ▼	–12
▲	+1	▷ ▲	+12
◀	–2		
▶	+2		

*A complete-octave musical scale is a geometric series of 12 audio frequencies, called half-steps. The 13th frequency is the octave—*double* the frequency of the first.

Solution: First, a little program to compute and sound the correct interval (for 1 second), given a starting frequency:

```
INTV:  « 2 12 INV ^ SWAP ^
         * DUP 1 BEEP »
```

Store this in HOME. Then, here's the key assignment list:

```
{ S « 0 INTV » 51
    « -1 INTV » 35 « -12 INTV » 35.2
    « 1 INTV » 25 « 12 INTV » 25.3
    « -2 INTV » 34 « 2 INTV » 36 }
```

Store this list as TONES in HOME, and then make it your User keyboard: [VAR] TONE [→][MODES] STOK.

Now test it: Key in a starting frequency, [4][4][0][ENTER], then press [←][USR][←][USR] and horse around with the [ENTER] and arrow keys.*

The point here is that you have saved these key assignments in the list named TONES, so you can reinstate them any time you want.

*Notice how it helps to use the existing labels of the keys: If your assignments are at all similar to keyboard functions, consider locating them there (as did the example on the previous page). If that isn't practicable, and if you use a lot of key assignments so that it isn't convenient to try to memorize what and where they are, you might consider plastic keyboard overlays (available from HP and/or their dealers). Notice also that although reassigning the [ENTER] key is certainly allowable, it's not too wise. After all, it's one of the most heavily used keys; if you need it—as [ENTER]—along with your key assignments, you'll find yourself constantly having to toggle in and out of USER mode. Not so handy.

You'll notice that the other keys still retain their standard definitions while you're in **USER** mode. Can you disable them so that only your reassigned keys work?

Sure: Just delete the standard key definitions, S: ⬅ USR ' α S ENTER ➡ MODES **DELK**. Now press **RCLK** to see the current user key assignments.... The S is gone.

But: Notice also that →Qπ is still defined as the ⬅ →Q key. How can that be? When you assigned TONES via **STOK**, didn't that wipe out the previous custom keyboard?

No: Custom *menus* use a VARiable (CST) to store the current menu list, so storing a new list into CST does indeed *replace* the previous custom menu. However, custom key assignments are stored in a reserved part of memory, and storing new key assignments *add* to the previous key assignments; only the specific keys designated in the new list get their assignments replaced. You must specifically delete any old key assignments that you don't want.

Do It: Delete the →Qπ user key assignment.

OK: Press 3 3 · 2 **DELK**. Confirm your work with **RCLK**.*

Finally, what if you now need some of the standard keys—say, ENTER, ←, CST, VAR, and the menu keys? How do you restore their standard definitions without restoring all of the standard keys?

Easy: Simply assign the name, 'SKEY', to each standard key you want to restore. Here's the list:

```
{ SKEY 51 SKEY 55 SKEY 23 SKEY 24 SKEY
11 SKEY 12 SKEY 13 SKEY 14 SKEY 15 SKEY 16 }
```

Store these additional user key assignments: **STOK**.

You now have a user keyboard where only some keys have definitions. Whenever you press a key that has no current definition, you'll hear the error beep to let you know that it's "dead."

*"Old", deleted key assignments still take up memory unless you periodically *repack* the way they're stored. This sequence accomplishes the repacking: **RCLK** 0 **DELK** **STOK**. If you use custom keyboards often, you should repack your keyboard memory regularly.

Custom Flag Settings

You know how to set and clear flags individually with **SF** and **CF**. Also, for some system flags (such as –3 or –31), you can use the special menu items (such as **SYM□** or **CNC□**) that toggle between set and clear. And here's a more in-depth reminder how—like the user-key assignments—you can store and recall a list of all the flag settings and save that list as a VARiable for later use.

Do This: Press (→)(MODES)(NXT) **RCLF**. You'll get a list of two binary integer objects (recall page 105). The first integer represents the states of all system flags (from –1 to –64); the second one represents the states of the user flags (from 1 to 64). Store this list as a variable, OLDF: (')(α)(α)(O)(L)(D)(F)(α)(STO).

Now change some flag settings: (6)(4)(+/–) **SF** (3)(←)(MODES) **FIX** **SYM■** (NXT) **CNC■** (NXT) **RAD** (NXT) **BIN**.
Recall the new flag settings: (6)(4)(MTH) **BASE** **STWS** (→)(LAST MENU)(→)(MODES)(NXT) **RCLF**.

In binary format, you can see (use (←)(EDIT) to explore) the 64 bits corresponding to the states of the 64 system flags:*

-64	-63	-62	-61	-60	-59	-58	-57	-56	-55	-54	-53	-52	-51	-50	-49	-48	-47	-46	-45	-44	-43	-42	-41	-40	-39	-38	-37	-36	-35	-34	-33
1	0	0	0	0	0	0	0	0	0	0	0	0	0	0	1	0	0	1	1	0	0	0	0	0	0	0	0	0	0	0	0
-32	-31	-30	-29	-28	-27	-26	-25	-24	-23	-22	-21	-20	-19	-18	-17	-16	-15	-14	-13	-12	-11	-10	-9	-8	-7	-6	-5	-4	-3	-2	-1
0	1	0	0	0	0	0	0	0	0	0	0	0	0	0	1	0	0	0	0	1	0	1	1	1	1	1	1	0	1	0	0

---

*You might have flags set other than the ones shown here. You may wish to refer to Appendix E (pp. 699-706) of your Owner's Manual to confirm why each of flags is set.

Notice that the user flag integer (the second value) isn't 64 bits long. The 48 doesn't display leading zeroes in its binary integers, so the binary format of the integer representing flag conditions will be only as long as the number of highest *set* flag (i.e. the left-most 1).*

To demonstrate this, clear flag –64 and press **RCLF** once again.... The result is only 50 bits long; all flags numbered above –50 are clear (0).

Now: You could, of course, store this list for later retrieval too—but don't bother. Suppose, however, that you do want to restore the original flag settings as saved in the list VARiable, OLDF.

Easy: (VAR) **OLDF** (↱)(LAST MENU) **STOF**.

So if you're using some program that requires a certain combination of system flag states, this is how to quickly set all those states—and preserve the previous flag states, too (so that you don't mess things up for the next task).

*You'll get all 64 bits only if flags –5 through –10 are set. That's the 64-bit default setting for the wordsize—recall page 103.

Customizing the Built-In Tools

SOLVE

To customize the SOLVR menu, you can:

- Specify the order in which the variables appear.
- Suppress certain variables from appearing at all.
- Add other non-variable objects.

You do all this with a SOLVR *list*.

Try It: Create a SOLVR menu for this formula:

$$V = \frac{h}{3b}\left[a\left(3R^2 - a^2\right) + 3R^2(b - R)\omega\right]$$

that includes—in order—the variables V, a, b, and h, and which adds a blank key, followed by FIX. R and ω are fixed and won't be needed in the calculations.

Solution: Create this list:

```
{ 'V=h/(3*b)*(a*(3*R^2-a^2)+3*R^2*(b-R)*ω)'
  { V a b h { } FIX } }
```

Notice that the list has two objects: the equation itself and a list of items desired on the SOLVR menu.
Now name the list: ⬅ SOLVE NEW U N G U L A ENTER.
And press SOLVR to see the resulting menu.

PLOT and STAT

You can't customize the PLOTR or STAT *menus* like that of SOLVR. But you can customize these tools with *parameter lists* that you can store in the reserved variables PPAR (for PLOT) and ΣPAR (for STAT). Each of these reserved variables stores a list of the key parameters used by their respective tools.

PPAR is a list of seven objects, in this order:

- A *complex number* representing the coordinates of the lower left corner of the display range;
- A *complex number* representing the coordinates of the upper right-hand corner of the display range;
- The *name* of the independent variable—or a *list* containing that name and two real numbers representing the horizontal plotting range;
- A *real number* or *binary integer* specifying (for most plot types) the plotting interval along the x-axis (for histograms, this value is the bin width; for bar graphs, the bar width);
- A *complex number* containing the coordinates of the intersection of the axes—or a *list* containing that complex number and two character strings, the labels for both axes;
- The plot type—a *name*;
- The *name* of the dependent variable—or a *list* containing that name and two real numbers specifying the vertical plotting range.

Similarly, ΣPAR is a list containing these five objects:

- A *real number*, designating which column of the current statistical array is the independent variable;
- A *real number*, designating which column of the current statistical array is the dependent variable;
- A *real number*, representing the intercept value, according to the current regression model;
- A *real number*, representing the slope value, according to the current regression model;
- The regression model *name*.

So, if you work frequently with certain graphs that require particular parameters, you can create your own plotting parameter list(s), store them under other names (such as PP1, or PP2), and simply store each into PPAR whenever you need it.

You can use that strategy for PPAR and ΣPAR within short programs, also—maybe called via custom menus—to save even more time and keystrokes in setting up your plots and/or analyses. And keep in mind that, as with CST, you can have different PPAR and ΣPAR VARiables in *each* directory. This allows you great latitude in customizing parameters for a number of specific uses.

Optimization: A Case Study

All right, you've seen certain hypothetical examples of lists that allow you to customize your calculator. Now, how will *you* use such ideas to save yourself labor and trouble?

First, go back to your original directory structure. Ask yourself which directories might benefit from custom menus or custom keyboards. If you find some likely candidates, build and store the custom lists for these goodies in the appropriate directories. And if there some custom lists—like CALG—that should be available more generally, put them in the **HOME** directory.

Next, refine the structure of your VAR menus by adding small touches.

For example, imagine that you're creating a VAR menu for your directory, **{ HOME PHYS DYNAM }**. When you select **DYNA** to enter that directory, you'll see its VAR menu.

What do you want in this menu? It's worth a little thought....

Suppose: You want a custom menu, MEN1, to use with your motion calculations—plus you want CALG available, too. Then you'd like to be able to push one key to set the flags and user keyboard for the kind of work you do in this directory—and another key to reset the flags and keys as they were before, when you've finished. And suppose you want these features always to appear on the *first* page of your VAR menu. How are you going to do all this?

Well: Here's one approach (you may think of others): First, in your **DYNAM** directory, create and name the programs that handle the various customizing details:

```
SET1:  « RCLF 'OLDF' STO RCLKEYS 'OLDK' STO
         CFL1 STOF 0 DELKEYS CKY1 STOKEYS
         CPP1 'PPAR' STO CΣP1 'ΣPAR' STO »

MEN1:  « CMN1 MENU »

ALGM:  « CALG TMENU »

QUIT:  « 0 DELKEYS OLDK STOKEYS OLDF STOF
         HOME 2 MENU »
```

Next, create and name your custom lists:

CMN1: { the items you want in your custom menu }
CFL1: { #system flags value #user flags value }
CKY1: { your custom key assignments }
CPP1: { your custom plotting parameters }
CΣP1: { your custom statistical parameters }

Finally, use the ORDER function to specify that SET1, MEN1, ALGM, and QUIT all appear on the first page of the VAR menu. Create a list of the names you want placed:

{ SET1 MEN1 ALGM QUIT }

Then press ⬅ MEMORY **ORDER**. Now anything not included in this list will be placed after these items.

Now your keystrokes are fairly well streamlined: As an engineering student, to get started with the dynamics problems in your physics class, starting at HOME, you would press **PHYS** **DYNA**, then **SET1** to configure your flags, keyboard and analysis parameters. At that point, you're ready to start on the problems themselves. You have all of your calculation variables available via VAR and your optimized menus via **MEN1** or CST or **ALGM**.

That's doing *a lot* in very few keystrokes. And you can use this same basic idea and structure in your other directories, too—even using the same names of variables and custom lists, if the consistency helps.

Notice the naming scheme for your customized lists. If you found yourself later needing, say, two different plotting parameter setups in the course of your analyses, you could name a second list CPP2, right?

Putting It All Together

The 48 workshop isn't difficult to learn how to use. But it takes a lot of practice to learn to use it well. The real challenge is to choose appropriately among its myriad options for tools and methods—to find the approach that works best for *you*.

This Easy Course has steered you through a rather densely-packed tour of the 48. To do so, it has pretended to "know" what's best for you in order to make certain points and cover certain features, albeit briefly. But the truth is, only you can decide what parts of the 48 are of interest to you; nobody uses it all. So be thinking about the possibilities as you take this final quiz....

Custom Questions

1. When and why might you not be able to use the "LAST" keys?

2. What are the differences between these three storage commands?

   STO STOKEYS STOF

3. What binary integer represents the default system flag states—the flag states as they would be after a system reset? (Don't do this, just think about it.)

4. As an engineering student, suppose that you do a large number of rigid-free-body analysis problems in your Statics class. You input vectors corresponding to forces, positions and moments acting on the body and then calculate the resultant sums of the forces and moments. You also do a great deal of "what-iffing," so you need to be able to store, retrieve, and edit specific descriptions for specific bodies. What strategy might you use to do all this on your 48?

Optimum Answers

1. LAST STACK, LAST ARG, LAST CMD, LAST MENU all allow you to recover information after you've moved on. But keeping these hidden records costs memory, and if you prefer not to spend that memory on some of these recovery features, you can specify that.

   LAST MENU is one of the built-in menu numbers (0), so it's always available; you can't turn this feature off.

   You can control LAST ARG via a toggle key in the MODES menu *or* with a flag (–55): When flag –55 is set, the 48 does not save the arguments of the most recently executed command—and so LAST ARG can't retrieve it.

   Also in the MODES menu are the toggle keys for enabling/disabling LAST STACK and LAST CMD. These two features can use a lot of memory, so if you're in need of more memory, these might be the first ones to forego, if it's appropriate.

2. Of these three, only STO allows you to control where in user memory (i.e. directory structure) you are storing an object:

   STO stores an object into the given name in the current VAR menu, overwriting the object (if any) previously stored there.

   STOKEYS stores a list of user key assignments into an unnamed place in the 48 memory. This overwrites the previous key assignments only for the specific keys in the given argument list, leaving all other key assignments intact.

STOF stores a binary integer (or list of two binary integers) into an unnamed place in the 48's memory. Each integer affects *all* of its 64 flags, overwriting all previous flag settings.

3. In the default settings, only flags –5 through –10 are set (to give a binary wordsize of 64). This value is

1111110000b or # 3F0h or # 1012d

4. First, you'd probably want to set up some custom configurations in your STATICS directory—similar to the approach you saw on pages 379-381.

In your flags, for example, you might want to clear flag –19 (so that you can build vectors rather than complex numbers with the ⬅ 2D and ➡ 3D keys) and set, say, ENG 2 display mode, DEGrees for angles and probably cylindrical vector mode.

As for your custom menu, before you can set that up, you need to envision the calculations themselves. For example, how are you going to build a complete description of each free body—with all its forces and moments acting upon it—into a single object that you can then name (FB1, FB2, etc.) for storage and use later? A *list* of some kind would do it, right?

Then what objects would be included in each body-description list? Vectors, probably, but how will you distinguish force vectors—with their corresponding position vectors—from moment vectors, which need no positional information? How about

three lists of vectors? The first two (forces and positions) would have the same number of vectors in them and correspond one-for-one; the third list would contain all the moment vectors.

Then you might want to build yourself some little editing tools—to make it easier to input, alter, delete and view the vectors in each of the lists. Such items would indeed be handy on your custom menu. And, of course, you'll need the calculation routines themselves—the summation of the forces and the summation of the moments—also good candidates for your custom menu.

Well, you get the idea. The point is, you can always find some way to customize and streamline a calculation pattern like this. The question that only *you* can answer is: How far should you go? When does the time you spend customizing start to outweigh the time it will ultimately save you? As you become more proficient in your 48 workshop, these tool-design and customizing decisions will come more smoothly; you'll gain more convenience from less time invested.

Foundation Completed

This is only the beginning—truly just a foundation of understanding—upon which you should continue to build and use your 48 workshop.

As you certainly realize by now, there's no way that any single book could give you an in-depth look at everything about the 48. You probably noticed on many occasions that this Course made just a passing, one-time reference to a certain function, keystrokes or calculation method. It was by necessity, not by neglect. So if you marked those spots or scratched your head over them, you might wish to use your HP manuals to explore those "breezed-over" features now.

Note also that this Course did not cover:

- Alarms and the alarm catalog;
- Printing;
- Transferring data into and out of the 48;
- Using plug-in cards;
- Using the LIBRARY features;
- Making backup objects.

Those topics are best handled by your HP manuals. In fact, now that you have a good "feel" for the machine overall, those manuals are indeed the sources to turn to for further exploration on all topics. They're thoroughly indexed and organized; you'll find their examples and coverage quite helpful.

So how did you like this Course? Do you find yourself wishing for more or less (or different) coverage of certain topics? Did you find any mistakes? Please let us hear from you. Your comments are our only way of knowing whether these books help or not.

Index

Item #	Book Title	Price
	Personal Computer & Consumer Books	
29	A Little **DOS** *Will Do You*	$ 9.00
32	Concise and **WordPerfect**	9.00
28	**Lotus** Be Brief	9.00
30	An Easy Course in Using **DOS**	18.00
37	An Easy Course in Using **WordPerfect**	18.00
38	An Easy Course in Using **LOTUS 1-2-3**	18.00
39	House-Training Your VCR	9.95
	Hewlett-Packard Calculator Books	
35	**The Answers** You Need for the **HP 95LX**	$ 9.00
34	**Lotus** in Minutes on the **HP 95LX**	9.00
19	An Easy Course in Using the **HP 19BII**	22.00
22	The **HP-19B Pocket Guide:** Just In Case	6.00
20	An Easy Course In Using The **HP-17B**	22.00
23	The **HP-17B Pocket Guide:** Just In Case	6.00
05	An Easy Course in Using the **HP-12C**	22.00
12	The **HP-12C Pocket Guide:** Just In Case	6.00
31	An Easy Course in Using the **HP 48**	22.00
33	**HP 48** Graphics	20.00
26	An Easy Course in Using the **HP-42S**	22.00
18	An Easy Course in Using the **HP-28S**	13.00
25	**HP-28S** Software Power Tools: **Electrical Circuits**	9.00
27	**HP-28S** Software Power Tools: **Utilities**	9.00
24	An Easy Course in Using the **HP-22S**	13.00
21	An Easy Course in Using the **HP-27S**	13.00
	Curriculum Books	
14	Problem Solving Situations: A Teacher Resource for the 90's	$ 15.00

(Prices are subject to change without notice)

To Order **Grapevine Publications** books:

☎ **Call** to charge the books on **VISA/MasterCard**, ***or***

✍ **Send** Form to: **Grapevine Publications, P.O. Box 2449 Corvallis, OR 97339**

Qty.	Item #	Book Title	Unit Cost	Total

Shipping Charges — Choose One

For orders of less than $8 (First class) .... **ADD $ 1.00**

For orders of $8 – $14 (First class)............................ **ADD $ 2.50**

For orders of more than $14

❑ **Surface Post** shipping and handling .... **ADD $ 2.50**
(allow 2-3 weeks for delivery)............................. *or*

❑ **Priority** ❑ **UPS** shipping and handling **ADD $ 4.00**
(allow 7-10 days for delivery) .... *or*

For International Mail: ....ADD $ ____
Add $5 per book to Canada and Mexico. Add $10 per book to all other countries. (Allow 2-3 weeks delivery)

Subtotal	
Shipping (See shipping charges)	
TOTAL	

Payment Information

❑ **Check** enclosed (Please **make your check** payable to **Grapevine Publications, Inc.**)
(International Check or Money Order must be in U.S. funds and drawn on a U.S. bank)

❑ **VISA** or **MasterCard #**________________________ Exp. date ________

Your Signature ________________________________

Name________________________ **Phone** ( ) ____________

Shipping Address________________________________

(Note: UPS will not deliver to a P.O. Box! Please give a street address for UPS delivery.)

City________________**State**_____ **Zip**__________ **Country**________

HP48 E.C. 8-92

Reader Comments

We here at Grapevine like to hear feedback about our books. It helps us produce books tailored to your needs. If you have any specific comments or advice for our authors after reading this book, we'd appreciate hearing from you!

Which of our books do you have?

Comments, Advice and Suggestions:

May we use your comments as testimonials?

Your Name: Profession:

City, State:

How long have you had your calculator?

Please send Grapevine Catalogues to these persons:

Name ____________________

Address ____________________

City ____________ State ______ Zip ______

Name ____________________

Address ____________________

City ____________ State ______ Zip ______